A Practitioner's Guide to the AIM Rules

A Practitioner's Guide to the AIM Rules

Consultant Editor

Tom Nicholls
Stephenson Harwood LLP

SWEET & MAXWELL

THOMSON REUTERS

First Edition	1999	by Tom Nicholls
Fifth Edition	2008	by Tom Nicholls
Sixth Edition	2011	by Tom Nicholls
Seventh Edition	2014	by Tom Nicholls

Published in 2014 by Thomson Reuters (Professional) UK Limited trading as Sweet & Maxwell, Friars House, 160 Blackfriars Road, London, SE1 8EZ (Registered in England & Wales, Company No.1679046.
Registered Office and address for service: 2nd floor, Aldgate House, 33 Aldgate High Street, London EC3N 1DL).

For further information on our products and services, visit *www.sweetandmaxwell.co.uk*

Typeset by Letterpart Limited, Caterham on the Hill, Surrey CR3 5XL

Printed and bound by CPI Group (UK) Ltd, Croydon CR0 4YY

No natural forests were destroyed to make this product; only farmed timber was used and re-planted.

A CIP catalogue record of this book is available for the British Library.

ISBN: 978-0-414-03402-0

Thomson Reuters and the Thomson Reuters logo are trademarks of Thomson Reuters.

Sweet & Maxwell ® is a registered trademark of Thomson Reuters (Professional) UK Limited.

Crown copyright material is reproduced with the permission of the Controller of HMSO and the Queen's Printer for Scotland.

Biographies

Marcus Stuttard is Head of AIM and has responsibility for Primary Markets in the UK across both AIM and the Main Market. He is responsible for the management and development of AIM, London Stock Exchange's international growth market for small and medium sized enterprises. He is a regular speaker on growth and business funding issues and sits on a number of industry and policy advisory bodies.

Elliot Shear is Managing Director of W Legal Limited. Elliot specialises in mergers and acquisitions for public and private companies and undertakes a full range of transactional and advisory work for corporate clients and financial institutions. His experience includes advising on corporate law and corporate governance as well as AIM admissions and joint ventures. Elliot's sector expertise is particularly in the Defence industry and also Financial Services. The strength of Elliot's growing reputation has been recognised through his inclusion in "The Lawyer" magazine's "Hot 100" lawyers.

Stephen Keys is Head of Growth Companies Corporate Finance at Cenkos Securities Plc, joining the company shortly after it was founded and having been a Director of Corporate Finance at Collins Stewart previously. During his career, Stephen has specialised in advising growth companies on both AIM and the Official List. He has acted for companies across a wide range of sectors and jurisdictions and has significant experience in advising Indian based companies. As well as completing a large number of IPOs and secondary fundraisings, Stephen is an experienced M&A practitioner. Prior to his career in the City, Stephen qualified and practiced as a corporate lawyer in Edinburgh.

Camilla Hume has been at Cenkos Securities Plc since February 2007, having previously worked at a boutique corporate finance house. Camilla has seven years' experience of advising on UK small and mid-cap transactions including numerous IPOs on AIM, secondary fundraisings, reverse takeovers and disposals across a broad range of industries. Her transaction experience also includes several transactions governed by the Takeover Code.

Linda Main is Head of KPMG LLP's Capital Markets Group which advises companies from all over the world who are considering an IPO in London. She joined KPMG in 1984 and has specialised in IPOs since 1997. She also has wide experience of other types of transactions. Linda spent two years on secondment to the Listing Group of the London Stock Exchange (now the UK Listing Authority) advising on the application of Listing Rules. Linda is a member of the UK Listing Authority's Listing Advisory panel and the London Stock Exchange's Aim Advisory Group.

Tom Nicholls is a corporate finance partner at Stephenson Harwood LLP and has wide ranging experience in capital raising and M&A. His practice includes advising on IPOs and secondary issues (Main Market and AIM) both in London and internationally, public company takeovers, investment funds, domestic and cross border M&A and advising quoted companies on their obligations to the UK Listing Authority and the London Stock Exchange. Tom also advises investment banks and financial advisers in their capacity as sponsors, nomads and brokers to listed companies. Tom has acted on over 50 IPOs on the London equity markets and numerous secondary fundraisings including placings, open offers and rights issues. Tom is recognised as a key individual for Capital Markets (mid-cap) by both the Legal 500 and Chambers and Partners directories.

John Bennett is an international business partner in the Corporate practice at Berwin Leighton Paisner LLP. He specialises in mergers and acquisitions, equity capital markets and company and securities law. John has 25 years experience in advising issuers and their sponsors, advisers and brokers on main market and alternative market transactions and was acknowledged in Chambers UK 2011 as a "leading individual". He is named as a leading corporate lawyer in the Chambers Guide to the Legal Profession and is also recommended as a leading M&A lawyer in PLC's *Which Lawyer?* Clients appreciate his "commitment, commerciality and expertise." (Chambers UK, 2013)

Nick Davis is a Partner in the Corporate Department at Memery Crystal LLP. He has experience in acting on a variety of capital market transactions for companies, nominated advisors and brokers and has advised on primary and secondary listings for many overseas companies. He also advises on acquisitions and disposals of public and private companies. Nick is a member of the AIM Advisory Group of the London Stock Exchange and is recognised as a leading individual for his capital markets and mining work by Chambers UK.

Kieran Stone is a Director in the Corporate Department at Memery Crystal LLP. He specialises in takeovers and flotations on AIM and the Main Market with experience in acting for companies, sponsors, nominated advisors and brokers. He has particular experience in working on overseas and multi-jurisdictional transactions.

Craig Lukins is an Assistant Director in Deloitte's PLC Advisory team, which acts as a nominated adviser to AIM companies and as an independent financial adviser to UK-quoted companies on a range of M&A, capital raising and restructuring transactions. He has seven years' experience of public and private company deals in a range of scenarios including public offers (buy and sell-side), IPOs, complex restructurings and private company processes.

Melanie Wadsworth is a Partner in the Corporate Department of Faegre Baker Daniels LLP. She has wide experience of public company work, including flotations, secondary fundraisings and public-to-private takeovers, for clients of all sizes and in a variety of sectors and jurisdictions. Melanie, who is recognised by Chambers as a "leading individual" in capital markets transactions, also serves on the Corporate Governance Expert Group of the Quoted Companies Alliance, an organisation dedicated to promoting and pursuing the interests of quoted companies outside the FTSE 350, including AIM companies.

Kristian Rogers is a partner in Wragge Lawrence Graham & Co's Corporate Team focusing on capital raising, including IPOs and secondary issues with particular emphasis on the investment funds sector (Private funds, Full List, AIM and the Specialist Fund Market) and fund restructurings. He also has experience on mergers and acquisitions (including public company takeovers), joint ventures and private equity.

John Reed is a partner in the Investment Funds Group at Wragge Lawrence Graham & Co. John specialises in investment funds and listed investment companies on the Main Market, AIM and the Specialist Funds Market as well as investment fund restructurings and financial and investment services. John also advises generally on capital raising and advising on IPOs and secondary issues together with public company takeovers.

Chilton Taylor is a Corporate Finance Partner and Head of Capital Markets at Baker Tilly who have been voted AIM Accountants of the Year a record five times in the Growth Company Awards. He is a graduate of Cambridge University and qualified at KPMG in 1977. He has over 25 years of corporate finance experience specialising in flotations, due diligence and fund raising. He has acted on over 130 flotations. He is a specialist on AIM IPOs and is one of only two practising accountants invited to the AIM Advisory Group of the London Stock Exchange. Although a Corporate Finance Partner, he is an acknowledged specialist in the VCT and EIS legislation and is the principal author of "A Guide to AIM Tax Benefits" a joint publication of Baker Tilly and the London Stock Exchange. Chilton is a member of the executive board of the Corporate Finance faculty of ICAEW.

John Wakefield is a Director of Corporate Finance at WH Ireland Limited. John was educated at Oxford University, following which he became a university lecturer and subsequently qualified and practised for five years as a solicitor with McKenna & Co, (now CMS Cameron McKenna) specialising in company and corporate work. In 1985 he joined stockbrokers Williams de Broe, in London and was instrumental in establishing their corporate finance department. He has considerable experience of sourcing capital for companies and has been involved in over 50 company flotations. He was a founder director of Rowan Dartington & Co Ltd in 1992 prior to its acquisition in 2006 by Blue Oar Group Plc. He was a member of the London Stock Exchange AIM Advisory Group from 2000-2004 and is the author of chapters on the Trading Rules of AIM and the Official List in two Practitioners' Manuals.

Nick Williams is a corporate partner at the law firm, Edwin Coe LLP. He advises listed and private companies and financial advisory firms on both domestic and international transactions. His expertise includes mergers and acquisitions, public takeovers, corporate finance, joint ventures, corporate governance and funds. In addition, Nick has a great deal of experience of capital markets work, and has advised UK and international companies and financial advisory firms on flotations and equity fundraisings and other transactions on the London Main Market and AIM. In recent years he has worked extensively with Chinese businesses listing on AIM.

Christopher Twemlow is Head of Legal Affairs at Euroclear UK, where he has been since 2007. The Euroclear group is a leading provider of post trade services and is the operator of the CREST securities settlement system.

Contents

3 The Role of the Nominated Adviser

Camilla Hume
Cenkos Securities Plc

Stephen Keys
Cenkos Securities Plc

4 The Role of the Accountant

Linda Main
Partner, KPMG LLP

5   The Role of the Solicitor

Tom Nicholls

Partner, Stephenson Harwood LLP

6   The Statutory Framework

John Bennett

Partner, Berwin Leighton Paisner LLP

7   The Admission Document and the Application Procedure

Nick Davis
Partner, Memery Crystal LLP

Kieran Stone
Director, Memery Crystal LLP

8   Continuing Obligations and Transactions

Craig Lukins
Assistant Director, Deloitte LLP

9   Directors' Dealings and Corporate Governance

Melanie Wadsworth

Partner, Faegre Baker Daniels LLP

10   Investing Companies

John Reed

Partner, Wragge Lawrence Graham & Co LLP

Kristian Rogers

Partner, Wragge Lawrence Graham & Co LLP

11   The Tax Regime

Chilton Taylor

Partner, Head of Capital Markets, Baker Tilly

12   The Broker and the Trading Rules

John Wakefield

Director, Corporate Finance, WH Ireland Limited

13   Overseas Companies on AIM

Nick Williams

Partner, Edwin Coe LLP

Chapter 1

AIM

Marcus Stuttard

Head of AIM, London Stock Exchange

1.1   Introduction

AIM, London Stock Exchange's ("LSE") international market for smaller, growing companies, was launched in June 1995. AIM's regulatory structure, tailored to the needs of growing businesses, allows companies to cost effectively raise capital at admission and throughout their life on AIM. As well as being geographically diverse, representing companies operating in over 90 countries, AIM supports the financing needs of businesses from over 40 different sectors.

1.2   A successful market for smaller growth companies

Since its launch, AIM has helped over 3,400 companies raise in excess of £85 billion. At the end of 2013, there were 1,087 companies on the market with an aggregate market value in excess of £75 billion. Around 20 per cent of companies on AIM are overseas incorporated and nearly 40 per cent have overseas operations.

As AIM has grown and wider market conditions have changed, the LSE has sought to ensure a balanced regulatory approach to meet the changing needs of companies and investors. This evolution of the rules has been critical to preserving the reputation of the market and maintaining investor confidence.

Institutional investment in AIM has continued to grow with around 50 per cent of the shareholdings in AIM companies being held by institutions over the last four years, compared to 30 per cent in 2003 (Source: GCI Institutional Investors In AIM 2011). This institutional support has allowed companies to seek further growth capital even throughout the difficult market conditions of recent years, evident from the £26.5 billion raised in further funds since the start of the financial crisis in the second half of 2007.

1.3 AIM's regulatory status

From October 2004 as AIM ceased to be classed as a "Regulated Market" as defined under European legislation, it is referred to as an "exchange-regulated" market. The LSE is responsible for the day to day regulation of the market. Additionally, under the UK's Financial Services and Markets Act, as AIM is operated by the LSE, a Recognised Investment Exchange, it is a Prescribed Market for the purposes of UK regulation and market abuse regime.

1.4 The AIM rules

The LSE is responsible for the development and enforcement of the rules for the market, which consist of the AIM Rules for Companies, AIM Rules for Nominated Advisers and the AIM Disciplinary Procedures and Appeals Handbook. In addition, there are sector specific rules for mining, oil and gas companies as well as for investing companies.

The rules, available from the LSE's website, are written in a clear and concise manner and are designed to be accessible to all types of companies. They include definitions and guidance notes to assist in the understanding of individual rules.

A company seeking admission to AIM is required to produce an admission document, which will contain disclosures about key areas including the company's directors, the company's strategy, its financial position and working capital.

Once admitted to AIM, a company is required to disclose certain matters on an ongoing basis, such as major contracts, the appointment of directors and all price-sensitive matters.

The admission rules and the continuing obligations for AIM companies are based on the principle of timely disclosure. Any failure to disclose material changes to a company's circumstances is treated very seriously by the LSE.

1.5   The role of the Nominated Adviser

A company seeking admission to AIM must appoint a Nominated Adviser ("Nomad"). A Nomad is the key adviser during the admission process and through a company's life on AIM, responsible for ensuring the applicant company complies with its obligations under the AIM Rules for Companies and for warranting to the LSE that a company is appropriate for AIM.

Throughout the admission process, Nomads are responsible for coordinating the due diligence process and involving external advisers as appropriate. This process includes understanding the company's financial position, assessing appropriateness of the board of directors, maintaining oversight and active involvement in the preparation of the admission document and ensuring adequate procedures are in place for the company to fulfil its obligations under the AIM Rules for Companies.

Financial due diligence will be carried out by suitably qualified accountants, and legal due diligence by appropriate lawyers. Should the company operate in a specific sector, such as mining, a specialist report may be commissioned to support the assertions and strategy which the company proposes to include in its admission document.

Notwithstanding the expertise of the other advisers involved in conducting due diligence on a prospective AIM company, the Nomad must ensure it has in place sufficiently robust procedures and checks to enable it to make the decision that the company is appropriate for the market.

The AIM admission process requires the pre-admission announcement (also known as Schedule 1) to be submitted to the LSE at least 10 business days prior to admission. The LSE will review and release the pre-admission announcement through a regulatory information service. It does not vet the AIM admission document but may discuss Schedule 1 with the Nomad to better understand how the Nomad has assessed the appropriateness of the applicant company.

In effect, Nomads act as the principal quality controllers for the market and therefore have their reputations to consider when confirming a company is suitable for the market. Consequently, they will carry out due diligence checks alongside other advisers on companies before they agree to provide such a declaration, and as such are central to the success of AIM.

The current list of approved Nomads includes investment banks, corporate finance boutiques and the corporate finance arm of specialist accountancy firms.

In order to be approved as a Nomad, the applicant firm must meet the LSE's criteria for eligibility as set out in the AIM Rules for Nominated Advisers. Broadly, the minimum criteria require that a prospective Nomad firm must have practised corporate finance for a minimum of two years, have undertaken, as a named principal corporate finance adviser, at least three major transactions on major stock exchanges and retain at least four similarly qualified full-time executives. Most importantly, the adviser must be able to demonstrate that it has a sound reputation for corporate finance and understanding of AIM.

Nomads have a number of specific responsibilities under the eligibility criteria. Above all, they have a duty to protect the reputation and integrity of the market. In short, this means that in addition to discharging their obligations under any specific rules, the adviser should use all reasonable endeavours to seek to ensure that the companies for which it acts conduct themselves in ways which befit AIM.

Nomads are subject to regular reviews by the LSE. Should a Nomad be found not to have acted with due skill and care or to be in breach of any of the rules for Nomads, the LSE has the authority to take appropriate disciplinary action.

A company must retain a Nomad at all times throughout its life on AIM. On an ongoing basis, the Nomad will maintain regular contact with a company to advise on its obligations under the AIM Rules for Companies. It is responsible for ensuring the company remains appropriate for market, liaising with the LSE as necessary.

Often companies admitting to AIM will have little experience of being admitted to a public market and will need help to understand what their obligations are as public entities. Nomads will normally charge a retainer fee for this ongoing service and it is in the interests of directors and their shareholders to ensure that they consult their Nomad on an on-going basis.

1.6   Further information

Details of recent and forthcoming admissions, market and trading statistics, company specific information, rules and regulations are available from the LSE's website.

AIM has an increasingly critical role to play as we emerge from the global financial crisis and are relying on growth companies to be the main contributors to economic growth, innovation and job contribution. The LSE remains committed to ensuring a favourable fiscal and regulatory regime continues to support the smaller, growing companies that seek to join AIM, helping to reinforce its reputation of an attractive platform for such businesses to raise capital to achieve their growth potential.

Chapter 2

An Overview of the AIM Rules

Elliot Shear

Managing Director, W Legal Limited

2.1 Introduction

After a relatively quiet period, unprecedented in its near 30-year history, the AIM Market of 2014 looks to be returning to better days – and it remains clear that one of the fundamental reasons for its prior success and recent upsurge is the nature of the rules of the AIM Market. The AIM Rules for Companies are generally considered to be principles-based. They are exceptionally brief (their main body currently covering only 12 pages and a mere 45 Rules) and have a specific focus on disclosure.

However, in an economic and political climate that continues to be somewhat hostile to "light-touch" regulation, it should be confidently stated that the AIM Rules for Companies were (and will again be) an essential element of what attracted many companies to the AIM Market – both UK and foreign. It would also be inaccurate to suggest that the challenges that the AIM Market has faced between 2008 and 2013 were a direct consequence of any key omissions or inadequacies in the AIM Rules for Companies. The fact that there were few new admissions to the AIM Market during that period can instead be seen as a consequence of global financial issues – often caused by companies in far more heavily regulated markets.

The underlying basis of the AIM Rules for Companies is that the relaxed regulatory approach works because every company applying and admitted to the AIM Market has to have a Nominated Adviser ("Nomad"). It is the role of the Nomad to ensure that not only is the company seeking admission an "appropriate" applicant for the AIM Market but also that the company is properly advised and guided on its responsibilities under the AIM Rules for Companies.

The AIM Rules for Companies act as the bare minimum that the London Stock Exchange ("LSE") demands and Nomads typically expect companies seeking admission to exceed the limited requirements of the AIM Rules for Companies in order to attract a reasonable class of investor. For example, although the AIM Rules for Companies make only one reference to corporate governance, many Nomads will require their companies to comply with certain recommendations of the UK Corporate Governance Code – and in a 2013 survey of AIM companies, it appears almost three quarters of companies "comply or explain" in accordance with the UK Corporate Governance Code.

The AIM Rules for Companies have often been referred to by the LSE as a form of regulation that is "market driven". This means that whenever the market has taken the view that the AIM Market is under-regulated, the LSE has stepped in with additional rules – for example, the AIM Rules for Nominated Advisers in February 2007; the AIM Note for Mining and Oil & Gas Companies and the AIM Note for Investing Companies in June 2009; and new rules added to the body of the AIM Rules for Companies which happens every couple of years. Although there have been no new formal Rules more recently, the LSE sends occasional Notices (one in July 2011 introduced "minor changes" to the Rules relating to the corporate action timetables in rr.24 and 25, and a second more recently in May 2014 made changes of "mainly an administrative and clarificatory nature". These deal with jurisdiction over companies that no longer trade on AIM, disclosure in r.11 based on a "significant" rather than a "substantial" movement in price and some changes to the Guidance Notes of the AIM Rules. Interestingly the LSE gives guidance to companies in an occasional publication called "Inside AIM" (most recently published in

February 2011, September 2011 and October 2012) and it is some of this guidance which has been added to those Guidance Notes).

2.2 Eligible applicants

Despite the introduction in 2010 of a new two-level approach to listing on the Official List of the FCA ("Premium Listings" and "Standard Listings" and the launch in 2013 of the High-Growth Segment, – the latter originally expected to be of significant competition to the AIM Market, but as of May 2014, there is only one company that is availing itself of such opportunity) the admission criteria for trading on the AIM Market continues to be less stringent, allowing young and growing companies easier access to a public investment market. Under the AIM Rules for Companies, for example, there is no minimum requirement for the number of shares to be held in public hands (although the company's Nomad will consider the proportion of shares in public hands when considering suitability for admission), nor is there a specific requirement to show three years of trading records. In fact, if the securities of a company have been traded on a market acceptable to the LSE, the company may seek to utilise an expedited process for its shares to be admitted to trading on AIM without even producing an admission document, by simply making a detailed pre-admission announcement.

2.2.1 *Suitability for admission:*

In assessing suitability for admission to the AIM Market under AIM r.1, the Nomad may consider factors such as whether there is a demonstrable market for the business of the company and whether it is likely to be profitable in the short term (e.g. within 12 months of its shares being admitted to trading on AIM). To some extent, the Nomad will rely on the reports of the company's lawyers and accountants who will need to carry out due diligence with the aim of satisfying the Nomad that the company is in good order and suitable for admission to AIM.

The information obtained during the due diligence process is also likely to form part of the admission document.

In order to comply with the admission criteria (below), it is sometimes necessary for a company to undergo a reorganisation, at least to some extent, and/or adopt constitutional amendments. For example, a UK incorporated private limited company is prohibited from offering its shares to the public (s.755 of the Companies Act 2006) so will need to re-register as a public limited company (requiring a minimum nominal share capital of £50,000 or the Euro equivalent). Also, a company with more than one class of shares is likely to want to reorganise its share capital into a single class of shares, and then to adopt articles of association that are suitable for a publicly traded company. Clearly such measures will require the consent of the shareholders, and so a lack of shareholder cohesion could therefore present a block to admission.

2.2.2 Standard requirements

Under the AIM Rules for Companies, a company is obliged to provide any information that its Nomad may reasonably request, and should seek advice from the Nomad and pay due consideration to such advice on any matters relating to the company's compliance with the AIM Rules for Companies (r.31).

If at any point the Nomad believes that the company is no longer suitable for its shares to be admitted to trading on AIM, the Nomad is under a duty to notify the AIM Regulation team.

Unless utilising the expedited procedure for admission, a company applying for admission to the AIM Market must produce an admission document (which, depending on how the shares in the company are being marketed, may also need to be a prospectus under the Prospectus Rules). A full prospectus is usually required where the company proposes to offer shares to the public and the offer does not fall within one of the following exemptions:

1. the total consideration for the offer is less than €2.5 million;
2. the offer is addressed only to certain qualified investors; or
3. the offer is addressed to fewer than 150 other persons per European Economic Area (EEA) state.

In most cases, companies seek to ensure they fall within one of these exemptions so that they do not have to produce a prospectus requiring approval from the Financial Conduct Authority ("FCA"), resulting in both time and cost savings.

The information required to be contained in the admission document is set out in Sch.2 to the AIM Rules for Companies. In summary, an admission document must provide all the information an investor would expect in order to be able to understand the assets and liabilities, financial position, profit and losses, and prospects of the company; and the rights attaching to its securities. The admission document will include the anticipated timetable for admission; details of the assets; liabilities and financial position of the business; a report on key business and market trends on the sector in which the company operates; details of what are considered the key risks for the company; details of the company's prospects; details of the management personnel; corporate registration information and the reasons for the company seeking admission of its shares to trading on the AIM Market.

The admission document must also contain a "working capital statement" by the directors. This is a statement that, in the directors' opinion, having made due and careful enquiry, the working capital available to the company and its group will be sufficient for its present requirements that is for at least 12 months from admission. In determining the available working capital, the amount of any concurrent fundraising may be taken into account.

The directors of the company (as well as the company itself) take responsibility for the contents of the admission document, confirming that it contains accurate and full information and that there are no material omissions.

2.2.3 Annual accounts and interim reports

An AIM company must produce, publish and send to its shareholders annual audited accounts within six months from the end of the financial year to which they relate. The content and form of such accounts will vary depending on the country of incorporation of the company, but must be in accordance with prescribed accounting practices and principles (as set out in r.19).

Also, an AIM company must publish a half-yearly report (including at least a balance sheet, income statement and cash flow statement with comparative figures for the corresponding period in the previous financial year) in respect of the six month period from the end of the financial period for which financial information was provided in its admission document. Subsequent half-yearly reports must then be published for every subsequent six month period thereafter (apart from the final six months preceding its accounting reference date for its annual audited accounts) but in each case are not required to be audited. All such reports must be notified no later than three months from the end of the relevant period.

2.2.4 Company website

To facilitate appropriate levels of transparency and communications between AIM companies and their shareholders, r.26 requires that each AIM company must make certain information available, free of charge, on its website. The information that must be available includes a description of its business and operations; details of its country of incorporation and main country of operation; copies of its constitutional documents; the names and biographies of its directors and their roles; details of the issued share capital and shareholders holding more than 3 per cent of issued shares (this information should be updated at least every six months – and the website should include the date on which this information was last updated) details of the corporate governance code being applied by the company, whether it is subject to the UK City Code on Takeover and Mergers and details of its Nomad and other key advisers. Additionally, the most recent annual accounts (and those for the past three years), all announcements through a Regulatory Information Service provider ("RIS") for the past 12 months and the company's most recent admission document (together with any circulars or similar publications sent to shareholders within the past 12 months) must be included on the website.

2.2.5 Transferability of securities

All securities traded on AIM (subject to limited exceptions) must be freely transferable (r.32). So, for example, the articles of association (or equivalent) of an AIM company should not contain pre-emption rights on transfer or provide for any minimum or maximum holdings of shares or restrict shareholders to, say, nationals of the country of incorporation. The exceptions to this are:

1. where, in any jurisdiction in which the AIM company operates, statute or regulation place restrictions upon transferability; or
2. where the AIM company is seeking to limit the number of shareholders domiciled in a particular country to ensure that it does not become subject to statute or regulation.

In order for a company to utilise these exceptions its Nomad will need to apply to the AIM Regulation team at the LSE for confirmation.

2.2.6 Securities to be admitted

A company must ensure that its application to admit securities for trading is in respect of all securities of that class, and that all such securities have been unconditionally allotted (r.33). The LSE may request evidence that the securities being admitted have been allotted, and although confirmation from the company's Nomad or copy board minutes resolving the allotment would be sufficient, in practice securities are commonly allotted in advance "subject to admission". Unless otherwise agreed by the LSE, confirmation of allotment must be received no later than 16:30 on the business day prior to the intended date of admission. Any change in the number of securities in issue requires liaison with the LSE's Admissions team.

2.2.7 *Retention of a Broker*

An AIM company must retain a broker at all times (r.35). The role of the broker is to encourage trading in the company's listed securities, and it must use its best endeavours to match buy and sell orders for the securities if there is no registered market maker. Any member firm of the LSE (subject to obtaining the requisite authorities from any other relevant regulator) may act as a broker, and a company's Nomad may also act as its broker.

A list of all member firms can be obtained from the LSE website where a separate list of firms which have already been appointed as brokers is also available. Any resignation, dismissal or change in a company's broker must be notified through its RIS.

2.2.8 *Settlement arrangements*

All AIM companies (pursuant to r.36) must ensure that appropriate arrangements are in place for the transfer and registration of, and payment for, their listed securities. Unless the LSE otherwise agrees (which will only be in exceptional circumstances such as where a company's local laws would prohibit it), the arrangements must permit electronic settlement.

Companies incorporated in the UK, Jersey and Guernsey, the Isle of Man and Ireland may be participants in the CREST settlement system. CREST is an electronic system allowing paperless settlement, and allowing shares to be held without hard copy certificates (although hard copy certificates can also be requested if required). CREST is operated by Euroclear UK & Ireland Ltd.

Shares settled through CREST can be held in a number of ways:

1. as a full member (provided the shareholder has the technological capacity to link to the system) where the member's name appears in the company's register of members;
2. as a sponsored member, where the member's name will appear in the register, but the member is not required to be linked to the system as the sponsor (who is likely to be a broker) will charge a fee to provide this link; and
3. as a client of a member or sponsored member who will act as nominee, where the nominee's name will appear on the register.

Alternative arrangements (such as CREST depository interests or settlement through Euroclear and/or Clearstream) will need to be considered where the applicant company is incorporated outside the UK, Jersey and Guernsey, the Isle of Man or Ireland.

2.2.9 *Administration*

An AIM company must pay fees as set by the LSE as soon as they become due, pursuant to r.37. An admission fee is payable by all applicants for admission (including the admission of an enlarged entity following a reverse takeover under r.14), and is payable no later than three clear business days before the anticipated date of admission. The admission fee is based on the market capitalisation of the company on the day of admission, and an AIM fees calculator is available on the LSE website.

A non-refundable annual fee is also payable by all AIM companies and the LSE issues invoices for this in the first week of April for the 12 months commencing 1 April. This fee must be paid within 30 days of the invoice date.

As at May 2014 the annual fee is £6,050 and a pro-rata annual fee is payable by all companies newly admitted. The pro-rata fee is calculated by taking the number of calendar days, including the date of admission to trading up to and including 31 March, dividing it by 365 and multiplying the result by the annual fee.

No admission fee is payable by companies transferring to AIM from the Official List, nor is a pro-rata annual fee payable on the admission of an enlarged company following a reverse takeover.

Details of an AIM company contact, including an e-mail address, must be provided to the LSE at the time of the application for admission and the LSE must be informed immediately of any subsequent changes to such details.

2.3   Special conditions for certain applicants

As well as the standard entry and ongoing criteria that a company must satisfy to trade its securities on the AIM Market, the AIM Rules for Companies impose additional requirements on certain types of company and provide scope for the LSE to impose further conditions where it may think it appropriate.

2.3.1   Lock-ins

If the company's main activity is a business which has not been independent and earning revenue for at least two years, r.7 requires that all "related parties" and "applicable employees" at the date of admission agree not to dispose of any interest in the applicant company's AIM securities for a period of 12 months from admission.

This requirement is designed to reassure investors as to the commitment of the management and existing shareholders of the company by ensuring that a company's management or existing shareholders do not use admission to the AIM Market as a means of realising their investment in, and exit from, the company.

The lock-ins will be evidenced by way of a lock-in agreement with each of the relevant related parties or applicable employees, and details of any such lock-in agreements should be included in the admission document.

2.3.1.1   *Persons required to be locked in*

Detailed definitions for the terms "related parties" and "applicable employees" are contained in the Glossary to the AIM Rules for Companies. These terms, which incorporate further defined terms of "family" and "substantial share-holder", are drafted widely and are designed to capture all individuals who may be involved in the personal or financial arrangements of key management and employees of the AIM company. In essence related parties include:

1.   any person who is a director of the applicant company or of any company within the same group as the applicant company;
2.   any person who holds any legal or beneficial interest (whether held directly or indirectly) in 10 per cent or more of any class of security (not including treasury shares) of the company seeking admission, or 10 per cent or more of the voting rights (not including treasury shares) of the company seeking admission; and
3.   any "associate" (meaning family, trustees, companies controlled by the person etc) of any person referred to in either (1) or (2) above.

Also, the Guidance Notes to the AIM Rules for Companies confirm that the LSE will not require a "substantial share-holder" (being the type of person described at (2) above) to be the subject of a lock-in under r.7 where that shareholder became a substantial shareholder at the time of the relevant company's admission and at a price which was more widely available, for example, as part of an offer to the public.

An "applicable employee" is any employee of the applicant company or any company within the same group as the applicant company who either individually or together with his or her family has a legal or beneficial interest (whether held directly or indirectly) in 0.5 per cent or more of a class of security of the applicant company.

2.3.1.2 Market practice

Before confirming an applicant company's suitability to be listed on the AIM Market, Nomads will often seek to impose lock-in arrangements on individuals who do not strictly fall under the remit of r.7, and/or longer periods of lock-in on those who do. For example, Nomads will frequently require management shareholders to enter into lock-in agreements under r.7 with a strict prohibition on the disposal of the company's AIM securities for a period of 12 months (a "hard lock-in"), followed by a further period of 6–12 months where the individual may only dispose of the company's AIM securities in certain limited circumstances (e.g. with the consent of the Nomad) which are in addition to the exception set out at Section 2.3.1.4 below (a "soft lock-in").

An arrangement similar to the "soft lock-in" is sometimes formalised into an orderly market agreement which seeks to ensure that an individual may only dispose of the company's AIM securities through the Nomad in his or her capacity as broker in order to ensure that investors do not sell shares in the market in a manner that may have a detrimental impact on their trading price.

2.3.1.3 Common issues

Given the wide remit of r.7, it is often difficult for a Nomad to identify all those persons who would technically be required to enter into lock-in arrangements, particularly where shareholders are part of complex financial arrangements involving trusts and/or foreign entities. Such complex arrangements can not only make it difficult to identify where lock-in arrangements should be put in place, but also to police those that are.

The Guidance Notes to the AIM Rules for Companies also recognise the risk to parties of lock-in agreements, if not properly drafted, that may constitute a concert party for the purposes of the City Code on Takeovers and Mergers. In order to minimise this risk, the Guidance Notes recommend that parties at risk should consult the Panel on Takeovers and Mergers before drafting any lock-in agreement.

2.3.1.4   *Exceptions to r.7*

Rule 7 will not apply in the event of an intervening court order, the death of a party who has been subject to the Rule, or in respect of an acceptance of a takeover offer for the AIM company which is open to all shareholders.

2.3.2   *Investing companies*

Where a company being admitted to AIM is, in the opinion of the LSE, an "investing company" (i.e. one whose primary business is of investing its funds in the securities of other companies or the acquisition of businesses) it is a special condition of that company's admission to AIM that it raises a minimum of £3 million in cash via an equity fundraising on, or immediately before, admission (r.8).

2.3.2.1   *Requirement for, and content of, investing policy*

An "investing company" is also required to have an investing policy in respect of asset allocation and risk diversification, which must contain sufficient detail to allow its assessment and, as a minimum, details of:

1. assets or companies in which it can invest;
2. the means or strategy by which the investing policy will be achieved;
3. whether such investments will be active or passive and, if applicable, the length of time that investments are likely to be held for;
4. how widely it will spread its investments and if applicable, its maximum exposure limits;
5. its policy in relation to gearing and cross-holdings, if applicable;

6.   investing restrictions, if applicable; and
7.   the nature of returns it will seek to deliver to shareholders and, if applicable, how long it can exist before making an investment and/or before having to return funds to shareholders.

The investing policy must be detailed in the company's admission document or, if utilising the expedited procedure for admission, in its pre-admission announcement, and in any announcement and circular produced pursuant to r.15.

2.3.2.2   Shareholder approval

If an "investing company" wishes to change its investing policy in any material way (taking into account the cumulative effect of changes made since the last shareholder approval – or if none, admission), it must first seek the prior consent of its shareholders in a general meeting (r.8). Also, where it has not substantially implemented its investing policy (usually the investment of at least in excess of 50 per cent of funds available to it) within 18 months of admission, an "investing company" should seek shareholder consent for its investing policy at its next annual general meeting and on an annual basis thereafter, until such time as its investing policy has been substantially implemented. This is to ensure that the company is putting those funds to use in the way that investors had anticipated when making the investment.

2.3.3   Other conditions

In addition to the prescribed requirements under the AIM Rules for Companies, where the LSE is aware of circumstances which could affect the applicant company's appropriateness for admission, or where the LSE considers that admission may be detrimental to the orderly operation or reputation of the AIM Market, it may make the admission of an applicant company subject to special conditions. The LSE must inform the Nomad of any such special condition, and may refuse admission if it considers that the applicant company does not or will not comply with the special condition. Such condition can impose a delay to admission of no longer than 10 working days, at which time the Nomad must make a decision as to whether to proceed, and if so when.

2.4   Disclosure

The AIM Rules for Companies are generally considered to be principles-based, with a focus on disclosure. Of the 45 AIM Rules for Companies, at least 16 of them deal with disclosure (rr.10–20 and rr.22–26). Each AIM company is required to retain a RIS through which it makes all notifications required under the AIM Rules for Companies. All such notifications must be made no later than when the same information is published elsewhere, and the company must take reasonable care to ensure that no notifications are misleading, false or deceptive and do not omit anything likely to affect the import of such information (r.10).

2.4.1   *price-sensitive information*

The key area of disclosure relates to price-sensitive information, and r.11 provides that a company must make an announcement through its RIS without delay of any new developments in its financial condition, its sphere of activity, the performance of its business or its expectation of its performance which, if made public, would be likely to lead to a significant movement in the price of its AIM securities. Until May 2014, the rules referred to a "substantial" movement but this has been changed in order to be more in line with Financial Services and Markets Act 2000. However, it need not announce information relating to impending developments or matters in the course of negotiation.

Whilst matters are in the course of negotiation and before a RIS announcement has been made, the company must keep the existence and detail of negotiations confidential, save that it may (providing it is satisfied that recipients of such information are aware that they must not trade in the company's AIM securities before the relevant information has been notified) give such information in confidence to its advisers, the other party's advisers, persons with whom it is negotiating any commercial, financial or investment transaction (including prospective underwriters or placees of its securities), representatives of its employees or trade unions acting on their behalf and any government department or statutory or regulatory body.

However, once information has been disclosed to such parties, if the company has reason to believe that a breach of confidence has occurred or is likely to occur in respect of that information, and that knowledge of it is likely to have a significant impact on the movement of its securities, it must issue a RIS announcement of such information without delay if that information has been made public. If it has not yet been made public, the company must at least issue a warning that it expects to release information regarding the matter shortly.

2.4.2   Corporate transactions

As well as the general obligation to disclose price-sensitive information, specific RIS announcements must be made in respect of certain transactions, including any transactions by any subsidiary of the company. The rules for transactions are set out in AIM Rules for Companies rr.12–16 and cover:

1.   Substantial transactions;
2.   Related party transactions;
3.   Reverse takeovers;
4.   Fundamental changes of business; and
5.   Aggregation of transactions during a 12-month period, in respect of (1), (2) and (3) above.

In order to determine whether a transaction is "substantial", a "reverse takeover" and so on, it is necessary to subject the transaction to the "class tests" which in each case compares a relevant aspect of the transaction against that of the AIM company. These tests are set out in Sch.3 to the AIM Rules for Companies and the tests are: (i) a Gross Assets Test; (ii) a Profits Test; (iii) a Turnover Test; (iv) a Consideration Test; (v) a

Gross Capital Test; and (vi) Substitute Tests (where the other five produce anomalous results).

Schedule 4 of the AIM Rules for Companies details the information which must be included in any corporate transaction announcements.

2.4.2.1 Substantial transactions

The definition of a "substantial transaction" for r.12 is quite straightforward – it is simply one which exceeds 10 per cent of any of the class tests referred to above.

However, it does not include any transactions of a revenue nature in the ordinary course of business, or any transaction to raise finance which does not involve a change in the fixed assets of the company or any of its subsidiaries.

2.4.2.2 Related party transactions

For the purposes of r.13, a transaction is a "related party transaction" when it exceeds 5 per cent of any of the class tests and is with a related party (as explained in Section 2.3.1.1 above).

In this case, the required notification would also have to contain a statement that the directors (other than any "interested" director) consider, having consulted with the Nomad, that the transaction is fair and reasonable insofar as the shareholders of the AIM company are concerned.

2.4.2.3 Reverse takeovers

A "reverse takeover" is a transaction which exceeds 100 per cent of any of the class tests (r.14).

In addition to the Sch.4 notification, a reverse takeover requires shareholder approval given in a general meeting. It also requires the publication of an admission document in respect of the proposed enlarged entity.

A reverse takeover is also deemed to have occurred in respect of an investing company, where it departs materially from its investing policy.

2.4.2.4 Fundamental changes of business

A "fundamental change of business" also requires shareholders' consent. It is deemed to have occurred when a disposal takes place (whether one disposal or a number over a 12-month period) which exceeds 75 per cent in any of the class tests.

The Sch.4 notification needs to be accompanied by a circular to shareholders.

Further, where the disposal divests the company of all, or substantially all, of its trading business, the company will be treated as an investing company and require shareholder consent for its formulated investing policy.

2.4.3 Miscellaneous information

Additionally, an AIM company must also issue a RIS announcement without delay of certain other matters relating to the AIM company, including:

1. any deals by directors;
2. any relevant changes to any significant shareholders;
3. the resignation, dismissal or appointment of any director;
4. any change in its accounting reference date, registered office or name;
5. any material change between its actual trading performance or financial condition and any profit forecast, estimate or projection included in the admission document or otherwise made public on its behalf;
6. any decision to make any payment in respect of its AIM securities;
7. the reason for the application for admission or cancellation of any AIM securities and consequent number of securities in issue;

8. the occurrence and number of shares taken into and out of treasury;
9. the resignation, dismissal or appointment of its Nomad or broker;
10. any change in the website address at which the information required by r.26 is available;
11. details of certain matters relating to directors; and
12. the admission to trading (or cancellation from trading) of the AIM securities (or any other securities issued by the AIM company) on any other exchange or trading platform.

The requirements of the AIM Rules for Companies in this regard are complex and the definitions of "deal" and "family" for these purposes are very wide.

2.4.4 Power of the LSE

In addition to the disclosure requirements detailed in AIM Rules for Companies rr.10–19, the LSE can require an AIM company to provide it with such information as it considers appropriate and may require the company to publish such information (r.22). Where the LSE has jurisdiction pursuant to r.43, r.22 shall continue to apply to a company which ceases to have a class of securities admitted to trading on AIM, as if it were an AIM company. The company must use all due skill and care to ensure that information provided to the LSE pursuant to r.22 is correct, complete and not misleading. If it comes to the attention of the company that information provided does not meet this requirement, the company should advise the LSE as soon as practicable. All communications between the LSE and the company are confidential to the LSE and the company's Nomad and should not be disclosed without the consent of the LSE, except to appropriate advisers to the company, or as required by any other regulatory body or agency.

The AIM Rules for Companies also allow the LSE to disclose any information regarding the company in its possession:

1. to co-operate with any person responsible for supervision or regulation of financial services or for law enforcement;
2. to enable it to discharge its legal or regulatory functions, including instituting, carrying on or defending proceedings; or
3. for any other purpose where it has the consent of the person from whom the information was obtained and, if different, the person to whom it relates.

2.5   Restrictions on deals

Directors and "applicable employees" (that is, employees who are likely to be in possession of price-sensitive information because of their employment in the AIM company, its subsidiaries or parent undertaking) are restricted from dealing in the AIM company's securities during a "close period".

"Dealing" is broadly defined in the AIM Rules for Companies and includes the acquisition, disposal or discharge of any financial product the value of which is determined directly or indirectly by reference to the price of the AIM company's securities (such as a contract for difference or a fixed odds bet). It would also include the granting of share options to the directors or employees.

However, dealing does not include undertakings or elections to take up entitlements under a rights issue or other pre-emptive offer, the actual take up of such entitlements, allowing such entitlements to lapse, the sale of sufficient entitlements nil-paid to allow take up of the balance of the entitlements, or undertakings to accept, or the acceptance of, a takeover offer.

A "close period" includes:

1. the period of two months preceding the publication of the AIM company's annual accounts pursuant to r.19 (or, if shorter, the period from the financial year end to the time of publication);

2. the period of two months immediately preceding the notification of its half-yearly report (and if it reports on a quarterly basis, one month immediately preceding the notification of its quarterly results);
3. any other period when the AIM company is in possession of unpublished price-sensitive information; and
4. any time it has become reasonably probable that such information will be required by the AIM Rules for Companies to be notified.

There are limited exceptions to the general r.21 restriction. It does not apply where a binding commitment was entered into before an AIM company entered into the close period and when it was not reasonably foreseeable that a close period was likely, provided that the commitment was notified at the time it was made.

The LSE also has discretion to permit a director or applicable employee to sell their AIM securities during a close period to alleviate severe personal hardship. The examples given in the Guidance Notes to the AIM Rules for Companies of severe personal hardship include the urgent need for a medical operation or having to satisfy a court order where no other funds are reasonably available. This would suggest that the severity of the personal hardship must be fairly high.

2.6 Responsibility for compliance

An AIM company must have in place sufficient procedures, resources and controls to enable it to comply with the AIM Rules for Companies. It must seek and take into account advice from its Nomad regarding its compliance with the AIM Rules for Companies whenever appropriate and it must provide its Nomad with any information the Nomad reasonably requests or requires in order to carry out its responsibilities under the AIM Rules for Companies and the AIM Rules for Nominated Advisers.

In addition, the Nomad should include in its engagement letter or Nomad agreement with an AIM company details of its specific requirements in connection with the dealing obligations set out above.

2.7 Ongoing requirements

The AIM Rules for Companies also specify that the following requirements must be complied with on an ongoing basis:

1. *Transferability of shares*: (r.32 – see Section 2.2.5 above).
2. *Securities to be admitted*: (r.33 – see Section 2.2.6 above).
3. *Electronic settlement*: (r.36 – see Section 2.2.8 above).
4. *Fees*: (r.37 – see Section 2.2.9 above).
5. *Contact details*: (r.38) – details of the company contact, including an e-mail address, must be provided to the LSE at the time of the application to admission and the LSE must be immediately notified of any changes thereafter.

2.8 Sanctions and appeals

The LSE's approach to regulation is aimed at maintaining the integrity, orderliness, transparency and good reputation of its markets and changing behaviour in those markets where necessary. If the LSE considers that a company has contravened the AIM Rules for Companies, any one or more of the following measures are available to it pursuant to AIM r.42:

1. issue the company with a warning notice;
2. fine or censure the company;
3. publish the fact that the company has been fined or censured and the reasons for that action; or
4. cancel admission of the company's securities to trading on AIM.

The factors which the LSE will take into account when considering what action to take in relation to a rule breach include the nature and seriousness of the breach, the actual or potential market impact of the breach, the extent to which it was deliberate or reckless, the compliance history of the company, the conduct of the company in relation to the matter under investigation and past precedent in relation to similar breaches.

Where, following investigation, the LSE wishes to commence disciplinary action against a company, it must refer the matter to either the AIM Executive Panel (which comprises members of the LSE's staff) or the AIM Disciplinary Committee (which comprises appropriately experienced non-LSE persons). In appropriate cases (including where a greater sanction than the AIM Executive Panel is authorised to impose is deemed appropriate by the AIM Executive Panel), the AIM Executive Panel may refer the case to the AIM Disciplinary Committee.

Companies have a right of appeal to the AIM Appeals Committee (which, like the AIM Disciplinary Committee, is drawn from a pool of appropriately experienced persons who are not members of the LSE's staff) against the findings of the AIM Disciplinary Committee and the AIM Executive Panel. The AIM Appeals Committee may uphold, quash or vary any decision it is asked to consider.

A new r.43 has been added to clarify the jurisdiction of the LSE, such that it can continue to investigate and take disciplinary action against an AIM company, even after it ceases to trade on the AIM Market.

Details of the disciplinary procedures and appeals process in relation to breaches of the AIM Rules for Companies are contained in the AIM Disciplinary Procedures and Appeals Handbook.

Any disciplinary actions resulting in public censure (for the most serious cases, generally involving significant market impact) will be published by the LSE in the form of AIM Disciplinary Notices. The LSE publishes anonymised details of private disciplinary actions in its *Inside AIM* newsletter. The purpose of this is to ensure that Nomads and companies understand the LSE's approach to the issues raised by its investigations.

Examples of the disciplinary issues the LSE has drawn attention to in *Inside AIM* are generally in relation to breaches of rr.10, 11 and/or 31. In relation to such breaches the LSE has made observations such as:

1. where a company's business is materially underperforming, it is not permissible for a company to delay updating the market based on the possibility that the year-end figures may be affected by possible accounting or tax changes, or one-off exceptional items;
2. a company should have regard to the fact that the procedures, systems and controls which might otherwise be regarded as industry standard for comparable non-quoted entities may not be sufficient for a company on a public market;
3. the Nomad must always be kept fully updated;
4. in appropriate circumstances, such as where some directors are aware of a material trading underperformance of which the rest of the board is unaware, resulting in a material delay in releasing the relevant information to the market, companies will be responsible for the individual, as well as collective, actions of its directors; and
5. companies should ensure that fundraising announcements accurately convey the purpose for which the funds are raised and update the market as to any material change in their use.

2.9 Conclusion

There are many commentators on the economic markets who have concluded that the challenges faced by the financial markets between 2008 and 2013 were a consequence of "light regulation". However, the AIM Rules for Companies, which are a good example of light, principles-based guidance, rather than strict, detailed, prescriptive rules cannot reasonably be seen as the reason for any difficulties faced by the AIM Market over that period. Many would argue that the AIM Rules for Companies themselves represent the essence of the success of the AIM Market – and are a particular draw to many foreign companies seeking to focus on building successful businesses, without the constraints of overly burdensome regulations.

While a small number of AIM companies may have proved to be less than successful, and may arguably have taken some advantage of the "light touch" regulatory environment, the vast majority of AIM companies are well-served by the AIM Rules for Companies and it is rare that investors are adversely affected by the lack of greater regulation.

Many reasons have been proffered by financial analysts as to why the global markets have endured such an adverse scenario – with one Nobel prize-winner for Economics (Professor Robert Aumann) suggesting the whole thing was simply the consequence of "an honest mistake" regarding sub-prime lending. Others may seek to argue that more regulation of the markets would have relieved some of the negative effects. However, companies on the AIM Market proved no more troublesome than those on more heavily regulated markets – and it would be unfair to point to the AIM Rules for Companies as being part of any of the problems that the AIM Market endured during that period.

It appears that the financial markets are "bouncing back" in 2014 and it is highly likely the AIM Rules for Companies will once again be seen as an effective and reasonable approach to regulating markets – and will return to being viewed as a fundamental part of the essential success of the AIM Market itself.

Chapter 3

The Role of the Nominated Adviser

Camilla Hume
Cenkos Securities Plc

Stephen Keys
Cenkos Securities Plc

3.1   Introduction

Pursuant to the AIM Rules for Companies, a nominated adviser ("Nomad") is a firm or company, which is responsible for assessing the appropriateness of an applicant for AIM, or an existing AIM company when appointed its Nomad, and for advising and guiding an AIM company on its responsibilities under the AIM Rules for Companies (the "AIM Rules"). It is the responsibility of the Nomad to ensure that the companies which have shares admitted to trading on AIM, or who are seeking to have their shares admitted to trading on AIM, are "appropriate" at the point of admission and that the company and its management are fully aware of their obligations under the AIM Rules on admission and on a continuing basis.

Accordingly, there is a high degree of responsibility on the Nomad to undertake extensive due diligence on the applicant company. The London Stock Exchange ("LSE") relies on the Nomad to screen applicant companies and confirm to them that the applicant company and its securities are, in the Nomad's opinion, appropriate to be admitted to AIM.

Once the applicant company has gained admission to AIM, it is the company's directors who are responsible for ensuring the company's ongoing compliance with the AIM Rules.

The AIM Rules for Nominated Advisers set out the eligibility, ongoing obligations and certain disciplinary matters in relation to Nomads, r.17 of which requires that Nomads be on hand at all times to advise and guide the company and its directors on their continuing obligations under the AIM Rules. In turn, the directors are required to seek advice from the Nomad regarding the company's compliance with the AIM Rules and to take that advice into account. Consequently, the role of the Nomad to an AIM company is essential to the well-established and continuing success of AIM and the relationship between the company and the Nomad should be close.

Given the importance of the Nomad role, each AIM company is required to retain a Nomad at all times and failure to do so will lead initially to suspension in trading of an AIM company's shares and ultimately (if the situation lasts for more than one month) their cancellation. The LSE maintains a list of those firms that they have approved to act in the capacity of Nomad.

Due to the importance of the Nomad role for all AIM companies, the LSE sets strict criteria for becoming and remaining a Nomad, so as to preserve the integrity of the market and to ensure that companies have ready access to high-quality advice. These criteria are enshrined in Part 1 of the AIM Rules for Nominated Advisers, which were introduced in February 2007 and which "codified" the previous market best practice.

Part 2 of the AIM Rules for Nominated Advisers, together with the Schedules to the Rules, set out the Continuing Obligations of a Nominated Adviser. These are the specific Nomad responsibilities, be it on engagement, admission, or on an ongoing basis. They also address other issues, such as Nomad independence, conflicts of interest and procedures and records.

As a result, there are very few more crucial relationships in business than between an AIM company and its Nomad. If a company is considering an admission to AIM, it should seek to appoint a Nomad as early as possible, as the Nomad is integral to the co-ordination of the admission process and its preparation. Similarly, both the AIM company and its Nomad must be able to trust each other, both in disclosing sensitive information about the AIM company and in providing advice to the AIM company. Additionally, the Nomad is required to confirm to the LSE that its client is suitable for admission to AIM at all times. Given the importance of this relationship, this chapter seeks to describe the role of the Nomad, the rules to which the Nomad is required to comply and the expected relationship between the Nomad and its client.

3.2   Nomads' responsibilities to the LSE

AIM is operated, regulated and promoted by the LSE and it is an overriding consideration that all Nomads should act so as to preserve the reputation and integrity of AIM (AIM Rules for Nominated Advisers, r.3). The Nomad's relationship with its corporate client will be set out in a contract, usually referred to as the "Nomad Agreement".

However, a Nomad's responsibilities are greater than those enshrined in the Nomad Agreement and the Nomad will have responsibilities to the LSE also. The LSE expects the Nomad to:

(a) be available at all times to advise and guide the board of its AIM-quoted clients; and
(b) to ensure that directors are aware of their continuing obligations, including when there are changes to the AIM Rules for Companies.

Whilst decisions of timing of disclosures is ultimately a Board decision, the AIM Team at the LSE expects the Nomad to be available to discuss the timing and content of information releases and ensure that the market is kept informed in a timely and informative manner.

In addition, a Nomad must ensure that it is independent of all its clients and that the Nomad is available to liaise with the AIM Team whenever required, including informing the AIM Team as soon as practicable if it believes that a client is in breach of the AIM Rules for Companies.

Further, the AIM Rules for Nominated Advisers state that a Nomad must provide each AIM company, to which it is the Nomad, with at least two appropriately qualified staff, one of whom must be a Qualified Executive (described in Section 3.5 below) and for such staff to be in regular contact with the AIM company.

The AIM Team also expects Nomads:

1. at the time of an application by a client to be admitted to AIM, or upon an appointment to act as Nomad to a company already admitted, to submit a Nomad's declaration form which, in summary, is the Nomad's confirmation that the company in question is appropriate to be on AIM;
2. to provide the LSE with any other information, in such form and within such time limits as it may reasonably require;
3. to liaise with the LSE where requested to do so by the LSE or an AIM company for which it acts;
4. to review regularly an AIM company's actual trading performance and financial condition against any published forecasts available to the stock market at large, or any estimate or projection included in the original admission document (or otherwise made public on behalf of the AIM company) in order to assist it in determining whether a notification is necessary under r.17 of the AIM Rules for Companies;
5. to inform the LSE when it ceases to be the Nomad to an AIM company;
6. to abide by the eligibility criteria for Nomads at all times; and
7. to act with due skill and care at all times.

3.3   Approval of Nomads

All Nomads are approved by the LSE, according to the eligibility criteria set out at Section 3.5 below and as described in the AIM Rules for Nominated Advisers. A complete list of approved advisers is maintained and published by the LSE on its website, *www.londonstockexchange.com*. Only those whose names are included on that list may act as Nomads.

3.4   The identity of Nomads

A Nomad is a firm or company and is usually an investment bank, the advisory arm of a stockbroker, or a firm of accountants.

3.5   Minimum criteria for approval as a Nomad

A Nomad must be a firm or company (individuals are not eligible); have practised corporate finance for at least the last two years; have acted on at least three "Relevant Transactions" during that two-year period; and employ at least four "Qualified Executives" ("QEs") and the LSE will take into account the overall experience of the QEs on an individual basis and as a team.

The LSE may waive its requirement for a two-year track record and/or three Relevant Transactions where it determines the applicant has highly experienced QEs. Typically, this occurs when a team of QEs transfers from one existing Nomad to another.

3.5.1   *Qualified Executives*

The AIM Rules for Companies and the AIM Rules for Nominated Advisers were recently amended to include the expansion of the definition of a QE.

The "expanded" r.4 of the AIM Rules for Nominated Advisers stipulates that a QE should be a full time employee of the Nomad who can demonstrate a sound understanding of the UK corporate finance market and AIM in particular, and who satisfies one of the following:

(a) in respect of a person applying to be approved as a QE, has acted in a corporate advisory role, for at least the last three years and who has acted in a lead corporate finance role on at least three "Relevant Transactions" in that three year period; or

(b) in respect of an existing QE who was approved as a QE within the last five years, and has been a QE on a continuous basis within that period, has acted in a lead corporate finance role on at least three "Relevant Transactions" with the last five years; or

(c) in respect of an existing QE who has been approved as a QE for five or more years on a continuous basis, has acted in a lead corporate finance role on at least one Relevant Transaction in the last five year period and can demonstrate to the satisfaction of the LSE that they are involved in an active capacity in the provision of corporate finance advisory work, and in relation to AIM in particular.

An individual will not be considered for approval as a QE (or be eligible to be a QE on a continuing basis):

(a) Where that person has been subject to disciplinary action or similar relating to corporate finance or financial services related work by a regulator or law enforcement agency in the context of corporate finance or financial services or has any unspent convictions in relation to indictable offences; or

(b) If in, or as a result of, an interview which it conducts, the LSE considers the individual has an inadequate understanding of corporate finance, market practice, or the prevailing legal or regulatory framework for corporate finance.

Where an individual who is a QE of a Nomad leaves the full-time employment of that Nomad, that executive will be taken off the register of QEs.

In addition, the LSE may remove an employee as a QE for a Nomad where that employee is subject to bankruptcy or disciplinary action by another regulator, is mentally incapacitated, or has been shown by formal review of the Nomad by the LSE to have failed to act with due skill and care in relation to his employer's role as a Nomad.

Either a Nomad or a QE may appeal against a decision to disqualify that executive in accordance with the procedures set out in the latest published version of the LSE's Disciplinary Procedures and Appeals Handbook.

3.5.2 Relevant Transactions

In r.5 of the AIM Rules for Nominated Advisers, the LSE describes qualifying transactions as:

1. a transaction requiring a prospectus or equivalent in any EEA country; or
2. a transaction involving acting for the offeror on the takeover of a public company within an EEA country which requires the publication of an offer document (or similar document where it is being effected by a scheme of arrangement).

In addition, the LSE will consider similar initial public offerings and major corporate transactions for publicly quoted companies, including mergers and acquisitions whether within the EEA or elsewhere in the world. It will also decide whether a transaction is relevant for the purpose of these eligibility criteria.

The LSE will not allow an adviser to claim a transaction as relevant unless that applicant acted as a principal corporate

finance adviser and was named prominently and unequivo-
cally in the public documentation pertaining to that transaction. Copies of this publicly available documentation must
be included with the application to become a Nomad.

3.5.3 *Preservation of the reputation and integrity of AIM*

The LSE reserves the right to reject an application where it
considers that the approval of the applicant might endanger
the reputation or the integrity of AIM. It reserves the right to
reject an applicant on these grounds alone, even if the
applicant otherwise meets the criteria stated at Sections 3.1, 3.2
and 3.5. In considering whether an applicant might endanger
AIM's reputation and integrity, the LSE will examine:

1.   whether the applicant is appropriately authorised and
     regulated;
2.   the applicant's standing with its regulators;
3.   the applicant's general reputation;
4.   whether the applicant or its executives have been the
     subject of disciplinary action by any legal, financial or
     regulatory authority;
5.   whether the applicant is facing such disciplinary action;
     and
6.   insofar as is relevant, the commercial and regulatory
     performance of its clients to whom it has given corporate
     finance advice.

3.5.4 *Independence*

A Nomad must be able to demonstrate to the LSE that both it
and its executives are independent from AIM companies for
which it acts such that there is no reasonable basis for
impugning its independence, typically as a result of conflicts of
interest.

Where the LSE requires a Nomad to demonstrate clearly that
neither its independence nor that of any of its executives has,
or could be, compromised by any potential conflict, the burden
of proof will be upon the Nomad.

If at any time a Nomad is in any doubt about its independence, it should consult the LSE immediately and certainly before entering into any commercial arrangement. In practical terms, a Nomad will usually identify any potential conflict of interest at the outset and, if appropriate, decline to act for the applicant company.

Whilst it is acceptable for Nomads with stock-broking branches to fulfil both roles for one company, the following points should be noted:

1. a Nomad may not act as both reporting accountant and/or auditor on the one hand and Nomad to the AIM company on the other, unless it has satisfied the LSE that appropriate safeguards are in place;
2. no partner, director or employee of a Nomad, nor an associate of any such partner, director or employee may hold the position of a director of an AIM company for which the firm acts as Nomad;
3. neither a Nomad nor a partner, director or employee of a Nomad, nor an associate of any such partner, director or employee either individually or collectively may be a substantial shareholder (i.e. hold 10 per cent or more, to include options and warrants) of an AIM company for which the firm acts as Nomad;
4. a Nomad or partner, director or employee of a Nomad or an associate of any such partner, director or employee may be a significant shareholder (i.e. hold 3 per cent or more, to include options and warrants, but not a substantial shareholder) of an AIM company for which the firm acts as Nomad, provided adequate safeguards are in place to prevent any conflict of interest;
5. during any close period for an AIM company, no partner, director or employee in a Nomad, nor an associate of any such partner, director or employee may deal in the securities of that company for which the firm acts as Nomad;
6. when calculating an interest in a client company, a Nomad is permitted to disregard any interest in shares pursuant to rr.5.1.3–5.1.5 of the Disclosure and Transparency Rules

published by the FCA (which includes shares the Nomad is holding in a capacity as custodian or nominee for a third party); and

7. where a Nomad breaches any of the above limits as a result of its underwriting activities, it must make best endeavours to sell down its holding to within these guidelines as soon as reasonably practicable.

3.5.5 Wider conflicts of interest

Under r.22 of the AIM Rules for Nominated Advisers, a Nomad must not have and must take care to avoid the semblance of a conflict between the interests of the AIM companies for which it acts and those of any other party. In particular, a Nomad must not act for any other party to a transaction or takeover other than its AIM client company.

3.5.6 Obligations under the AIM Rules

Rule 15 of the AIM Rules for Nominated Advisers states that, at all times, a Nomad must abide by its responsibilities under the AIM Rules for Nominated Advisers and the AIM Rules for Companies, as published by the LSE. It is also incumbent upon the Nomad to ensure that the directors of its client are appraised of changes to the AIM Rules for Companies in a timely fashion, including where applicable the AIM Note for Investing Companies and the AIM Note for Mining and Oil & Gas Companies.

3.5.7 Proper procedures

Under r.23 of the AIM Rules for Nominated Advisers, a Nomad must ensure that at all times it maintains procedures which are sufficient for it to discharge its ongoing obligations under prevailing rules. In particular, it must ensure that any members of staff who are not approved as QEs are properly supervised by those who are.

3.5.8   Adequacy of staff

A Nomad must ensure that it has sufficient QEs to discharge its obligations as a Nomad under these rules at all times (AIM Rules for Nominated Advisers r.24). In determining what constitutes a sufficient level of staffing, a Nomad must have regard to the number and type of AIM companies for which it acts and the experience in relevant corporate finance matters of the corporate finance team as a whole. As a minimum, the LSE states that the Nomad must retain at least four QEs who would have sufficient experience for that Nomad to be approved by the LSE were it a new applicant.

3.5.9   Suitable expertise in mining and oil & gas

In the view of AIM, mining and oil & gas companies require a different knowledge base from many other companies and therefore AIM has issued a specific set of rules in relation to these industries. Where a Nomad is adviser to a mining and/or oil & gas company, the AIM Rules for Nominated Advisers state that the Nomad should ensure that it has access to suitably experienced and qualified individual(s) in the relevant sector. These do not need to be full time employees and may be engaged on a consultancy basis.

3.5.10   Ongoing experience of corporate finance

A Nomad must ensure that it continues to meet the minimum approval criteria for Nomads. In particular, a Nomad must have been involved in sufficient recent Relevant Transactions to allow it to qualify were it a new applicant at any time.

The LSE reserves the right to conduct further tests to ensure that QEs maintain an understanding of corporate finance and the responsibilities of being a Nomad.

It is the responsibility of the Nomad to ensure that QEs receive appropriate levels of training to ensure they are fully equipped to fulfil their roles. It is also the Nomad's responsibility to inform the LSE if this is not the case.

3.5.11 Maintenance of records

Rule 25 of the AIM Rules for Nominated Advisers states that a Nomad must retain sufficient records to maintain an audit trail of the discussions held and advice which it has given to those AIM companies for which it acts. It is also obliged to retain these records for a minimum of three years after it ceases to be a Nomad.

3.5.12 Annual fees

A Nomad must pay the annual fees as set by the LSE from time to time in respect of each year it wishes its name to be maintained on the register of approved Nomads.

3.5.13 Additional qualified executives

Application to have further employees registered as QEs may be made to the LSE at any time. The LSE must also be notified without delay of any QEs leaving the Nomad's full-time employment.

3.5.14 Performance review of Nomads

Under r.26 of the AIM Rules for Nominated Advisers, a Nomad may be subject to formal review by the LSE to ensure that it has fully discharged its responsibilities under these criteria. A Nomad must ensure that its QEs cooperate fully with the LSE and that the appropriate partner or director for a transaction is available to answer any questions by the LSE about those transactions. A Nomad must allow LSE officers access to its records and business premises when so requested by the LSE.

Similarly, r.4 of the AIM Rules for Nominated Advisers (as part of the QE approval process), allows the LSE to conduct interviews in order to assess the competence and suitability of the individual as a QE.

3.5.15 Moratorium on acting for further AIM companies

Where, in the opinion of the LSE, a Nomad is not meeting the requirements to be a Nomad, is not meeting their responsibility as a Nomad, has insufficient staff and/or is the subject of disciplinary action taken by the LSE, or if there is a reasonable likelihood of a change of control or there has been a change in its financial position or operating position that may affect its ability to act as a nominated adviser, the LSE may prevent that Nomad from acting as a Nomad for any additional AIM companies until that situation is resolved to the LSE's satisfaction. The LSE may choose to make the imposition of any moratorium public by way of a published AIM notice and/or by marking the Nomad register accordingly.

3.6 Responsibilities of the Nomad

Part Two of the Rules for Nominated Advisers covers the "Continuing Obligations of a Nominated Adviser", whilst Schedule 3 (Nominated Adviser Responsibilities) of the AIM Rules for Nominated Advisers sets out a range of numbered principles that must be satisfied, in all cases, in respect of Admission Responsibilities ("AR"), Ongoing Responsibilities ("OR") and Engagement Responsibilities ("ER").

3.6.1 Admission Responsibilities

At admission, *AR1 Applicant and its securities*, states that, in assessing the appropriateness of an applicant and its securities for AIM, a Nomad should achieve a sound understanding of the applicant and its business.

AR2 Directors and board stipulates that a Nomad should: (i) investigate and consider the suitability of each director and proposed director of the applicant; and (ii) consider the efficacy of the board as a whole for the company's needs, in each case having in mind that the company will be admitted to trading on a UK public market. Part of this process will typically involve each director being required to fill in the Nomad's standard due diligence questionnaire, standard know your client checks and, where applicable, the AIM Team would expect Nomads to undertake further investigative due diligence.

AR3 Due diligence states that the Nomad should both oversee the due diligence process and satisfy itself that it is appropriate to the applicant and the transaction and that any material issues arising from it are dealt with or otherwise do not affect the appropriateness of the Applicant for AIM. Part of this will typically involve at least one site visit to the proposed AIM company's primary sites of business.

AR4 Admission document demands that the Nomad should oversee and be actively involved in the preparation of the admission document, satisfying itself that it has been prepared in compliance with the AIM Rules for Companies, with due verification having been undertaken.

AR5 AIM Rule compliance states that a Nomad should satisfy itself that the applicant has in place sufficient systems, procedures and controls in order to comply with the AIM Rules for Companies and should satisfy itself that the applicant understands its obligations under the AIM Rules for Companies.

In practical terms, the Nomad will also usually be responsible for some if not all of the following with respect to admission:

1. assisting with the appointment and coordination of the company's advisers, including solicitors, reporting accountants, public relations advisers and registrars (and, if a separate company or firm, its brokers);
2. helping the applicant evaluate alternative fundraising options should an initial public offering ("IPO") not be viable;
3. managing the entire admission process, to include setting and controlling the timetable, as well as guiding the company through the necessary paperwork and documentation, including the 10 business-day announcement (or 20

business-day pre-admission announcement in the case of companies moving to AIM from the Official List or other designated market under the fast track process);

4. co-ordinating the drafting of the admission document, to include overall responsibility for content and the distribution of revised versions;

5. liaising with the company's legal advisers, reporting accountants and auditors, particularly in terms of the working capital review, long form report, legal due diligence, the overall verification process, and the placing agreement (if there is to be one);

6. in parallel with the development of the admission document, assuming overall responsibility for the development of the marketing presentation to be used in any fundraising; and

7. in the event of fundraising, advising the company on the pricing of shares on admission (in conjunction with the broker).

3.6.2   Ongoing Responsibilities

These apply on a continuing basis in respect of any Nomad who acts for an AIM company:

OR1 Regular contact between company and Nomad states that the Nomad should maintain regular contact with an AIM company for which it acts, in particular so that it can assess whether: (i) the Nomad is being kept up to date with developments at the AIM company; and (ii) the AIM company continues to understand its obligations under the AIM Rules for Companies.

OR2 Review of notifications says that the Nomad should undertake a prior review of relevant notifications made by an AIM company, with a view to ensuring compliance with the AIM Rules for Companies. Where possible, AIM companies should aim to send important announcements to the Nomad a few days in advance to ensure that announcements are compliant with the AIM Rules for Companies, as well as allowing for views on likely investor reactions.

OR3 Monitor trading stipulates that the Nomad should monitor the trading activity in securities of an AIM company for which it acts, especially when there is unpublished price-sensitive information in relation to the AIM company.

OR4 Advise the AIM company on any changes to the board of directors states that the Nomad should advise the AIM company on any changes to the board of directors which the AIM company proposes to make, including: (i) investigating and considering the suitability of proposed new directors; and (ii) considering the effect any changes have on the efficacy of the board as a whole for the company's needs, in each case having in mind that the company is admitted to trading on a UK public market. An AIM company should provide a Nomad with adequate notice of a director appointment to enable the Nomad to discharge its due diligence duties.

3.6.3 Engagement Responsibilities

The ERs apply to a Nomad when it is taking on an existing AIM company as a client and when it is bringing a company to AIM as its Nomad. Upon entering into an engagement as the company's Nomad, the Nomad has to confirm the following to the AIM Team:

ER1 The AIM company and its securities states that in assessing the appropriateness of an AIM company and its securities for AIM when taking on an existing AIM company, a Nomad should achieve a sound understanding of the AIM company and its business.

ER2 Directors and board stipulates that, in assessing the appropriateness of an existing AIM company and its securities for AIM, a Nomad should: (i) investigate and consider the suitability of each director and each proposed director of the company; and (ii) consider the efficacy of the board as a whole for the company's needs, in each case having in mind that the company is admitted to trading on a UK public market. Typically, including in the case of taking on an existing AIM company as a client, a Nomad will ask each director to complete a director's questionnaire to ensure there compliance with the AIM Rules for Companies.

ER3 AIM rule compliance states that the Nomad should satisfy itself that the AIM company has in place sufficient systems, procedures and controls in order to comply with the AIM Rules for Companies and should satisfy itself that the AIM company and its directors understand their obligations under the AIM Rules for Companies.

3.7 Transfer to AIM from Official List or AIM Designated Market

Where a company is transferring to AIM from the Official List, or another AIM Designated Market, where it has had a quotation for at least 18 months, the admission process is a lot less onerous than a new entrant to the public markets. In such circumstances it is not necessary for the company to produce an admission document but the company is required to make a detailed pre-admission announcement 20 business days prior to admission, the announcement being drafted in close consultation with its Nomad and other professional advisers and also submit to the LSE an electronic version of its latest annual accounts. The Nomad will also submit the Nomad declaration form and will be required to continue to act for the AIM company on an ongoing basis. Further details of the AIM designated market provisions are described in Chapter 3.

3.8 Sanctions and appeals (AIM Rules for Companies Rules 42–45)

The LSE considers it important that the AIM Rules for Companies are carefully observed, not only to build investor confidence in the companies on AIM, but also for the protection of investors and the credibility of the market as a whole.

3.8.1   *Disciplinary action against a Nomad*

If the LSE (in accordance with the procedures set out in the Disciplinary Procedures and Appeals Handbook) considers that a Nomad is in breach of its responsibilities under these criteria or under the AIM Rules for Nominated Advisers, or has failed to act with due skill and care, or that the integrity and reputation of AIM has been or may be impaired as a result of its conduct or judgment, the LSE may:

1.   issue a warning notice;
2.   fine the Nomad;
3.   censure the Nomad;
4.   remove the Nomad from the register; and/or
5.   publish the action it has taken and the reasons for that action.

3.8.2   *Disciplinary process*

Where the LSE proposes to take such steps, it will follow the procedures set out in the Disciplinary Procedures and Appeals Handbook.

3.8.3   *Appeals by Nomads*

In the event of the LSE taking steps against a Nomad, that Nomad may appeal against the LSE's decision in accordance with the procedures in the LSE's Disciplinary Procedures and Appeals Handbook.

3.9   Retention of a Nomad

Pursuant to r.1, an AIM company must retain a Nomad at all times. If a company ceases to have a Nomad, the LSE will suspend trading in its shares, regardless of whether the loss of Nomad relates to a termination of the engagement by either party or the Nomad losing its Nomad status. If, within one month of that suspension, the company has failed to appoint a replacement Nomad, the admission of the company's shares to trading on AIM will be cancelled.

Similarly, an AIM company must retain a broker at all times (r.35) and whilst in many cases the same firm provides the role of Nomad and broker to an AIM company, this is not a requirement. Additionally, an AIM company can appoint joint brokers if it believes that is in its best commercial interests. The broker liaises with shareholders, promotes awareness of the company in the market place, assists in the raising of finance and attempts to ensure that there is a market for the shares. The main responsibilities of a broker are:

1. providing equity research coverage and institutional sales support for that company;
2. acting as a point of contact between the investment community and the company and using its reasonable endeavours to generate investor interest in the securities of the company;
3. advising the company on investment conditions and in the event of a share issue, managing the equity fund raising element and assisting in the pricing of the securities; and
4. using its best endeavours to match buyers and sellers of the company's shares if there is no registered market maker (although often the broker will act as a market maker in the AIM company's shares).

3.9.1 Fees

The Nomad Agreement will usually provide for the engagement of the Nomad to be entitled to:

(a) a fee for assisting in the preparations for admission;
(b) a separate fee and commission based upon funds raised for arranging for the placing of the company's shares on admission (if applicable); and
(c) reimbursement of the Nomad's expenses, including legal fees and other expenses with respect to admission.

A Nomad will also charge an annual retainer in relation to its continuing role as Nomad.

In addition, the Nomad will often be engaged on a transactional basis. Examples of this include a fee for assisting with the preparation of admission to AIM and fees in respect of fundraisings (both commissions and corporate work such as producing a circular).

3.9.2   Termination

Given the consequences of a company ceasing to have a Nomad, it will usually want the Nomad to give at least one to three months' notice of termination. The Nomad is likely to require the company to give similar notice.

Both parties typically retain the right to terminate the relationship with immediate effect if either side (including any director in the case of the company) is in material breach of any legal or regulatory requirement or standard, or, in the case of the Nomad, if it is removed from the register of Nomads maintained by the LSE.

3.9.3   Changing Nomad

Subject to considerations in its Nomad engagement letter, a company is free to change its Nomad, although frequent changes may lead to public scepticism. An incoming Nomad will need to go through the procedures described above in the Engagement Rules which can take several weeks. In addition, the new Nomad should speak with the existing Nomad to confirm that there are no ongoing investigations or any other regulatory issues with the AIM company. Following this and signature of the engagement letter, the new Nomad submits a form to the AIM Team to state that it has taken on the new client and an announcement is made to the market. Shortly afterwards, the outgoing Nomad should provide AIM with an explanation as to why it is no longer Nomad to the AIM company.

3.10   Conclusion

The Nomad has responsibilities and obligations, both to the LSE and to its clients. In effect, the Nomad has delegated authority on behalf of AIM to ensure that its clients continue to be suitable for admission to AIM. A good Nomad will have a well-established relationship with the AIM Team and will assist the Nomad's clients through a detailed knowledge and practical application of the AIM Rules for Companies.

Above all, the key role of the Nomad is to develop and maintain close relationships with both its corporate clients and the AIM Team so as to ensure proper adherence to, and application of, the rules by companies on AIM, thereby protecting the integrity of the market.

Chapter 4

The Role of the Accountant

Linda Main
Partner, KPMG LLP

4.1 Introduction

This Chapter deals with the role of the reporting accountant and the financial reporting requirements for listing on AIM. It also touches on practical points covering:

1. the accountant's long-form report;
2. presentation of financial information in the admission document;
3. the working capital statement; and
4. financial position and prospects procedures.

The reporting accountant is involved throughout the AIM admission process. The role encompasses reporting on certain financial information in the admission document and other due diligence in relation to the contents of the admission document and the company. Some aspects of the role are driven by the AIM Rules for Companies, whereas others are designed to assist the Nominated Adviser ("Nomad"). The precise scope of the work to be carried out by the reporting accountant is agreed at the outset between the accountant, the company and the Nomad and is set out in a detailed engagement letter.

4.2 Accountant's long-form report

There is no regulatory requirement for a company to commission a long-form report prior to admission to AIM. However, this type of due diligence is typically requested by the Nomad to help discharge his responsibilities under the AIM Rules for Nomads.

The long-form report is a detailed due diligence report covering all aspects of the business and usually incorporates commentary on the company's operations including its products and markets as well as a detailed analysis of its recent financial performance. The company's management structure and system of internal control are also key areas covered as part of the exercise.

The due diligence process is time consuming and requires input from the directors and management team. It is important that sufficient attention is given to this process as the long form report provides much of the information which is subsequently used to draft the admission document itself.

4.3 Presentation of financial information in the admission document

A company wishing to join AIM must produce an admission document unless it is already quoted on one of the AIM Designated Markets. The admission document must contain the financial information specified by the AIM Rules for Companies which require the presentation of information consistent with that set out in Annexes I and III of the Prospectus Directive Regulation, subject to certain disapplications and modifications. If an offer is being made to the public a prospectus that is fully compliant with the Prospectus Directive Regulation is required.

Annex I of the Prospectus Directive Regulation requires the inclusion of the financial statements for each of the last three years which must have been independently audited or reported upon. If the company has been in existence for a shorter period then the accounts should be presented from incorporation.

In practice, this means that either the financial statements will be reproduced in full including each of the auditors' reports which were issued at the time, or a new "accountant's report" will be prepared, with a new opinion from the reporting accountant covering all three years.

No guidance is given as to which approach is preferred, although an accountant's report is usually prepared where there have been changes in the accounting policies or group structure during the period under review, or there will be changes in the next financial statements to be published by the company.

The reproduction of the previously published annual accounts is generally a less costly option, but can also be more cumbersome, as the three years comprising the track record are presented sequentially rather than in a single document as with an accountant's report.

The format of an accountant's report is not dissimilar to an audit opinion on a set of financial statements. The Standards for Investment Reporting issued by the Auditing Practices Board (SIR 2000 Revised) clarifies that the underlying financial information on which the accountant's report is based is the responsibility of the directors of the company, and the accountant's responsibility is to form an opinion as to whether the information gives, for the purposes of the admission document or prospectus, a true and fair view of the state of affairs and profit or loss of the company.

The financial information in the admission document should contain all the information typically found in a set of annual accounts (including the income statement, statement of financial position, statement of changes in equity, cash flow statement and notes).

A company incorporated in the EU should prepare its financial statements in accordance with IFRS as adopted by the EU (or local standards, if it is a standalone company). For companies from outside the EU, in addition to IFRS, US, Canadian and Japanese GAAP and Australian IFRS are also permitted. Since it is still relatively uncommon for private companies to prepare full IFRS financial statements, this requirement (plus the fact that it is a more attractive presentation) tends to mean that presentation of restated financial information, and therefore an accountant's report is more common than the reproduction of existing audit reports.

If the admission document is to be published more than nine months after the end of the company's financial year, the AIM Rules for Companies require the inclusion of interim accounts covering at least six months of the new financial year.

The interim accounts need not be audited, but must otherwise be prepared to the standard applicable to the accounts for a financial year. In practice, it is relatively unusual for unaudited interims to be included in an admission document; most companies and their Nomads choose to have the interims audited.

Where previously published financial information is restated an accountant's report is required. The nature of adjustments that may be made is limited, but some examples of the circumstances where adjustments can be made are:

1. to ensure that the same accounting policies have been applied throughout the period covered by the report (e.g. if new accounting standards have been introduced during the period) or they apply new accounting policies for the historical period (e.g. IFRS where the original accounts were under the UK GAAP);
2. to correct a departure from an accounting standard that has led to an audit qualification in the original accounts; or
3. to correct fundamental errors which have come to light since the original accounts were produced.

The overriding objective is to arrive at a set of figures which presents a fair picture of the results of the business in which people are asked to invest.

The application of the same accounting policies throughout the period is, in theory, a relatively simple matter, but it can give rise to practical complications if the information necessary to enable the accounts of previous years to be restated on the current policies is not easily available. The important issue is the question of materiality. The company may have to decide whether it believes that, whilst the figures cannot be computed precisely, reasonable estimates can nevertheless be arrived at which are acceptable and which enable a true and fair opinion to be given.

The issue of considering fundamental errors is more difficult. There can well be circumstances in which the company will say that the historical figures are clearly wrong and in its view were clearly wrong at the time. This is important. The preparer of financial information always has to avoid the excessive use of hindsight and has to put himself in the position of judging whether or not the view taken on a particular issue was reasonable at the time, even though subsequent events may cause a different view to be taken.

It is an unavoidable part of accounts preparation that estimates have to be made. Each year's accounts contain the adjustments made to the previous years' estimates as well as the estimates made at that year end. Subject to the overriding need to present a true and fair view, it is not the purpose of making adjustments to historical financial information to substitute more accurate information subsequently ascertained in place of reasonable estimates made at the time. A useful maxim in these circumstances might be, "if in doubt, do not adjust".

A company applying to join AIM which is already quoted on another exchange (one of the AIM Designated Markets) is not required to prepare an admission document. In this case, the AIM Rules for Companies require the publication of a website address where the latest published annual accounts (and interims if it is more than nine months since the year end) can be viewed. These accounts should be prepared using IFRS, Australian IFRS or one of the acceptable GAAPs mentioned above. Although this route dispenses with the need for an accountant's report, the Nomad may still require the preparation of a long-form report.

4.4   Pro forma financial information

Pro forma financial information is not required by the AIM Rules for Companies, but is sometimes included to satisfy the requirement to illustrate the effect of a transaction such as a fund raising on the assets and liabilities and earnings of a company. Other circumstances where a pro forma net asset statement may be included are where a group is coming together for the first time or an issuer is making a significant acquisition or disposal.

The Institute of Chartered Accountants in England & Wales ("ICAEW") has published a technical release (and latterly an Exposure Draft in October 2013) which gives detailed guidance on the preparation of pro forma financial information. This guidance is particularly useful in determining when it is appropriate to make adjustments.

If the admission document also constitutes a prospectus pursuant to the Prospectus Directive Regulation and the company has had a "significant gross change", pro forma financial information must be included in compliance with Annex II of the Regulation. Further, a report from the reporting accountant must be published in the admission document stating whether, in its opinion, the pro forma financial information has been properly compiled on the basis of preparation stated therein and whether, in its opinion, such basis is consistent with the accounting policies of the company. Where an admission document which is not a prospectus includes pro forma financial information, the accountant may provide a private comfort letter to the Nomad.

4.5   Working capital

The AIM Rules for Companies require the issuer to make a statement in the admission document that, in the opinion of its directors, having made due and careful enquiry, the working capital available to it and to the group is sufficient for its present requirements (i.e. 12 months from admission). The Nomad typically asks the reporting accountant to review the underlying projections and prepare a comfort letter.

This comfort will take the form of a private letter from the reporting accountant to the company and the Nomad. In order for the reporting accountant to be able to give such comfort, it is necessary for the company to prepare a board memorandum setting out the cash flow projections and the assumptions which underlie them. The board memorandum will be reviewed by the reporting accountant. The level of detailed work that has to be done in carrying out a working capital review will vary, to a certain extent, depending upon the margin between the working capital resources available (cash at bank and other facilities) and the requirements shown by the projections. Although the period has to be a minimum of the next 12 months, in practice a longer period may need to be covered and it is particularly necessary to consider any known circumstances beyond that time.

Confirmations of available facilities should be obtained from banks. Typically, these will expire during the period covered by the review. In these circumstances, the banks should be asked to confirm that they would expect, in normal circumstances, to renew the facilities at the review date.

4.6   Financial position and prospects procedures

The directors of new applicants to AIM are required to confirm that they have established procedures which provide a reasonable basis for them to make proper judgment as to the financial position and prospects of the issuer. The ICAEW

Technical Release "Guidance on financial position and prospects procedures" contains practical guidance for directors on how they might approach giving this confirmation. The reporting accountant is usually asked to provide comfort to the Nomad in this area which it will also undertake having regard to the ICAEW Technical Release. The reporting accountant will usually also be asked to provide a commentary on the company's financial position and prospects procedures. It will nevertheless be for the directors of the company to form a conclusion on whether the procedures are a reasonable basis for their judgments about the financial position and prospects.

4.7 Other comfort letters

There are a number of other areas where the Nomad may request comfort letters from the reporting accountant. The most common are:

- a request for the accountant to review the disclosures in the admission document relating to the tax effects of the transaction on UK shareholders;
- confirmation that certain financial information included in the document has been accurately extracted from the various source documents; and
- a request for the accountant to perform certain procedures in relation to the statement by the Directors that there has been no significant change in the financial or trading position of the company since its last published financial statements.

4.8 Other requirements of the Prospectus Directive

In addition to the points mentioned above, there are two other areas where additional information must be included if the admission document also constitutes a prospectus. The first is the need to include a statement of indebtedness showing the total indebtedness of the group as at a date not more than 90 days before the date of publication of the prospectus.

The second is the formalisation of the requirement to include an "operating and financial review" setting out, in narrative form, the key factors influencing the performance of the company during the period covered by the financial statements. In practice, this requirement is simply formalising what had already become common practice. There is no standard format for an operating and financial review, but it typically takes the form of a discussion of the reasons for the movements in revenue, profits and net assets in each year compared with the one before, as well as discussion of the key accounting policies adopted by the group and how these have been applied.

4.9 Conclusion

Overall, as can be seen from the above, the accountant's role is wide-ranging and goes far beyond the presentation of the basic financial information in the admission document. It is important not to underestimate the amount of time the various tasks will take.

Chapter 5

The Role of the Solicitor

Tom Nicholls

Partner, Stephenson Harwood LLP

5.1   Introduction

The role of the solicitor in an AIM flotation, or in any secondary issue, will depend on whether the solicitor is acting for the company or the Nominated Adviser ("Nomad") and/or broker. These roles are typically known respectively as, "Solicitor to the company" and "Solicitor to the issue". The solicitor to the company normally has a wider role which will include the initial advice on all structuring issues and advice on all aspects of the documentation involved. The solicitor to the issue usually concentrates on the drafting of and advice to the Nomad/broker on any placing or underwriting agreement and otherwise generally has a secondary role overseeing the whole process from the Nomad/broker perspective.

5.2   Solicitor to the company

5.2.1   *Principal functions of the solicitor to the company*

The responsibility of the solicitor to the company is to work as part of the team advising the company and its directors, liaising with the company's auditors and other advisers, including the Nomad, broker and reporting accountants.

The principal functions include:

- handling the pre-flotation legal due diligence;

- reviewing and advising on any necessary corporate restructuring;
- advising on the drafting of the admission document (which may also comprise a prospectus under the Prospectus Directive) which will be required to be published, with principal responsibility for the statutory sections of that document and managing the process of the verification of the contents of the admission document;
- negotiating the terms of any placing, underwriting or introduction agreement between the company, the directors, the Nomad/broker and any other relevant party;
- preparing directors' service contracts and appointment letters, if required;
- preparing employees' share participation schemes, if required;
- advising the directors of the company on their responsibilities as directors of a company whose securities are traded on AIM, particularly in relation to the flotation arrangements;
- advising on corporate governance matters including the creation of the various governance committees of the board and agreeing their terms of reference;
- negotiating the terms of the ongoing advisory agreements between the Nomad and the company and the broker and the company; and
- giving general advice which may be required in relation to matters arising out of the flotation.

5.3   Pre-flotation legal due diligence

5.3.1.   *Reasons for the legal due diligence*

It is common for the professional team to insist that a comprehensive legal due diligence exercise is conducted by the solicitors to the company in respect of the business of the company prior to flotation. They will generally be expected to address the due diligence report to the Nomad and broker as well as to the company. Together with the reporting accountant's long-form report, the legal due diligence report is particularly relevant to the Nomad, who owes certain duties to the London Stock Exchange ("LSE") in its capacity as a Nomad, not least confirming that it is satisfied that the company and its shares are appropriate to be admitted to AIM.

It is important to try not to overlap to any significant degree with the work that the reporting accountants will undertake in compiling the long-form report. Unnecessary duplication will waste the time of the directors charged with the task of collating information, who are often under considerable pressure in any event. For this purpose, it is vital that there is early dialogue between the reporting accountants, the solicitors to the company, the Nomad and the solicitors to the issue to coordinate the scope of the accounting and legal due diligence. The scope of the work to be undertaken by each for the company should be agreed at an early stage in engagement letters for the purpose.

At the outset, the solicitors to the company typically send a legal due diligence questionnaire to the company covering all aspects of its business. This questionnaire is similar in nature to a pre-acquisition due diligence enquiry form which a buyer (or its solicitors) would send to a seller. The questionnaire will contain questions designed to elicit the information, which will be required to compile the statutory and general information to be included in the admission document. Inaccurate or incomplete responses to the legal due diligence questionnaire have a profound influence on the ability of the solicitors to the company to prepare and complete the statutory and general information in the admission document quickly, accurately and efficiently. The directors need to be made aware of this if cost and timing over-runs are to be avoided. It is usually of great benefit if one person at the company (company secretary, financial controller, finance director or any other single director) is designated with and/or assumes direct and full-time responsibility for dealing with the due diligence issues. This serves to aid the consistency and flow of the information provided to the professional team.

5.3.2 What information is required for the due diligence?

The pre-flotation legal due diligence questionnaire will request details of:

- the basic corporate history and current corporate information on the company including its full name and company number, registered office, details of its directors, company secretary, shareholders and subsidiaries and copies of its memorandum and articles of association all of which will be checked against the relevant public records of the company (as the two will not necessarily be consistent);
- the existing issued share capital and existing shareholders, particularly directors' shareholdings and details of any existing shareholder agreement(s) or any other similar arrangements between shareholders (which will, most likely, need to be brought to an end immediately prior to, or consequent upon, admission of shares to trading on AIM);
- principal customers of, and suppliers to, the company together with copy contracts in order that a review of such contracts can take place. This is not only to check if any such contracts have, for example, change of control provisions in them, unduly onerous terms or abnormally short notice provisions, all of which would clearly have a potentially significant effect on the flotation, but also to check to see that such principal contracts are legally enforceable;
- service contracts between the company or any subsidiary company and the directors and employment details for all the employees and consultants in the business, including entitlements under bonus schemes and pension schemes and other benefits in kind as well as details of share incentive schemes, together with complete records of current share capital under option. Care should be taken in reporting details of employees, to avoid infringement of data protection legislation (normally by anonymising the information);
- in respect of each of the directors, details of his or her current directorships and former directorships in the

previous five years, unspent convictions, bankruptcies or individual voluntary arrangements, public criticisms, details of any receiverships, compulsory liquidations, creditors' voluntary liquidations, administrations, company voluntary arrangements or any composition or arrangement with creditors of companies generally where such director was a director at the time of or within the 12 months preceding such events, as well as the information otherwise required by para.(g) of Sch.2 to the AIM Rules for Companies. This of itself can be a very time-consuming exercise if the directors have extensive current and former directorships to disclose, particularly where numbers of overseas companies are involved, where the information will not be readily ascertainable through UK Companies House, nor in the equivalent authority in the relevant overseas jurisdiction;

- any material contracts of the business entered into by the company or any group company. These do not need to include contracts entered into in the ordinary course of the business of the company. Acquisition or disposal documentation entered into by the company or financing documentation of significance to the company including any placing or underwriting agreement entered into by the company as part of the flotation would generally be considered outside the ordinary course of business;

- any governmental, legal or arbitration proceedings being brought by or against the company or any subsidiary. Where any such matters are active, pending or threatened they must be disclosed in the admission document covering a period of up to one year if it is having or may have a significant effect on the company's financial position or profitability. An assessment as to whether any disclosures are required can be made, based on the information given, if any, in answer to the due diligence enquiries; and

- any person or entity, other than the professional advisers named in the admission document, who has received cash, shares or any other benefit with a value of £10,000 or more in the year prior to the application for admission or will or may receive any such benefit on or after admission, as required by para.(h) of Sch.2 to the AIM Rules for Companies.

These are some of the standard areas of questioning in a pre-flotation due diligence exercise. Complete and accurate answers with all supporting documentation will ease the preparation of the due diligence report and, ultimately, the admission document.

5.3.3   *Examples of actions consequent upon the legal due diligence*

Inevitably, the results of the legal due diligence exercise may give rise to a number of other eventualities. For example, it may be that arrangements have to be put in place to terminate a shareholders' agreement, which is not appropriate for a public company, or to restructure the share capital in order to convert different classes of share into one single class in readiness for flotation.

It may transpire that an important part of the company's business is not properly dealt with in the legal documentation that it uses. Whilst this may not preclude the flotation, the recommendation may be that the flaw needs immediate rectification. The solicitors to the company will need to draft appropriate documentation.

It may be that the legal due diligence reveals that documentation does not exist at all, or for part of the business of the company. This could be, for example, either that service agreements or terms of employment for directors and employees have never been prepared, or a part of the day-to-day means of doing business between the company and its customers has just not been committed to writing. This is not wholly unusual for young and growing companies. Once again, the solicitors to the company will need to create and agree the documentation with the company, as appropriate.

It is critical that the solicitors to the company have a very clear understanding of the business of the company and how it operates. It is equally important that the operation of the business is consistent with the underlying legal documentation. It is also worth noting here that specialist reports may also be commissioned in certain circumstances if the legal due diligence exercise uncovers some particular specialist issue or if the nature of the company requires it. These reports may be reproduced in the admission document. If the business of the company is heavily reliant on, for example patents, then a patent agent's report may be required. Likewise, if the company has significant property interests, a valuation report may be required and/or a solicitor's report or certificate on title commissioned. A mining, oil or gas company will require a competent person's report from an appropriately qualified professional in accordance with the AIM Note for Mining and Oil & Gas Companies of June 2009.

5.3.4 Draft and final legal due diligence report

An interim or draft form of the legal due diligence report should be circulated to the professional team involved at as early a stage as possible. This is usually extremely useful for the Nomad in getting an early indication of any problems or any areas which may require attention before the flotation process progresses any further. It also may assist the reporting accountants and inevitably also help on the task of verification. Certain aspects identified may need to be high-lighted in the admission document by means of specific risk factors or disclosures.

At the end of the legal due diligence process, the report will be signed off by the solicitors to the company. This is usually immediately before publication of the admission document itself. As mentioned above, the report will be addressed to the company and to the Nomad. It will have covered the entire business, as scoped out at the outset, and will highlight certain issues or problems as well as making recommendations.

5.3.4.1   Pre-flotation corporate matters

A number of changes may need to take place in the corporate structure of the company prior to its flotation. This may have been planned as part of the flotation agenda, or it may only have become apparent because of the legal due diligence exercise. Corporate structural changes may include some or all of the following:

- a UK company may be required to be re-registered as a public limited company in accordance with the requisite provisions in Pt 7 of the Companies Act 2006 ("CA")) (or if that is not possible, for example, because the net assets of the company are less than its called up share capital and undistributable reserves, then a new public holding company will need to be formed and a share exchange agreement entered into between the shareholders of the limited liability company and the newly formed plc);
- there may need to be a reorganisation of the capital of the company, in order to comply with the public company share capital requirements in Pts 17 and 20 of the CA and/or to create a uniform share structure appropriate for flotation (i.e. to convert different classes of share into a single class of ordinary shares, all of which will be admitted to trading on AIM);
- the company's articles of association are likely to need to be amended so as to be in a form appropriate for a publicly quoted company, not least to include provisions stating that the shares and any other securities to be admitted to AIM are freely transferable (r.32); and
- in order to be able to raise new money on flotation and subsequently, power may need to be given to the directors to allot new shares, if necessary excluding the statutory pre-emption rights, to give flexibility to issue new shares for cash in appropriate circumstances in the future.

Once the changes have all been identified and agreed, the solicitors to the company will prepare the necessary documentation. Normally, this would then be signed and any filings to

Companies House, or the equivalent authority in the relevant overseas jurisdiction, made in advance of publication of the admission document.

5.3.5 *The admission document and the verification of its contents*

5.3.5.1 *Drafting the admission document*

Once sufficient work has been undertaken on the long-form report by the reporting accountants and on the legal due diligence report by the solicitors to the company, work can commence on the drafting of the narrative section and the other parts of the admission document. The Nomad generally leads the drafting team, with the solicitors to the company being primarily responsible for the "statutory and general information" section of the admission document. In addition, the solicitors to the company review the main descriptive sections of the admission document, which are prepared by the Nomad together with the company.

The solicitors to the company will need to make sure that every applicable part of the AIM Rules for Companies have been complied with. A "tick test" of these rules is essential to ensure full and proper compliance. A considerable number of these rules are satisfied by means of the information which is contained in the "statutory and general information" section. In contrast, it is interesting to note that this "tick test" exercise would be agreed between the United Kingdom Listing Authority and the Nomad in the context of a prospectus required under the Prospectus Directive, or the sponsor in the context of a flotation on the Official List. The AIM team at the LSE has no such involvement in relation to an AIM admission document and the responsibility of the solicitors to the company is therefore more onerous. Ancillary ticklists will also be required for natural resource companies and investing companies in relation to the respective AIM guidance notes for such companies.

5.3.6   *Verification of the admission document*

After a number of iterations of the draft of the admission document, it will eventually reach a certain state where the text is settled enough in order sensibly to allow the verification process to begin. The solicitors to the company will prepare verification notes to check the accuracy of the admission document. These verification notes take the form of questions to which answers must be given by the directors to verify the relevant statements of fact and opinion and to provide supporting material.

The actual verification usually falls into two distinct areas within the admission document, although the process is a composite exercise.

First, the narrative sections describing the company and its business, which are typically agreed between the Nomad and the company, need to be verified. This is the sales pitch within the admission document and therefore, by its very nature, is likely to contain more subjective statements of opinion about the company, its business and the market in which it operates. Great care is needed properly to verify all subjective statements.

Second, the factual, more objective statements in the admission document also need to be verified. These are typically matters in the control of the solicitors to the company and the other professional members of the advisory team. This area could and should be capable of verification with relative ease. This is particularly so if sufficient attention has been paid to the preliminary due diligence enquiries and the responses to those enquiries and has included the provision of full documentation by the company to its solicitors.

5.3.7   *Relevance of the verification process*

It is true to say that the verification process often receives "bad press" and "its reputation goes before it". However, its importance cannot be stressed enough. The company and its directors are responsible for the admission document. The directors are personally responsible for the accuracy of the admission document and can incur personal liability to pay compensation to investors in the company if the admission document is inaccurate, untrue or misleading. Each director must therefore be satisfied on reasonable grounds that each statement of fact or opinion is not only accurate, but also is not misleading in its context. The verification process is designed to eradicate any statement incapable of substantiation by the company and its directors. It is also designed factually to test all significant statements. Together with the "tick test", the verification process therefore represents a vital sieve through which the admission document must pass, thus protecting the company and its directors and the Nomad. The verification process is not, in itself, a defence, but it is intended to provide the evidentiary basis for establishing that reasonable care has been taken by the persons responsible for the admission document.

5.3.8   When should verification have been completed?

The verification process should generally be substantially completed by the time the broker to the company sets up presentations to be made by the company to potential institutional investors or any other third party. Depending on the type of business, its maturity and the experience of its management, among other things, a "teaser" or "pathfinder" admission document may be sent out to prospective investors early in the process before any formal presentations are made. Exactly the same concerns exist regarding the accuracy of the information in any teaser or pathfinder document, as well as in any presentational slides shown to prospective investors. The solicitors to the company will be responsible for making sure that this process is properly completed in respect of any pre-flotation material paying particular attention to ensure that no additional information is contained in presentational materials which is not contained in the public admission document.

5.4 Placing/underwriting or introduction agreement

5.4.1 Parties to the placing agreement

If it is proposed to raise "new money" as part of the flotation process, part of the role of the solicitors to the company will be to negotiate and advise the company and the directors in relation to the placing or underwriting agreement. Any such agreement is the prime responsibility of the solicitors to the issue. The parties to the placing or underwriting agreement will be the company, possibly also the directors, and the party which is carrying out the placing or underwriting (namely the Nomad and/or broker). It is not uncommon for there to be existing investors in the company who wish to exit the company as part of the flotation arrangements. Quite apart from director shareholders, private equity investors, venture capitalists or banks with part of their investment in equity may wish to sell shares upon the flotation. It is likely that the terms of any such arrangements will also need to be negotiated with such investors and their advisers subject to any lock-in requirement as discussed below.

5.4.2 Contents of the placing agreement

Other than the pure mechanics of the placing or underwriting, a number of key issues will need to be negotiated by the parties. These may include some or all of the following:

- the conditions attaching to the obligations of the Nomad, including, ultimately, assisting the company in connection with the admission of its existing issued, and to be issued, shares to trading on AIM;
- the placing obligations of the broker and whether the broker is, for example, going to use its reasonable endeavours to find subscribers for new shares but not otherwise subscribe itself, or whether it will underwrite the issue and subscribe for new shares to the extent that it cannot find subscribers for some or all of the intended issue;

- the fees, commissions and expenses to be paid by the company to the Nomad and/or broker;
- the warranties, undertakings and indemnities to be given by the company and its directors to the Nomad and/or broker in respect of the admission document, the company and its business;
- the events which entitle the Nomad and/or broker to terminate the placing or underwriting agreement, including breach of agreement, breach of warranty and an event of force majeure (11 September 2001 is often cited as an example of an event of force majeure) which is outside the control of the company;
- the limitations on future activities and the obligations imposed on the company to consult with the Nomad and broker;
- the lock-in provisions restricting directors and other parties from selling their shares (as to which see below).

5.4.3   Negotiation of the placing agreement

Certain issues can become very emotive topics in the course of negotiations, particularly on the subject of whether directors will be required by the Nomad and/or broker to give warranties and indemnities alongside the company. If directors are required to do so, then there is the further issue of whether, and if so what, limitations on liability should apply to those warranties and indemnities given by the directors. Common limitations on liabilities might include a limitation on how long the directors remain liable and for how much they are liable. Whilst practice does develop and change, every flotation is different and it is the task of the solicitors to the company to guide and advise the company and its directors according to the circumstances prevailing at the time.

If no "new money" is being raised then an introduction agreement will be prepared by the solicitors to the issue. This will be similar to a placing agreement but with the deletion of references to any placing of shares!

5.4.4 Requirement for "lock-in" of shares in placing agreement

The AIM Rules for Companies impose special conditions on companies where the main activity of the company is a business that has not been independent and earning revenue for at least two years. In such a case, the company must ensure that all directors, substantial shareholders (owning 10 per cent or more of the voting share capital) and employees (owning 0.5 per cent or more of the voting share capital) agree not to dispose of any interest in their AIM shares for a year from admission. Certain others may be required to lock in their shares if they are associates of a director or substantial shareholders. This "lock in" can sometimes be contained in the placing agreement. Alternatively, a separate agreement will be prepared, typically between the company, the Nomad and the shareholder in question. This may occur, for example, where there are quite a number of shareholders who fall within the ambit of the rule and where therefore it is not necessarily appropriate for all of them to be a party to the placing agreement. The solicitors to the company will want to draft this document as the obligation in the AIM Rules for Companies is primarily imposed on the company to ensure compliance by directors and applicable employees. It will often be the case, even when a company has traded for two years, that the Nomad or broker will still require a form of "lock in" from the same group of people, albeit that the level of exceptions and carve-outs to the lock in may be greater than permitted in the AIM Rules for Companies. The exceptions or carve-outs for a mandatory lock in under the AIM Rules for Companies only include an intervening court order, death or a takeover offer.

5.4.5 Directors' service contracts

The AIM Rules for Companies, the CA, together with the requirements of the institutional investor protection committees, lay down certain criteria relating to directors' service contracts and certain matters which need to be disclosed in the admission document. These govern what is acceptable in such contracts and also the circumstances in which such contracts must be disclosed to shareholders and approved by them. The solicitors to the company will advise the company and draft the necessary contracts (and letters of appointment for non-executive directors) accordingly. The Nomad will want to ensure that key directors and employees are sensibly tied in to the business, as well as being sensibly remunerated.

5.4.6 Employee share participation

A flotation offers the company the opportunity of adopting one or more of the share incentive and share option schemes which are capable of approval by UK HM Revenue & Customs (HMRC) and which allow employees to obtain an equity participation in the company on a beneficial tax basis. The existence of share option packages can dovetail with the overall employment package properly to incentivise staff. There are three types of scheme that can be approved by HMRC:

- executive share option schemes (Enterprise Management Incentives ("EMI") Schemes or company share ownership plans, known as "CSOPs");
- save as you earn schemes; and
- share incentive plans.

In addition to HMRC-approved schemes, it may be appropriate to set up particular share option schemes which are outside HMRC's rules. These may, depending on the size of the company and the views of the Nomad, need to conform to the guidelines laid down by the institutional investment protection committees.

If management do have plans to grant options then it is highly advisable to give early consideration to drafting and implementing the appropriate scheme. In the context of approved schemes, HMRC are paying increased attention to schemes where a flotation is in the offing. The closer to flotation, the less likely it is to be able to achieve a discount to the float price when valuing the options and therefore the option price and the tax consequences for the option holder are less advantageous.

5.4.7 Directors' duties and responsibilities on flotation and afterwards

The directors of the company already have significant responsibilities under the CA and the insolvency legislation in their role as directors of a company. However, with the introduction of outside public shareholders and inevitable greater public scrutiny of the actions of the board of a company which has its shares traded on a public share market, these responsibilities are significantly increased.

The directors of the company will be accepting new responsibilities under:

- the Financial Services and Markets Act 2000 ("FSMA") and, if the admission document constitutes a prospectus, the Prospectus Directive;
- the AIM Rules for Companies relating to the continuing obligations;
- the insider dealing legislation in the Criminal Justice Act 1993;
- the misleading statements legislation in the Financial Services Act 2012;
- the City Code on Takeovers and Mergers; and
- the reports upon corporate governance, including the constitution of the board of directors and the terms of reference of remuneration, audit, risk and nominations committees.

As part of the flotation process, the solicitors to the company will give formal advice to the directors on their new responsibilities and will prepare for them a detailed reference memorandum covering all these topics. The formal advice is usually given at a full board meeting of the company either by the solicitors to the company or the Nomad. The memorandum, together with the oral explanation, effectively allows the company to give the first of six declarations it has to make on the AIM application form signed by the company before flotation. This particular declaration states that "we have received advice and guidance ... as to the nature of our rights and obligations under the AIM Rules and the Rules of the London Stock Exchange and we understand and accept these rights and obligations".

5.4.8   Nomad agreement and broker agreement

The AIM Rules for Companies require that a company whose securities are traded on AIM must retain a Nomad and a broker at all times. Accordingly, part of the role of the solicitors to the company will be to negotiate and advise the company and the directors in relation to the Nomad agreement and broker agreement. These agreements may be combined into one agreement (particularly so if the Nomad and broker is the same investment bank), or alternatively they may take the form of two separate agreements. A practice has developed to include the appropriate terms that would otherwise be contained in the Nomad and broker agreement in the original engagement letter with the company.

Whatever the form of agreement, the main provisions that will be included to govern the relationship between the company and the Nomad and broker are:

- the appointment of the Nomad and related obligations (such obligations typically include making the Nomad's declaration (as required by r.5 of the AIM Rules for Companies and Sch.2 to the AIM Rules for Nominated Advisers), ensuring compliance by the company with the AIM Rules for Companies, liaising with the AIM team in relation to the continued trading of the company's shares on AIM, reviewing the trading performance and financial condition of the company against any profit forecast, estimate or projection included in the admission document and releasing to a regulatory information service all information received by the company which is required to be announced under the AIM Rules for Companies);

- the appointment of the broker and related obligations (such obligations typically include advising and coordinating an appropriate investor liaison programme for the company, maintaining an orderly market in the company's shares and consequently coordinating transactions in the company's shares, advising the company on investment conditions, the pricing of its securities and significant movements in its share price and providing advice to the company on anticipated market reactions to matters such as finance raising, acquisitions and disposals);
- the obligations of the company and its directors, which will typically include complying with the AIM Rules for Companies on a timely basis, adhering to all statements of intent contained in the admission document, informing the Nomad and/or broker of any material changes affecting the financial or trading position or prospects of the company and providing the Nomad with the information that the company is required in accordance with the AIM Rules for Companies to notify to a regulatory information service;
- the fees and expenses to be paid by the company to the Nomad and broker;
- the undertakings and indemnities to be given by the company and, as appropriate, its directors to the Nomad and broker in respect of their appointments; and
- the events which entitle a Nomad or broker to terminate their appointment.

5.4.9 *General advice on the flotation given by the solicitors to the company*

The solicitors to the company will also be responsible for providing general advice to the company, which may be required in relation to matters arising out of the flotation. Such general advice would include drafting and negotiating ancillary documentation. These documents will comprise:

- Directors' responsibility statements (pursuant to which directors agree, amongst other things, to accept responsibility for the admission document);

- powers of attorney (pursuant to which each director of the company appoints any other director of the company to be his attorney to agree and execute any documents required for admission);
- comfort letters (these would usually include letters from the company and/or the directors addressed to the Nomad confirming the company's financial position and prospects procedures, confirming that the directors understand the nature of their responsibilities and obligations as a director of an AIM company and confirming that the admission document includes all information which investors and their professional advisers would reasonably expect to find there for the purpose of making an informed assessment of the assets and liabilities, financial position and prospects of the company and of the rights attaching to its shares); and
- engagement letters to be entered into by the company with its registrar, printers and public relations firm.

5.4.9.1 Solicitor to the issue

The principal responsibilities of the solicitor to the issue are generally to advise the Nomad and/or broker in relation to admission and specifically to ensure the company and its directors comply with the AIM Rules for Companies and to ensure that the Nomad has fulfilled its responsibilities in relation to the AIM Rules for Nominated Advisers.

The principal functions include:

- reviewing and advising on the drafting of the admission document;
- reviewing the legal due diligence report;
- reviewing and advising on the verification notes which will be prepared by the solicitors to the company;
- reviewing, commenting on and (if necessary) negotiating the ancillary documentation (such documentation would include lock-in agreements, the directors responsibility statements, powers of attorney and comfort letters);

- drafting and negotiating the placing, underwriting or introduction agreement;
- drafting and negotiating the Nomad agreement and broker agreement; and
- providing general advice to the Nomad regarding research notes, presentation slides, any "pathfinder" or teaser admission document, placing letters and any other communication by the Nomad and/or broker on behalf of the company with potential investors or any third party, particularly in respect of the financial promotion restrictions contained in the FSMA.

These functions have been discussed above in relation to the responsibilities of the solicitors to the company. However, the solicitors to the issue will clearly be looking at these documents from a different perspective to the solicitors to the company as they act for the Nomad and broker.

In similar fashion to the declaration given by the company in its application to AIM, the Nomad has to declare, among other things, that the directors have received advice and guidance as to the company's responsibilities and obligations under the AIM Rules for Companies. Moreover, the Nomad has to confirm to the AIM team that all applicable requirements of the AIM Rules for Companies and the AIM Rules for Nominated Advisers have been complied with and that it is satisfied that the company and its securities are appropriate to be admitted to AIM. These are serious declarations and ones on which the Nomad and broker need legal input and assistance from their solicitors.

5.5 Conclusion

The roles of the solicitors to the company and to the issue are complex and far reaching. They are central to the process of achieving admission to AIM. Fulfilling their roles properly requires great experience of the flotation process, an ability to display significant manpower and to understand the extensive teamwork required.

Chapter 6

The Statutory Framework

John Bennett
Partner, Berwin Leighton Paisner LLP

6.1 Introduction

6.1.1 The prospectus regime

The current regime for UK securities laws was introduced on 1 July 2005 when the EU Prospectus Directive (2003/71/EC) ("Prospectus Directive") and the Market Abuse Directive (2003/6/EC) (together the "EU Directives") were implemented. These had the broad aim of harmonising investor protection and the requirements relating to the issue of a prospectus when securities are offered to the public, or are admitted to trading on a regulated market in any European Economic Area (EEA) state. A regulated market for this purpose means a securities market recognised by a Member State for the purposes of the Markets in Financial Instruments Directive (2004/39/EC) ("MiFID"). The revised prospectus regime was implemented through the EU Prospectus Regulations 2005 (SI 2005/1433) (the "Regulations").

Section 85 of the Financial Services and Markets Act 2000 (the "FSMA 2000") (as amended by the Regulations) requires a prospectus approved in advance by the Financial Conduct Authority (formerly the Financial Services Authority) ("FCA") to be published (unless an available exemption applies) in two distinct circumstances:

1. before a company offers its transferable securities to the public; or

2.   before a company requests the admission of its transferable securities to trading on a regulated market.

The Regulations also authorised the FCA to make the Prospectus Rules (see Section 6.2.3).

At the same time, the revised market abuse regime was implemented in the UK through the Financial Services and Markets Act 2000 (Market Abuse) Regulations 2005 (SI 2005/381). Among other things, these authorised the FCA to make rules relating to the publication and control of inside information for companies with securities admitted to trading on a regulated market in the UK.

6.1.2   AIM and the prospectus regime

There had been a general concern that the implementation of the EU Directives would damage AIM on account of the "one size fits all" requirements which were to apply to all regulated markets. Accordingly, with effect from 12 October 2004, AIM ceased to be a regulated market and instead became an exchange-regulated market. The goal was to preserve AIM's regulatory regime and market structure with continued regulatory oversight by the FCA, whilst avoiding some of the more onerous requirements of the EU Directives.

As a consequence, AIM companies and prospective AIM companies have been less affected by the regulatory regime introduced in 2005 than companies on the main London Stock Exchange ("LSE") market for listed securities. A fundamental difference is that an AIM company is not required to issue a prospectus approved by the FCA just because its securities are trading, or are to be admitted to trading, on AIM. It only has to issue an approved prospectus where any marketing of its securities constitutes an offer to the public under the Prospectus Directive and no relevant exemption applies. Many AIM issues will fall within one or more of the exemptions such as the exemptions for an offer made to or directed at:

1.   qualified investors only; or

2.   fewer than 150 persons (increased from 100 persons in July 2011), other than qualified investors, per EEA State.

Following consultation, and to reflect the nature of AIM, LSE adopted the Prospectus Directive requirements with certain carve-outs as the standard of information required for an admission document required to be produced by an AIM company or applicant where an approved prospectus is not required. This standard is referred to as AIM-PD (see Section 6.5 for more detail). It recognised that the full Prospectus Directive was not appropriate but, whilst maintaining broadly equivalent standards to those which applied under the pre-Prospectus Directive regime, it wished to ensure consistency in the type and format of information seen by investors, adopt an up-to-date and well recognised standard (albeit with carve-outs) and simplify the process for companies wishing to move across to an EU-regulated market in due course.

The change from being a regulated market had other implications beyond the scope of the Prospectus Directive. For example, the treatment of AIM companies under the Disclosure and Transparency Rules differs from those companies on the main market. This also used to be the case for the Directive on Takeover Bids (2004/25/EC). However, on 30 September 2013, the Takeover Panel amended the Takeover Code, extending its application to companies which have their registered offices in the UK, Channel Islands or the Isle of Man and which have securities admitted to trading on a multilateral trading facility such as AIM (not just a regulated market), regardless of where such companies are managed or controlled.

6.2   Legislation

6.2.1   *The Prospectus Directive and related EU measures*

The Prospectus Directive sought to harmonise the requirements for the drawing up, scrutiny and distribution of prospectuses to be published when transferable securities are:

1.   offered to the public; or
2.   admitted to trading on a regulated market situated or
      operating within an EU Member State.

The Prospectus Directive introduced the concept of a "single passport" for issuers, making it easier to raise capital throughout the EU. This means that once a prospectus has been approved by the competent authority of the home Member State, it must be accepted throughout the EU subject only (if the relevant host state authority requires) to translation of the summary into the official language of the host state and to certain notifications to the host state authority.

The Prospectus Directive, like many of the measures under the EU's so-called Financial Services Action Plan, was adopted and implemented through the so-called Lamfalussy approach. This introduced a four-level legislative approach to the harmonisation of financial services regulation in the EU that deals with framework principles, implementing measures, regulatory cooperation and finally enforcement. The Prospectus Directive, as a piece of framework legislation, did not specify the form and content of prospectuses, but instead these were prescribed in a detailed EU Level 2 implementing regulation known as Commission Regulation 809/2004 of 29 April 2004 ("EU Prospectus Regulation"). The EU Prospectus Regulation became directly applicable as law in Member States from 1 July 2005. Alongside the EU Prospectus Regulation, the Committee of European Securities Regulators (the "CESR") published recommendations setting out detailed guidance on how the provisions of the Prospectus Directive and the EU Prospectus Regulation should be interpreted. On 1 January 2011, the CESR was replaced by the European Securities and Markets Authority (the "ESMA"), which is part of the European System of Financial Supervision. These recommendations are now referred to as "ESMA update on the CESR recommendations". The ESMA continues to publish FAQs in response to questions posed to it on prospectuses.

6.2.2   *The Financial Services and Markets Act 2000*

The Regulations implemented the Prospectus Directive in the UK under s.2(2) of the European Communities Act 1972. The Regulations amended the FSMA 2000 by setting out, among other things, the basic circumstances in which an approved prospectus is required. Section 85 of the FSMA 2000 states the general rule that a person may not make an offer of securities to the public in the UK or seek admission to trading on a regulated market in the UK unless a prospectus approved by the FCA has first been published. The Regulations implemented some of the important exemptions from the Prospectus Directive, and authorised the FCA to make the Prospectus Rules (which incorporated further exemptions from the Prospectus Directive). The FSMA 2000 (as amended) also deals with the procedure for dealing with an application for approval of a prospectus. The period for consideration of an application is, except in the case of a new issuer, 10 working days starting with the first working day after the date on which the application and all required information is received by the FCA. In the case of a new issuer, the equivalent period is 20 working days.

6.2.3   *The FCA's Prospectus Rules*

The FCA's Prospectus Rules made in exercise of powers granted under the FSMA 2000 set out further detailed requirements relating to prospectuses and incorporated some of the permitted exemptions from the prospectus requirements. The relevant provisions of the FSMA 2000 must therefore be read in conjunction with the Prospectus Rules.

As the Prospectus Directive is a "maximum harmonisation" Directive, it does not permit Member States to require additional disclosure in a prospectus and there was therefore little scope for the UK to apply discretion in the way it was implemented. Section 84 of the FSMA 2000 sets out the matters that may be dealt with by the Prospectus Rules through rules (labelled "R" in the Prospectus Rules), including the form and content of a prospectus, the period of validity of a prospectus and the ways in which a prospectus may be published. Under s.157 of the FSMA 2000, the FCA can also give guidance (which is labelled "G" in the Prospectus Rules) with respect to the operation of the Prospectus Rules. Paragraphs 1.1.6G and 1.1.8G of the Prospectus Rules state that, in determining whether the prospectus regime has been complied with, the FCA will take into account whether a person has complied with the ESMA update on the CESR recommendations. As a result, the Prospectus Rules must be read in conjunction with the ESMA update on the CESR recommendations.

6.2.4   The Companies Act 2006

A domestic private company limited by shares is prohibited by ss.755 and 756 of the CA 2006 from offering its shares or debentures to the public, or from allotting or agreeing to allot its shares or debentures with a view to all or any of them being offered for sale to the public. Under s.756 of the CA 2006, an offer is not made to the public for this purpose if it can properly be regarded, in all the circumstances, either as not being calculated to result in the shares or debentures becoming available for subscription or purchase by persons other than those receiving the offer, or as being a domestic concern of the people receiving and making it. This definition of an "offer to the public" differs from the definition of an "offer of transferable securities to the public" in the FSMA 2000 (see Section 6.3.3 below). It will be necessary to consider each of these tests in context.

Although the Government had previously stated that it was its objective to align, as far as possible, the statutory meaning of "offer to the public" (and in particular the related exemptions) with the definition and exemptions which apply in relation to an offer to the public for the purposes of the FSMA 2000, ss.755 and 756 of the CA 2006 substantially re-enact ss.81 and 742A of the Companies Act 1985 ("CA 1985"), save that the consequences of breaching this prohibition have changed.

In addition to ss.755 and 756 of the CA 2006 one residual provision, re-enacted from the CA 1985, still applies to any offer of unlisted securities (including securities admitted or to be admitted to AIM) to the public by a domestic UK company, whether or not it is required to publish a prospectus in accordance with Pt VI of the FSMA 2000. Under s.578 of the CA 2006 no allotment can be made of any share capital of a public company offered for subscription unless the issue is fully subscribed or the offer states that, even if it is not fully subscribed, the actual amount of capital subscribed may be allotted in any event or in the event of specified conditions being satisfied. If a minimum level of take up is stipulated in the offer, that minimum level must be achieved within 40 days, otherwise any money received from those who did apply for shares must be returned to them.

6.2.5 *Financial promotion*

The financial promotion regime contained in s.21 of the FSMA 2000 prohibits a person "in the course of business", from communicating "an invitation or inducement to engage in investment activity" unless he is an authorised person under the FSMA 2000, or an authorised person approves the content of the communication, or the communication is exempt.

In order to avoid any regulatory overlap, the financial promotion regime does not apply to a prospectus or supplementary prospectus, any other document required or permitted to be published by the Prospectus Rules or any non-real time or solicited real time communication required or permitted to be communicated by the rules of a relevant market or a body which regulates the market. For this purpose, AIM constitutes a relevant market and accordingly an AIM admission document which is not a prospectus but which is produced pursuant to the AIM Rules for Companies, and any other document required or permitted to be communicated by the AIM Rules for Companies is exempt.

A pathfinder prospectus will not be covered by these exemptions, but the distribution of the pathfinder by an AIM company will typically take advantage of the professional, sophisticated and high net worth investor exemptions. Any other advertisement which is used in conjunction with the marketing of an AIM company's securities but which is not an approved prospectus or an AIM-PD document or a document required or permitted to be communicated by the AIM Rules for Companies will generally need to comply with the financial promotion regime, unless it can also take advantage of these exemptions.

6.3 The prospectus regime and AIM companies

6.3.1 When is a prospectus required to be issued by AIM companies?

An AIM company will not be required to issue a prospectus approved by the FCA just because its securities are admitted to trading on AIM. However, it will have to issue an approved prospectus when any marketing of its securities constitutes an offer of transferable securities to the public in the UK which is not an exempt offer to the public.

6.3.2 What if a prospectus is not required?

If the transaction does not involve an offer of transferable securities to the public in the UK or an exemption from the requirement for an approved prospectus applies, an applicant (whether or not its shares are already quoted) will be required under the AIM Rules for Companies to prepare an admission document (complying with the Prospectus Directive with carve-outs).

6.3.3 Is there an "offer of transferable securities to the public"?

This concept is significant, because unless an exemption is available, an FCA-approved fully compliant prospectus will have to be published by an AIM company if there is an offer of transferable securities to the public in the UK, as defined in s.102B of the FSMA 2000. In practice, many AIM companies seek to fall within one or more of the exemptions to the requirement to prepare a prospectus in order to avoid the obligation to have a prospectus approved by the FCA, even if there is an offer of transferable securities to the public.

An "offer of transferable securities to the public" is defined widely as a communication to any person in any form and by any means which presents sufficient information on the transferable securities to be offered and the terms on which they are offered, to enable an investor to decide to buy or subscribe for the securities in question. It includes the placing of securities through a financial intermediary. To the extent that an offer of transferable securities is made to a person in the UK, it is an offer of transferable securities to the public in the UK unless an exemption applies. Transferable securities include shares, bonds or other forms of securitised debt which are transferable securities (for the purposes of MiFID) other than money-market instruments which have a maturity of less than 12 months. An option granted under an employee share option scheme which is not transferable is not caught by the regime.

6.3.4 Does an exemption apply?

There are a number of exemptions from the requirement to publish a prospectus. Exemptions are contained both in s.86 of the FSMA 2000 and in the Prospectus Rules (rr.1.2.2R and 1.2.3R) and must be considered separately in relation to public offers and the admission of securities to trading. Where a transaction involves both a public offer and the admission of securities to trading on a regulated market, an exemption from both requirements would be needed to avoid a prospectus. For example, a rights issue of less than 10 per cent of an existing class of listed shares would benefit from the 10 per cent exemption from the requirement to produce a prospectus for admission to trading on a regulated market, but a prospectus would nevertheless be required because there is a public offer of the securities and the 10 per cent exemption does not apply to a public offer. In the context of the AIM market, only the exemptions which apply to a public offer will be relevant.

One of the most significant exemptions from the requirement to produce a prospectus where shares are offered to the public relates to an offer made to "qualified investors" only. There is no longer the ability for investors to self-certify as "qualified investors" under the FSMA 2000. The definition was amended to include only those persons considered to be or treated on request as professional clients in accordance with Annex II of MiFID or recognised as eligible counterparties in accordance with art.24 of MiFID.

There is also an exemption for offers made to or directed at fewer than 150 persons (other than qualified investors) per Member State, and an exemption for offers where the minimum consideration per investor for, or the minimum denomination of, the securities is at least €100,000.

An offer to a qualified investor who can accept offers of securities without referring to the underlying clients (which would include a discretionary private client broker) will not be treated as an offer to those underlying clients when applying the qualifying investor or the 150 persons exemptions.

Prospectus Rules r.1.2.2R(2) contains an exemption from the requirement to produce a prospectus where securities are offered in connection with a takeover made by means of an exchange offer, if a document is available containing information which is regarded by the FCA as being equivalent to that of a prospectus, taking into account the requirements of EU legislation. The FCA applies the full vetting process to any such takeover document to determine whether it is equivalent to a prospectus. There is a degree of discretion about what is acceptable as equivalent, but it is limited. While a prospectus can be passported for use in other EU states which may be useful if the target has a significant number of retail shareholders in different EU countries, the advantage of an equivalent document is that there is no requirement to produce a supplementary prospectus (where relevant) which in turn avoids the problem of withdrawal rights for target shareholders.

Sub-paragraph (h) of article 1(2) of the Prospectus Directive excludes from the scope of the Prospectus Directive securities included in an offer where the total consideration under the offer is less than €5 million, calculated over 12 months, and this is reflected in s.85(5) and para.9(1) of Sch.11A to the FSMA 2000.

Somewhat confusingly there is also an exemption from the requirement for an approved prospectus which applies to an offer of securities with a total consideration of €100,000 or less, which limit is calculated over a 12-month period (article 3(2) of the Prospectus Directive and s.86(1)(e) and (4) of the FSMA 2000). However this limit is not relevant in the context of UK legislation as HM Treasury has decided not to require prospectus style documents to be produced for offers of less than €5 million.

In July 2012, as a result of European legislation, a new proportionate disclosure regime was introduced in the UK which provides for reduced disclosure requirements for prospectuses prepared in connection with rights issues on the Main Market and AIM.

6.4   Format of an admission document

If a prospectus is required, it may be drawn up as a single document containing all the requisite information or as a three-part document consisting of a registration document (which is valid for 12 months from its approval and can be used for a number of issues of securities during that period), a securities note (containing information relating to the securities), and a non-technical summary containing "key information" that will help investors decide whether to invest. Key information includes the essential characteristics of, and risks associated with, the issuer, the general terms of the offer and an estimate of the expenses charged to an investor by an issuer. The summary must not exceed 7 per cent of the prospectus or 15 pages, whichever is longer. The detailed requirements for the summary are set out in a new Annex XXII to the EU

Prospectus Regulation. These format requirements do not apply if a prospectus is not required. In practice, a single document in a similar format tends to be used whether or not a prospectus is required.

6.5 Content requirements for an admission document

The Prospectus Rules introduced a number of changes to the content requirements for prospectuses. The principal changes were to require inclusion of a summary, referred to in 6.4 above, risk factors specific to the issuer or its industry, disclosed prominently in a section headed "risk factors", and an operating and financial review of the issuer's business. This should include the causes of material changes from year to year in the financial information to the extent necessary for an understanding of the issuer's business as a whole. A statement of board practices is also required.

Where a prospectus is being prepared, the relevant Annexes to the EU Prospectus Regulation (Annexes I–III) should be followed, but supplemented by any additional or more stringent requirements set out in Sch.2 to the AIM Rules for Companies.

Where a prospectus is not required, a new applicant to AIM will be required to produce an admission document containing the information specified in Sch.2 to the AIM Rules for Companies, essentially AIM-PD. The AIM Rules for Companies refer to the information required by Annexes I–III of the EU Prospectus Regulation. These have been reproduced and colour-coded in the AIM Rules for Companies to indicate the carve-outs relevant to AIM-PD. Carve-outs were chosen with the overall objective of preserving the previous admission process in terms of the level of detail required within admission documents whilst ensuring that AIM maintains high standards of regulation and transparency and keeps up to date with best practice.

Some sections of Annexes I–III represent areas which overlap with more rigorous disclosure requirements for an AIM admission document under Sch.2 to the AIM Rules for Companies. In these cases, the LSE has maintained its existing higher standards. These relate to profit forecasts or estimates, directors' disclosures and working capital statements.

In addition, Sch.2 to the AIM Rules for Companies requires that an admission document must include certain additional information including a standard risk statement regarding AIM, a statement of compulsory 12-month lock-ins for directors and certain employees where the issuer's main activity is a business which has not been independent and earning revenue for at least two years, and details of its investing strategy where it is an investing company.

The Prospectus Rules contain a general requirement, that a prospectus must contain all information which is necessary to enable investors to make an informed assessment of the assets and liabilities, financial position, profits and losses, and prospects of the issuer (and of any guarantor) and of the rights attaching to the securities. However, there is arguably a more stringent general duty of disclosure under Sch.2 to the AIM Rules for Companies requiring the inclusion in the admission document (whether or not it constitutes a prospectus) of any other information which the applicant reasonably considers necessary to enable investors to form a full understanding of:

1. the assets and liabilities, financial position, profits and losses, and prospects of the applicant and its securities for which admission is being sought;
2. the rights attaching to those securities; and
3. any other matter contained in the admission document.

The FCA may authorise the omission of information from a prospectus on the grounds that its disclosure would be seriously detrimental to the issuer (provided that the omission would be unlikely to mislead the public with regard to any facts or circumstances which are essential for an informed assessment), or that the information is only of minor importance for a specific offer to the public or admission to trading and unlikely to influence an informed assessment. Where the admission document is not a prospectus, the LSE can, without FCA approval, authorise the omission of information in similar circumstances where the applicant's Nominated Adviser ("Nomad") confirms that those circumstances exist.

6.6 Filing and publication requirements

At least three business days before the expected date of admission, an applicant must submit to the LSE a completed application form and an electronic version of its admission document accompanied by a Nomad's declaration required by the AIM Rules for Nominated Advisers. If the admission document is a prospectus, the document must be approved by the FCA and then filed with the FCA and made available to the public (in the manner required by the Prospectus Rules (r.3.2.4)) as soon as practicable, and in any case at a reasonable time in advance of, and at the latest at the beginning of, the offer or the admission to trading of the securities involved.

6.7 Supplementary admission documents and withdrawal rights

If between the date of publication of the admission document and the date of admission of the company's shares to AIM, any material new factor, mistake or inaccuracy arises or is noted relating to the information contained in the admission document, a supplementary admission document containing details of the new factor, mistake or inaccuracy must be published. If the admission document is a prospectus, any supplementary document must comply with the Prospectus Rules in the same way as the prospectus. Under the Prospectus Rules, a supplementary prospectus must be submitted to the UKLA for approval as soon as practicable after the new factor, mistake or inaccuracy arose or was noted (r.3.4.3).

If the admission document is a prospectus and a supplementary prospectus has been published, a person who has agreed to buy or subscribe for securities may under s.87Q of the FSMA 2000 withdraw his acceptance within two working days after the publication of the supplementary prospectus or such later time specified in the supplementary prospectus. The right to withdraw acceptance of an offer only applies to an offer to the public and ends when the offer closes and the securities are delivered. It is worth noting that the FCA considers it to be best practice in offer situations for the offer to be suspended between the trigger event and the publication of a supplementary prospectus in certain circumstances e.g. in situations where securities are allotted immediately thereby preventing investors that have completed their purchase before the supplementary prospectus was published from benefitting from the withdrawal rights (see the UKLA Technical Note on supplementary prospectuses).

6.8 Further admission documents and secondary issues

A further admission document will be required for an AIM company only when it is:

1. required to issue a prospectus under the Prospectus Rules for a further issue of AIM quoted securities; or
2. seeking admission for a new class of securities; or
3. undertaking a reverse takeover.

There is an obligation on AIM companies to prepare and publish a prospectus (where an exemption is not available) in relation to open offers, rights issues and takeover offers where AIM securities are used as consideration.

As noted above, there is an exemption in relation to takeovers where a document is available containing information that is regarded by the FCA as being equivalent to that of a prospectus, but this tends not to make much difference in practice.

6.9 Responsibility for admission document

The Prospectus Rules set out the persons responsible for an approved prospectus (r.5.5). Those responsible include the directors of the issuer. Where the prospectus relates to non-equity securities, the Prospectus Rules do not expressly make the directors responsible. However, in practice they are likely to be responsible in their capacity as persons stated in the prospectus as having authorised the contents of the prospectus.

The Guidance Notes to the AIM Rules for Companies confirm that the persons responsible for the information provided in the admission document are the same persons that would be responsible for the information in a prospectus under the Prospectus Rules (Guidance Notes to Sch.2(a)). The admission document also needs to include a declaration of responsibility from those responsible for the document.

6.10 Liability

6.10.1 *Criminal liability*

Section 85(3) of the FSMA 2000 makes it a criminal offence for a person to offer transferable securities to the public in the UK unless an FCA-approved prospectus has been made available before the offer is made or an exemption from the requirement to publish a prospectus applies. Section 89 of the Financial Services Act 2012 (previously s.397 of the FSMA 2000) also imposes criminal liability on any person who: (i) makes a statement which he knows to be misleading or false in a material respect; (ii) recklessly makes a statement which is misleading or false in a material respect; or (iii) dishonestly conceals any material facts, for the purpose of inducing (or is reckless as to whether it may induce) another person to enter into or offer to enter into, a contract for the subscription or purchase of an investment.

6.10.2 Civil liability

Liability for the admission document can also arise under the civil offence of market abuse contained in ss.118–131 of the FSMA 2000. Under s.118(7) of the FSMA 2000, behaviour involving the dissemination of information which gives, or is likely to give, a false or misleading impression as to a qualifying investment traded (or for which a request for admission to trading has been made) on a prescribed market (including AIM) by a person who knew or could be reasonably expected to have known that the information was false or misleading is an offence.

Where market abuse is committed, the FCA may impose sanctions, but the enforceability of any contract is not affected. The sanctions include the imposition of a financial penalty, or the publication of a statement that the person concerned has engaged in market abuse.

Civil liability can also arise under common law. Those who suffer as a result of untrue or misleading statements and omissions in the admission document may be able either to claim damages or to rescind their contract. Directors and others who authorised the issue of the admission document may be liable at common law and under the Misrepresentation Act 1967 for a fraudulent or negligent misstatement made in the admission document.

6.11 Financial promotion

An admission document is exempt from the financial promotion regime whether or not it constitutes an approved prospectus. Any other communication which is published in conjunction with the marketing of an AIM company's securities, but which is not an admission document or a prospectus and is not otherwise required or permitted to be communicated by the AIM Rules for Companies will need to be approved by an authorised person for the purposes the financial promotion regime unless it falls within one or more of the exemptions contained in the Financial Services and Markets Act 2000 (Financial Promotion) Order 2005 (as amended) (e.g. communications to sophisticated investors).

6.12 Disclosure obligations

AIM companies incorporated in the UK must comply with Chapter 5 of the Disclosure Rules and Transparency Rules published by the FCA ("DTR"). Subject to certain exemptions, the DTR requires a person to notify the relevant issuer if the percentage of voting rights which he holds as shareholder or through his direct or indirect holdings of financial instruments reaches, exceeds or falls below three per cent or any whole percentage figure above three per cent. In addition, all AIM companies must comply with r.17 of the AIM Rules for Companies which requires disclosure of relevant changes to significant shareholders (being holders of any legal or beneficial interest, whether direct or indirect, of three per cent or more of any class of AIM security). Non-UK incorporated AIM companies which are not subject to the DTR are required to use all reasonable endeavours to comply with r.17, notwithstanding that the local law applicable to some AIM companies may not contain provisions similar to the DTR. Such AIM companies are advised, in the guidance notes to r.17, to include provisions in their constitutions requiring significant shareholders to notify the relevant company of any relevant changes to their shareholdings in similar terms to the DTR.

6.13 The future

AIM has now been in operation since 1995. In early 2014 the London Stock Exchange introduced further changes to the AIM Rules for Companies and AIM Rules for Nominated Advisers. However, none of these has altered the statutory framework under which AIM operates.

The European Commission has published a proposal to repeal the Market Abuse Directive (2003/6/EC) and replace it with a regulation on insider dealing and market manipulation and a directive on criminal sanctions for insider dealing and market manipulation. The regulation on insider dealing and market manipulation awaits final adoption. Once it has been approved, the UK will have 24 months to implement it into UK law. In February 2012, the Government announced that it had decided not to opt in to the Directive on criminal sanctions at present, although it hopes to opt in at a later stage, once the proposals are "better progressed".

Chapter 7

The Admission Document and the Application Procedure

Nick Davis

Partner, Memery Crystal LLP

Kieran Stone

Director, Memery Crystal LLP

7.1 Introduction

The process of applying for admission to AIM primarily seeks to ensure that the applicant company, its directors and management are prepared for life as a quoted company, that the company has a credible and robust business strategy going forward and that all material information about the company and its quoted securities is disclosed to the market.

This Chapter explains the legal, regulatory and other requirements and procedures which are involved in the admission process.

7.2 AIM Rules for Companies

The admission process is governed by the AIM Rules for Companies. Under these rules, (and save in certain circumstances dealt with elsewhere in this Chapter), new applicants are required to publish an admission document which complies with the content requirements set out in Sch.2 to the AIM Rules for Companies.

Schedule 2 to the AIM Rules for Companies requires an admission document to contain information equivalent to that which would be required by Annexes I, II and III of Regulation 809/2004 of the European Commission (known as the "PD Regulation" in the Financial Conduct Authority ("FCA") Handbook), as reprinted in the Prospectus Rules published by the FCA, other than the information specified in para.(b)(i) of Sch.2 and as amended by para.(b)(ii) of Sch.2. In addition, paras (c)–(k) of Sch.2 set out additional information which must also be included in the admission document.

In addition, a company may be required by s.85 of the Financial Services and Markets Act 2000 (the "FSMA 2000") to produce a prospectus. A prospectus must be approved by the FCA (acting in its capacity as the United Kingdom Listing Authority (the "UKLA")) and comply with the Prospectus Rules. In practice, if a company is required to produce both an admission document and a prospectus, it should produce a single document which meets the more stringent requirements of the Prospectus Rules. As the prospectus will also be an admission document, it must also contain the information specified in paras (c)–(k) of Sch.2 to the AIM Rules for Companies.

In the context of a company seeking admission of its securities to trading on AIM, a prospectus is required if a company offers its transferable securities to the public. There are a number of circumstances set out in s.86 of the FSMA 2000 where such an offer will be deemed to be an "exempt offer" and therefore no requirement to produce a prospectus will arise. These include where an offer is directed at "qualified investors" only, or at fewer than 150 persons, other than "qualified investors", per European Economic Area (EEA) state.

As a general guide, where an offer is made to a retail broker and then offered by that retail broker to its discretionary private clients, it is treated as having been made to one person for the purposes of establishing whether it is directed at more than 150 persons. It is therefore likely that for such offers, few companies will be required to produce a prospectus in connection with an application for admission to AIM.

Applicants must also comply with the various administrative procedures set out in the AIM Rules for Companies, including the payment of a fee and the submission to the London Stock Exchange ("LSE") of certain application forms and other information.

7.3   The Nomad and the broker

Under the AIM Rules for Companies, all new applicants must appoint a nominated adviser ("Nomad"). All AIM companies must retain a Nomad and a broker at all times (although often a company's Nomad will also act as the company's broker).

The LSE does not itself generally seek to vet applicants for admission to AIM and will not comment on the admission document. Instead, it seeks the assurances it requires from the company's Nomad who is responsible for assessing that the company and its directors have complied with the AIM Rules for Companies and that the company and its securities are suitable for admission to AIM. The role and responsibilities of the Nomad in connection with the admission process and its ongoing role are set out in the AIM Rules for Nominated Advisers, issued in February 2007. These rules impose a number of responsibilities on a Nomad to:

1. achieve a sound understanding of the applicant and its business by assessing the appropriateness of an application and its securities for AIM;
2. investigate and consider the suitability of each director and proposed director and the efficacy of the board as a whole for the company's needs;
3. oversee the due diligence process and be satisfied that any material issues arising from it are dealt with and do not otherwise affect the appropriateness of the application;
4. oversee and be actively involved in the preparation of the admission document, satisfying itself that it has been

prepared in compliance with the AIM Rules for Companies, with due verification; and

5.   satisfy itself that the applicant understands and has in place sufficient systems, procedures and controls to comply with the AIM Rules for Companies.

Therefore, the Nomad will effectively be acting as the company's regulator as well as adviser in relation to the admission process. In order to be able to give the required assurances to the LSE, the Nomad will need to seek its own assurances from the company and its directors and other professional advisers. It may also impose a number of additional requirements on the company and its directors beyond those set out in the AIM Rules for Companies.

Where admission is accompanied by a fundraising, the company's broker (if separate from the company's Nomad) may also impose its own additional requirements for the protection of its investors and the after-market in the company's shares.

On top of the requirements of the AIM Rules for Companies therefore, an applicant may need to comply with a number of additional requirements and procedures which have been developed by its advisers, partly by reference to the requirements for Main Market companies and partly by reference to general market practice, as a benchmark for ensuring best practice.

7.4   Initial steps

7.4.1   *Engagement letters*

The first step in the admission process will normally be for the new applicant to appoint, and sign engagement letters with its professional advisers, including reporting accountants, lawyers, printers, financial public relations advisers and its Nomad and broker. The engagement letters should confirm the fact that such advisers are acting on behalf of the company (as well as, in the case of the reporting accountants, the Nomad) and set out the scope of work that each party will undertake in the admission process and their estimated fees. Companies will usually seek to negotiate a reduced fee in the event that admission does not take place or any proposed fundraising is not completed and such an arrangement is usually complemented by an "uplift" on the quoted fee in the event the transaction is successful.

7.4.2 Administrative documents

Lists of parties and documents and a timetable will be produced at an early stage in the admission process, usually by the Nomad with input from the directors and other professional advisers. The timetable will act as a means of coordinating the activities of the various professional advisers and should assist the company's directors and advisers in prioritising their various commitments at different stages of the process.

7.5 Admission document

7.5.1 When is an admission document required?

An admission document is generally required for all new applicants, whether or not money is being raised on admission. However, unless a company is required to publish a prospectus under s.85 of the FSMA 2000, or is carrying out a transaction classed as a "reverse takeover" under the AIM Rules for Companies, it will not need to publish an admission document if it already has securities of the same class admitted to AIM.

Exemptions are also available for new applicants transferring from the Official List or whose securities (of the same class) are already listed on one of the other AIM Designated Markets. In practice, however, the Nomad or broker may, in any event, require some form of (modified) admission document or information memorandum for investors, particularly where there is to be a fundraising on admission.

The admission document must be available publicly, free of charge, for at least one month from the date of admission of the company's securities to AIM.

7.5.2 Content requirements – overview

Where an admission document is required, r.3 of the AIM Rules for Companies requires that it must disclose the information set out in Sch.2 to the AIM Rules for Companies. In practice, the document will typically be divided into sections relating broadly to:

1. a description of the company and its group, including its share capital, its business, assets and strategy, its directors, employees and organisational structure, its policies regarding corporate governance, its dividend policy, any fundraising and how the proceeds are to be applied and the group's current trading and prospects;
2. prominent disclosure of the risk factors which should be considered by investors when purchasing the company's securities;
3. historical financial information relating to the group – usually the last three years' audited accounts and where appropriate a pro forma statement of the group's net assets and liabilities; and
4. an additional information section setting out, amongst other things, the rights attaching to the company's securities, summaries of material contracts, material litigation, details of the directors' terms of engagement and directors' and major shareholders' interests in the company's securities, and details of any option schemes or warrants.

7.5.3 General duty of disclosure

There is a general duty of disclosure set out in Sch.2 which states that, in addition to any specific content requirement, an admission document must contain all such information as the company reasonably considers necessary to enable investors to form a full understanding of:

1. the assets and liabilities, financial position, profits and losses, and prospects of the issuer and its securities for which admission is being sought;
2. the rights attaching to those securities; and
3. any other matter contained in the admission document.

This catch-all provision means that, effectively, any information which might reasonably be considered to be material by a potential investor should be disclosed in the admission document and the company and/or the directors will typically be expected to warrant to the company's Nomad and broker (if separate) that this is the case at the point of admission (typically in the placing agreement).

7.5.4 *Equivalent information to the Prospectus Rules*

As discussed, the AIM Rules for Companies require an admission document to contain information equivalent to that which would be required by Annexes I–III of the Prospectus Rules (subject to certain carve-outs), unless a prospectus is required, in which case the document must comply fully with Annexes I–III of the Prospectus Rules. In all cases, the admission document will need to be carefully checked against the content requirements of the three annexes to ensure compliance. Among other things, an admission document must include the following:

1. prominent disclosure of risk factors specific to the group and its business or its industry;
2. description of any significant change in the financial or trading position of the group that has occurred since the last financial period or a negative statement that, since the date to which the last published audited financial information or interim financial information have been prepared, there has been no significant change in the group's financial or trading position;
3. information on the most significant recent trends since the end of the last financial year to the date of the admission

document and any known trends, uncertainties, commitments or events which are reasonably likely to have a
material effect on the issuer's prospects for at least the
current financial year; and

4. detailed information regarding the company's share capi-
    tal and the securities being offered and/or admitted to
    AIM, along with any dilution effects if a fundraising is
    being carried out.

7.5.5 *Additional specific content requirements*

Schedule 2 goes on to list a number of additional specific
content requirements, including:

1. a statement by the company's directors that, in their
    opinion, having made due and careful enquiry, the
    working capital available to the company and its group
    will be sufficient for its present requirements, that is for at
    least 12 months from the date of admission of its securities
    to AIM;
2. where the document contains a profit forecast, estimate or
    projection:
    (a) a statement from the directors that this has been made
        after due and careful enquiry;
    (b) a statement of the principal assumptions for each
        factor which could have a material effect on its
        achievement;
    (c) confirmation from the Nomad that it has satisfied
        itself that such statement has been made after due and
        careful enquiry by the directors; and
    (d) such profit forecast, estimate or projection must be
        prepared on a basis comparable with the historic
        financial information.
3. prominently and in bold on the first page, warnings to
    prospective investors that:
    (a) AIM is a market designed primarily for emerging or
        smaller companies to which a higher investment risk
        tends to be attached than to larger or more established
        companies;

(b) AIM securities are not admitted to the official list of the UKLA;

(c) a prospective investor should be aware of the risks of investing in such companies and should make the decision to invest only after careful consideration and, if appropriate, consultation with an independent financial adviser;

(d) each AIM company is required pursuant to the AIM Rules for Companies to have a Nomad. The Nomad is required to make a declaration to the LSE on admission in the form set out in Sch.2 to the AIM Rules for Nominated Advisers; and

(e) the LSE has not itself examined or approved the contents of the document.

4. where directors or other related parties or employees of a company are required to be "locked-in" under r.7 of the AIM Rules for Companies (for which see Chapter 2), a statement that the relevant persons agree not to dispose of their interests in the relevant securities for a period of at least 12 months from the date of admission. In practice, this statement will usually set out the full extent of any lock-in and orderly market restriction required by the Nomad or broker in addition to the lock-in requirements of the AIM Rules for Companies;

5. information relating to each director (including shadow directors) and proposed directors, including:

(a) their full name and age;

(b) the names of all companies and partnerships of which each has been a director or partner at any time in the past five years (including whether or not each appointment is current at the date of the admission document);

(c) any unspent convictions in relation to indictable offences;

(d) details of all bankruptcies or individual voluntary arrangements;

(e) details of any receiverships, compulsory liquidations, creditors' voluntary liquidations, administrations, company voluntary arrangements or any composition or arrangement with its creditors generally or any class of its creditors of any company where such director was a director at the time of or within 12 months preceding such events;

(f) details of any compulsory liquidations, administrations or partnership voluntary arrangements of any partnerships where such director was a partner at the time of, or within the 12 months preceding, such events;

(g) details of any receiverships of any asset of such director or of a partnership of which the director was a partner at the time of or within the 12 months preceding such events; and

(h) details of any public criticisms of such director by statutory or regulatory authorities (including recognised public bodies) and whether a director has ever been disqualified by a court from acting as a director or from acting in the management or conduct of the affairs of any company.

6. the name of any person (except for professional advisers disclosed in the admission document and trade suppliers) as well as the relationship of any such person to the company who either has received (directly or indirectly) within the 12 months preceding the application for admission, or has entered into contractual arrangements to receive (directly or indirectly) on or after admission fees, securities or other benefits in the company having a total value of £10,000 or more as well as details of such fees, securities or benefits;

7. the name of any director or member of a director's family who has a related financial product referenced to the company's AIM securities or securities being admitted, together with details of such financial product;

8. in the case of an investment company, details of its investment strategy;

9. the company's Nomad may also require specific additional information to be included in the admission document, which is not expressly required under the AIM Rules for Companies.

As long as it does not also constitute a prospectus, the LSE can authorise the omission of information from an admission document that would otherwise be required if the Nomad confirms that such information is minor or could be seriously detrimental to the company if disclosed and in either case is not likely to influence an investor's assessment of the company or its securities.

7.5.6 Public document

The admission document will, from the date of its publication, be a public document. An electronic version of the admission document must be sent to the LSE along with the completed application form (for further details see Section 7.17.2), and copies must be made available to the public, free of charge, at an address in the UK for a period of not less than one month from the date of admission.

There is no requirement under the AIM Rules for Companies to register a copy of the admission document with Companies House or with any other entity.

7.5.7 Display documents

The Nomad will often require the company to make certain documents referred to in the admission document available for inspection by investors. This will normally include the company's memorandum and articles of association (or equivalent documents), the directors' service contracts and letters of appointment, the last three years' statutory accounts and material contracts. Sometimes, it will not be possible or desirable to display a material contract due to confidentiality clauses, or for reasons of commercial sensitivity. There is no requirement under the AIM Rules for Companies to put any such documents on display and the Nomad may, therefore, agree to relax the requirement in appropriate cases, unless the admission document is a prospectus, in which case the company's memorandum and articles of association (or equivalent documents), historical financial information for the two preceding years and any documents prepared by an expert at the company's request and included or referred to in the admission document must be made available for inspection.

7.6 Legal considerations

7.6.1 *General*

It is the responsibility of the company and its directors to ensure that the admission document complies with all relevant legal and regulatory requirements, although the Nomad must itself asses the appropriateness of an applicant for AIM and confirm to the LSE that to the best of its knowledge and belief, having made due and careful enquiry, all requirements of the AIM Rules for Companies and AIM Rules for Nominated Advisers have been complied with. The AIM Rules for Companies also state that a company must ensure its directors accept full responsibility collectively and individually for its compliance with the AIM Rules for Companies and the disclosure without delay of all relevant information which is necessary for the company to comply with the AIM Rules for Companies. What these requirements are will, in part, depend upon:

1. whether or not the company is using the admission document to raise money; and
2. the number and nature of the proposed investors.

The relevant requirements and the potential liability for the company and its directors are summarised below and are more fully set out in Chapter 6.

7.6.2 *Financial promotion*

The admission document will normally constitute a financial promotion for the purposes of s.21 of the FSMA 2000. This means that it will need to be issued or approved by an "authorised person" under the FSMA 2000, such as the company's Nomad or broker, unless it constitutes an "exempt communication". In practice, exemptions will normally be available under the Financial Services and Markets Act 2000 (Financial Promotion) Order 2005 (SI 2005/1529) (the "Order") because the document is required to be published under the AIM Rules for Companies (art.68), or because it comprises a prospectus (art.72).

It should be noted that a "pathfinder" or similar draft of the admission document circulated to potential investors prior to admission, if not approved under s.21 of the FSMA 2000 will not fall within the exemption set out in art.68 of the Order and it is usual to rely on further exemptions contained in arts 19, 49 and 50 of the Order, relating to promotions to, respectively: "Investment Professionals"; "High Net-worth Individuals"; and "Sophisticated Investors".

7.6.3   Prospectus liability

If the admission document also constitutes a prospectus under the FSMA 2000, strict statutory liability (known as "prospectus liability") will apply where a person suffers loss as a result of any inaccuracy in, or omission from, a prospectus. Persons responsible for the prospectus (and so subject to such potential liability) include the company, its directors, the Nomad and any expert whose report is included in the prospectus.

7.6.4   Liability under general law

Even in the absence of prospectus liability, liability may still arise under general law. Claims may, for example, be brought for misrepresentation, negligence or deceit in circumstances where it can be demonstrated that an investor has suffered loss as a result of having relied upon an inaccurate or misleading statement in the admission document or other public documentation supporting the company's admission (i.e. any investor presentation).

7.6.5 Directors' responsibility statement

The admission document must include a declaration by the directors taking responsibility for the information contained in the document that, having taken all reasonable care to ensure that such is the case, the information contained in the admission document is, to the best of their knowledge, in accordance with the facts and contains no omission likely to affect its import.

Even in the absence of prospectus liability, it may be possible for investors to bring claims successfully against the directors in their personal capacity if the admission document is inaccurate or misleading.

7.6.6 Section 89 of the Financial Services Act 2012

In all cases, the requirements of s.89 of the Financial Services Act 2012 will be relevant. Under this section it is a criminal offence for a person (including a company and its directors) to make a statement, promise or forecast, which the person making it knows to be (or is reckless as to whether it will be) false or misleading in a material respect, or dishonestly conceals any material facts for the purpose of inducing (or being reckless as to whether making it or concealing it will induce) another person (whether or not the person to whom the statement is made) to enter into or offer to enter into, or to refrain from entering or offering to enter into, a relevant agreement, or to exercise, or refrain from exercising, any rights conferred by a relevant investment.

7.6.7 General

It is therefore crucial to ensure that, in all material respects, the admission document is fair, accurate and not misleading, whether or not it is being used in connection with a fundraising. The usual ways of seeking to ensure this is the case is for the company and its advisers to conduct comprehensive due diligence on the company and its subsidiaries and their business, financial position, prospects and risks and for the directors to satisfy themselves, again with the assistance of the company's advisers, that every statement in the admission document is true and accurate and, if necessary, can be independently verified and that they have not omitted information which ought to be disclosed.

7.7 Verification

In order to help ensure that the admission document is accurate and not misleading, the company's solicitors will assist the directors in an exercise to verify the information contained in the admission document. This verification process will normally be reviewed by the Nomad's lawyers. Depending on the nature of the admission/fundraising and the Nomad's individual requirements, the verification process will typically involve the preparation of a comprehensive set of notes which take the admission document and turn it into a series of statements and questions, the answers to which will both seek to confirm the accuracy of each statement of fact on a "line by line" basis; and to confirm that there are reasonable grounds for each statement of opinion contained in the admission document, where possible by reference to independent documentary evidence. Where a statement cannot be verified, the board may decide to alter or qualify that statement in the final admission document or delete it entirely. The verification notes and supporting documents may also later provide the directors with the basis for a defence against possible future claims that a statement which is later found to be incorrect was, at the time, made on reasonable grounds and in good faith.

Where costs and timing are a consideration (especially in relation to small fundraisings) it is common for a less stringent approach to be taken to verification with the process focusing on key statements of fact and opinion as opposed to a comprehensive "line by line" review.

7.8   Due diligence

7.8.1   *General*

Financial, accounting, commercial and legal due diligence will be conducted by the company's reporting accountants, Nomad and solicitors.

By convention, the Nomad has usually overseen the due diligence process. This responsibility now forms part of the AIM Rules for Nominated Advisers, which require a Nomad to oversee the due diligence process, satisfying itself that it is appropriate to the application and transaction and that any material issues arising do not affect the appropriateness of the company for admission to AIM. The Nomad is required to:

1.   be satisfied that appropriate financial and legal due diligence is undertaken by an appropriate professional firm(s);
2.   be satisfied that appropriate working capital and financial reporting systems and controls reviews are undertaken (usually including reports or letters from the reporting accountants to the company);
3.   consider whether commercial, specialist and/or technical due diligence is required and be satisfied that it is undertaken where required;
4.   agree the scope of all due diligence and reports (including assumptions and sensitivities); and
5.   review and assess all due diligence, reports and adviser comfort letters and be satisfied that all appropriate actions have been taken to resolve any matters or be satisfied that it does not affect the company's appropriateness for AIM.

7.8.2   *Financial due diligence*

The due diligence conducted by the reporting accountants will normally form the basis of long-form and short-form accountants' reports and reports on working capital and cash flow forecasts and the company's financial reporting systems and procedures, all of which will usually be addressed to the company and its Nomad.

The long-form report will take the form of a comprehensive financial and commercial analysis of the group and its business over a typical period of three years. It will focus on a number of areas, including internal management and structure, financial and risk control mechanisms, the market in which the group operates and the group's competitors. It will also highlight material risk factors relating to the group and its business which can then be brought to the attention of potential investors in the admission document.

The short-form report will usually contain the group's last three years' statutory audited accounts (or cover such shorter period that the group has been in operation) together with the auditors' reports thereon and notes relating thereto. This will be included in the admission document. The report includes an opinion by the reporting accountants as to whether or not, for the purposes for which it is prepared, it gives a true and fair view of the financial information set out in it.

The working capital report addresses the group's financial requirements for the 12 months following admission. This report will form the basis of the directors' working capital confirmation in the admission document.

7.8.3   Commercial due diligence

The Nomad and broker (if separate) will conduct their own commercial assessments in relation to the group and its business in order to gauge what value investors are likely to attach to the company's securities and whether or not the company is appropriate for admission to AIM. Guidance as to what steps a Nomad should take in assessing the appropriateness of a company for AIM is set out in Sch.3 to the AIM Rules for Nominated Advisers.

The Nomad will also send each director a personal questionnaire which focuses on the matters referred to at Section 7.5.5 point (5) above.

7.8.4 *Legal due diligence and title opinions*

The purpose of the legal due diligence exercise will be to examine the core assets comprising the group's business and discover whether any steps need to be taken to prepare the group or its structure in connection with admission, and to elicit relevant information for the purpose of drafting the additional information section of the admission document. Moreover, any key risks or liabilities unearthed in the legal due diligence report (e.g. invalid patents, licences or major litigation) could question the valuation or indeed the whole basis for the proposed flotation.

In addition and, specifically with regard to resource companies, it is common for a Nomad in conducting the legal due diligence exercise to request that the company provide a suitable legal opinion (to be prepared by local lawyers in each relevant jurisdiction) examining its title to its assets (i.e. licences conferring exploration and/or production rights) and the consequential obligations and requirements arising from such rights, binding the members of the group in the local jurisdiction in which it operates. Accordingly the title opinion will often be used to supplement and support the competent person's report.

The company's solicitors will normally send a legal due diligence questionnaire to the company's directors tailored to reflect the nature of the group and its business and assets and may then be asked to compile a report addressed to the company and its Nomad based upon the company's responses. Depending on the nature of the transaction, the report may be fairly informal, focusing only on issues for resolution or key elements of the transaction (i.e. an "exceptions only" report). Alternatively the report may be comprehensive and, depending on the nature of the group's business, further specific reports may also be required, such as reports on title relating to the company's properties, a patent report from the company's patent agent or an independent patent agent, and counsel's opinion on material litigation affecting the company. The Nomad's lawyer will review this due diligence report and actively contribute to the due diligence process to ensure that the Nomad is satisfied from a "suitability" point of view.

7.8.5 *Competent person's and specialist reports*

Pursuant to the guidance note for mining, oil and gas companies issued in June 2009 by the LSE, a resource company is expected to include in any admission document a competent person's report ("CPR") setting out all material assets and liabilities of the applicant. The CPR should be prepared by a professionally qualified member in good standing of an appropriate recognised professional association of engineers and/or geoscientists who, amongst other requirements, is independent of the company, its directors and advisers and has at least five years' relevant experience in estimation, assessment and evaluation of the resource.

In certain other circumstances, the Nomad may require the company to obtain an independent expert's report on its business or market or technology. This is particularly likely to apply to companies operating in specialist fields such as biotechnology and the Nomad may wish such a report to be disclosed to investors in the admission document.

It should be noted that pursuant to Annex I of the Prospectus Rules, all persons responsible for information given in the admission document (including the CPR or any other specialist report) should take responsibility in the admission document for such information and confirm that it is in accordance with the facts and does not omit anything likely to affect the import of such information.

7.9 Financial and accounting procedures

7.9.1 Working capital

The board will be responsible for compiling working capital and cash flow forecasts, usually for a longer period (such as 18 or 24 months) than the 12 months working capital statement required to be made in the admission document.

7.9.2 Financial reporting procedures

A review by the reporting accountants of the group's financial reporting systems and controls will be of particular relevance where the company is raising new money. In any event, however, the AIM Rules for Nominated Advisers require the Nomad to ensure that the company has appropriate financial reporting systems and control procedures in place.

7.9.3 Forecasts and projections

Where the admission document is to contain a profit forecast, estimate or projection, the assumptions on which this is based will need to be reviewed by the reporting accountants and disclosed in the admission document along with a confirmation from the directors that such profit forecast, estimate or projection has been made after all due and careful enquiry. There is no formal requirement under the AIM Rules for Companies for the report of the reporting accountants on such matters to be disclosed (as there is under the Prospectus Rules). The Nomad will be required to confirm in the admission document that it has satisfied itself that the forecast, estimate or projection has been made after due and careful enquiry by the directors and will normally, as a minimum, require a report to be compiled and addressed to them. Companies are usually advised not to include profit forecasts in the admission document on the grounds that investors may bring claims, or the company's share price may suffer, where these are not fulfilled. This advice can however present a dilemma for a very young company with no financial track record but potentially impressive growth prospects.

7.9.4 Indebtedness

Unless the admission document also constitutes a prospectus, there is no express requirement under the AIM Rules for Companies to include a statement in the admission document relating to the group's indebtedness. The Nomad will, however, often require a review to be undertaken by the reporting accountant of the group's loan capital, term loans and other borrowings, commitments and obligations (e.g. under hire purchase contracts) as part of the due diligence process, and for the reporting accountants to report on this in the long-form report and/or by way of a separate report. Obviously, indebtedness will be one of the factors that contribute to the valuation.

7.9.5 No material adverse change

The company and its directors will often be required to provide the Nomad with written comfort that they are not aware that there has been any material adverse change in the group's financial position or prospects since the date of its last audited accounts, save as disclosed in the admission document; and the admission document itself must contain details of any significant change in the group's financial or trading position which has occurred since the end of the last financial period, or an appropriate negative statement. This opinion will normally be based on monthly management accounts produced in respect of this period, as well as on the general awareness of the directors.

7.9.6 Taxation

The admission document should contain information relating to tax on income from the securities withheld at source, along with an indication as to whether the company assumes responsibility for such withholding. Additionally, although not expressly required by the AIM Rules for Companies, the admission document will usually include a section on taxation generally. This will generally, among other things, summarise the UK tax position on holding and selling shares, including liability to chargeable gains and stamp duty and in respect of dividends. It may also include a section relating to taxation of overseas shareholders which a taxation specialist will need to draft or review.

7.10   Legal restructuring

7.10.1 General

A number of different issues may arise out of the legal due diligence exercise, and these will require attention before admission. The following are some of the most common.

7.10.2   Re-registration as a public company

A private company incorporated in England and Wales will need to be re-registered as a public limited company prior to admission. Where the company fails to meet the share capital or net asset requirements set out in the Companies Act 2006 ("CA 2006") re-registration will not be permitted. It will instead be necessary to incorporate a new public holding company and effect a group reorganisation, usually by way of a share-for-share exchange, with the new public company acquiring the existing trading company.

7.10.3   De-merger

It may be desirable for part of the group's business to be de-merged or "hived off" prior to admission. This may be the case where, for example, the group owns a business which represents a non-core activity, or which would not be suited to a company admitted to AIM, or which would not be of interest to investors. It will be important, however, to ensure that any arrangements put in place for future relations between such businesses avoid potential conflicts of interests and are entered into on an arm's-length basis.

7.10.4   *Termination rights and consents*

The company may have entered into banking facility arrangements and other material contracts, under which consent requirements or termination rights arise on a flotation or an issue of new shares. This may require consents or waivers to be obtained, or even a refinancing to be effected, prior to admission.

7.10.5   *Shareholders' agreements*

The company's shareholders may have entered into a shareholders' agreement with the company. Any such agreement will need to be terminated prior to admission, unless termination will occur automatically in accordance with its terms.

7.11   Shareholder resolutions

It will often be necessary for the company to seek the approval of its shareholders for a variety of matters prior to admission. Such shareholder resolutions may be passed in advance and made conditional upon admission taking place by a certain date.

Shareholders may need to allot and authorise the directors to issue new shares to investors free from pre-emption rights.

A capital reorganisation may sometimes be required in order to ensure that the opening price of the company's shares on admission is at a level which will assist liquidity in the shares. This may involve a consolidation, share split or a bonus issue of shares.

It will also often be necessary to alter the company's articles of association, or for the company to adopt a new set of articles of association. These should be suitable for a public company admitted to AIM, and should allow for the holding of shares in dematerialised form and for shares to be traded electronically via the CREST system. In particular, any provision hindering free transfer of shares under the articles would have to be changed.

In the case of companies not subject to The City Code on Takeovers and Mergers (the "Code") it may also be necessary to amend the company's articles of association to include provisions comparable to those that would otherwise be offered to shareholders of companies that would be subject to the code, although the effectiveness of such provisions is debatable.

It may be possible for some companies to pass written resolutions signed by all shareholders, or to hold a general meeting on short notice (usually requiring the written consent of the holders of 95 per cent in nominal value of the company's ordinary shares). Otherwise, the admission timetable will need to allow for a meeting to be held on the requisite notice (being 21 clear days in respect of a meeting which is the annual general meeting and 14 clear days for any other general meeting).

7.12   Employee share schemes

Companies will often want to set up executive and/or employee share schemes or share option schemes prior to admission. Consideration will need to be given at an early stage as to which form of scheme is most appropriate, having regard to the jurisdiction of the applicant and any applicable tax advantages and administrative considerations. If the approval of HM Revenue and Customs ("HMRC") is required for an approved scheme, then allowance may need to be made for this in the timetable. The extent to which HMRC are willing to approve an exercise price which is less than the share price on admission may also depend on the length of the period between the date on which the options are granted and the date of admission. The Nomad should be consulted as to the numbers of options to be granted, both on and following admission, and as to the exercise price. Investors will want to be able to identify the maximum level of dilution arising from share options and the circumstances (e.g. are there performance criteria?).

7.13 The board and corporate governance

In addition to its obligations under the CA 2006 (or for companies incorporated outside of England & Wales, any applicable legislation) and the AIM Rules for Companies, there are two further indicative sources of corporate governance that have been prepared for AIM companies:

- the Corporate Governance Code for Small and Mid-Size Quoted Companies published by the Quoted Companies Alliance (QCA) in May 2013; and
- the Corporate Governance and Voting Guidelines for Smaller Companies published by the National Association of Pension Funds (NAPF) in December 2012.

In addition, although the UK Corporate Governance Code (the "UK Code") does not strictly apply to AIM quoted companies, the company's Nomad will generally want the company to have regard to the UK Code as a means of reflecting "best practice".

The admission document must contain a statement as to whether or not the company complies with its country of incorporation's corporate governance regime(s). In the event that the company does not comply with such a regime, a statement to that effect must be included together with an explanation regarding why the company does not comply with such regime.

For companies incorporated in England and Wales it is usual to see a broad qualification in the admission document that the company complies with the UK Code in so far as is considered practical, having regard to its size and resources.

Consideration will need to be given as to the balance of the board, in terms of numbers of executive and non-executive directors and as to the role of the latter in relation to various board committees, including audit, remuneration and nomination committees. The board will need to consider whether it has adopted appropriate systems to control and manage risk internally and with its customers and suppliers. The company should seek guidance from its Nomad in each case. Where new non-executive directors are to be appointed, it will be important to identify them and include them in the admission process at an early stage, so that they are able to become familiar with the group and its business, since they will be jointly responsible for the admission document.

7.14   Placing agreement

If the company is intending to raise money on admission, then one of the documents required will be a placing or underwriting agreement. This will normally be entered into by the company's directors, as well as the company, with the Nomad and its broker (if separate). It will usually be prepared by the solicitors acting for the Nomad and broker.

The principal purpose of the placing agreement is to provide the Nomad with the comfort it needs to make its declaration to the LSE, and the broker with the authority and comfort it requires to place shares in the company with its placees. The broker will then agree to use its reasonable endeavours to procure such placees and, in the case of an underwritten fundraising, itself to subscribe for any shares not so placed.

Underwriting usually occurs where shares are also being offered to the company's existing shareholders by way of a rights issue or open offer, as the company may then want the comfort that the fundraising is guaranteed once the admission document or prospectus has been published, whatever the level of take-up by shareholders under such an offer. Underwriting on admissions to AIM is unusual given the high cost and risks involved in underwriting (and sub-underwriting), a more common alternative is to make the offer to shareholders conditional upon a successful placing with institutional and other placees procured by the broker, or structure the offer as a placing, subject to claw-back to satisfy acceptances under the offer.

The placing agreement will include a series of undertakings in favour of the Nomad and broker relating to the conduct of the group's business going forward which are designed to protect the Nomad in its role of de facto regulator and the broker and its placees in the after-market. However, some or all of these may instead be incorporated into a separate Nomad and broker agreement, which will also be entered into prior to admission (see Chapter 3 Section 3.9, and Chapter 5 Section 5.4.8 of this Guide).

The company and its directors will normally be required to give representations and warranties in favour of the Nomad and the broker which relate to the accuracy and completeness of the admission document and the quality of the information contained in that document.

There will also be a broad indemnity in favour of the Nomad and the broker in respect of any losses which they may suffer (e.g. where placees bring a claim against them). Normal carve-outs will include where the Nomad or the broker (if separate) have been negligent, acted in bad faith or in breach of the conduct of business rules of the FCA. Some Nomads will require an indemnity from both the company and its directors and some from only the company.

A key negotiating issue will often be the level of any "cap" on warranty or indemnity liability, and what other limitations should apply to the directors' and company's liability under the agreement. As a matter of current market practice, executive directors' liability will often be capped by reference to a multiple of between two to four times their annual salary or fee from the company. Where higher levels of liability are agreed, directors may wish to arrange to put in place warranty and indemnity insurance (usually at the cost of the company).

The responsibilities of the Nomad and the broker under the placing agreement will often remain conditional upon a number of factors, including there having been no material breach of the warranties prior to admission and the company not being required under the AIM Rules for Companies to publish a supplemental admission document. The Nomad and the broker will also normally have the right to terminate the agreement in certain circumstances, such as in the case of a force majeure event occurring prior to admission. These are hardly ever invoked.

The Nomad's and broker's fees and commissions for the placing (and any underwriting commitment) will also be dealt with in the placing agreement. There will often be a fixed corporate finance fee payable to the Nomad, plus a variable commission payable to the broker based upon the amount raised in the fundraising (often excluding amounts raised from investors introduced by the board). These may often be supplemented by an option or warrant granted or issued to the broker to subscribe for shares at the placing price following admission.

Where existing shareholders are selling shares as part of a placing, they will usually also be parties to the placing agreement, so as to authorise the broker to sell their shares. They will generally also be required to give limited warranties, principally relating to title to their shares and their ability to sell. Stamp duty and commissions will usually be deducted by the broker from the sale proceeds.

The lock-in provisions set out in r.7 of the AIM Rules for Companies are often supplemented or increased in their scope by additional lock-in requirements of the Nomad and the broker (often extending the lock-in period beyond one year and/or extending to persons not required to be locked in under the AIM Rules for Companies) to ensure an orderly market for the securities post admission. Such lock-in arrangements may be included in the placing agreement or, where the scope of the lock-in extends beyond the directors of the company, set out in separate lock-in agreements entered into with the company and its Nomad and the broker.

7.15   Directors' documents

7.15.1   General

The company's directors will be required to sign a number of documents reflecting their responsibility for the admission document and for managing the company's affairs following admission. Under its obligations under the AIM Rules for Nominated Advisers the Nomad will need to satisfy itself that the directors have been properly advised of their responsibilities and that they have conducted a thorough review of the admission document and all underlying documents. Normally the Nomad will attend a formal briefing given by the company's solicitors to the board in this regard.

7.15.2   Responsibility memorandum and statements

The company's solicitors will advise the directors generally as to their responsibilities and continuing obligations as directors of a public company admitted to trading on AIM. This advice will usually be given by reference to a memorandum setting out such responsibilities and obligations, including relevant areas of civil and criminal liability. The Nomad will need to confirm to the LSE that the directors have received such advice and guidance and will, therefore, usually require some form of written comfort from the company's solicitors that this is the case, usually in the form of a confirmation to the Nomad that they have given the directors appropriate legal advice on the AIM Rules for Companies and in relation to their responsibilities as directors and that, having done so, they are not aware that the admission document excludes any information which it is required to contain under the AIM Rules for Companies. The Nomad will also usually require each director to sign a responsibility letter addressed to it and the company acknowledging that he has read and understood the memorandum and that he takes responsibility for the information contained in the admission document and for the other documents connected with admission.

7.15.3 Dealing rules

In addition to the restrictions imposed under insider dealing and market abuse legislation (for which see Chapter 12 Section 12.9 and Chapter 6 Section 6.10 of this Guide), directors and employees who hold shares in the company are required under the AIM Rules for Companies to adhere to strict dealing restrictions (similar, in part, to those under the Model Code in the Listing Rules), which provide, among other things, that they may not deal in shares in the company during a "close" period of two months prior to publication of the company's interim and final results or when the company is in possession of unpublished price-sensitive information. Further details of these restrictions are set out in Chapter 9 of this Guide.

7.15.4 Service agreements

As part of the due diligence exercise, the Nomad will review the existing service agreements and levels of remuneration and benefits of the directors, and the notice periods which apply on termination. Changes may need to be made, for example to ensure that the agreements contain enforceable restrictive covenants preventing the directors from competing with or soliciting employees from the group. The Nomad may also want to review the letters of appointment of non-executive directors.

7.15.5 Board meetings

The board of directors of the company will not only have to approve the admission document, but also all of the other key documents relating to the application for admission. Detailed board minutes will need to be prepared for this purpose to ensure that each document is considered carefully and that the directors are fully aware of their individual and collective responsibilities. Board meetings will also need to be held to approve any pathfinder or placing proofs of the admission document and any circular sent to shareholders. The board will often appoint a committee of directors at the pathfinder stage to finalise all documentation, approve the allotment of any new shares on admission and complete the admission process on behalf of the board.

7.15.6 *Powers of attorney*

The directors will usually be required to grant powers of attorney authorising any of their co-directors (or another suitable person) to sign on their behalf any document required for admission. In addition to stating that the power of attorney is given with regard to a company's proposed admission to AIM, the powers of attorney will usually list (on a non-exclusive basis) the main documents which will need to be signed by the directors and give a general power relating to any other ancillary documents required to be signed in relation to admission. Authority may also be given to allow non-substantive amendments to be made to those documents already reviewed by the directors. The giving of a power of attorney means that admission need not be delayed due to the absence of any director.

Such powers of attorney, whilst typically being irrevocable, usually expire around three months after the date on which they are given. It is also usual for the director to indemnify any attorney for any action properly taken by such attorney in the director's name pursuant to the authority set out in the power of attorney.

Powers of attorney may also be sought from existing shareholders proposing to sell their shares as part of the fundraising on admission. These will facilitate the execution of placing agreements and share transfer forms as required to effect the sale of their shares.

7.16 Financial public relations

A public relations ("PR") agency will sometimes be appointed by the company, initially to help ensure that presentations to potential investors run smoothly, as well as releasing announcements to the LSE and the media, and generally dealing with the press. Following admission, the PR agency will make announcements on behalf of the company and distribute these as appropriate to the LSE, media and analysts. The PR agency will also help the company form relationships with the media, analysts and the City in general.

7.17 Application

7.17.1 Ten-day announcement

A company seeking admission of new shares must notify the LSE of certain matters (set out in Sch.1 to the AIM Rules for Companies) at least 10 business days prior to the expected date of admission. These matters include, inter alia:

1. the name, address/registered office and country of incorporation of the company;
2. the website address at which the information required by r.26 of the AIM Rules for Companies will be available;
3. a brief description of its business (or in the case of an investing company, details of its investment strategy);
4. the number and nature of the securities (including details of any treasury shares) and the amount of any fundraising occurring with admission;
5. the percentage of AIM securities not in public hands on admission;
6. the full names and functions of all directors (including any shadow and proposed directors);
7. insofar as is known, the name of any person who is interested directly or indirectly in three per cent or more of the company's securities before and after admission, together with the percentage of such interest; and
8. the name and address of the Nomad and the broker.

If any of the details above alter, then the company must advise the LSE immediately.

7.17.2 Three-day announcement

The company must then submit to the LSE not fewer than three business days prior to the expected date of admission:

1. An application (together with an electronic version of the admission document). The application contains various declarations from the company relating to working capital, any profit forecast made in the admission document, the company's financial procedures and other such matters. It will be signed by a duly authorised officer of the company.
2. A Nomad declaration. The Nomad will sign a declaration (to be submitted with the application form and electronic version of the admission document) confirming its appointment and also that the directors have received guidance as to the nature of their responsibilities and obligations, that to the best of their knowledge and belief all relevant requirements of the AIM Rules for Companies have been complied with and that they are satisfied that in their opinion, the company and its securities are "appropriate" to be admitted to AIM. The required contents of this declaration are set out in Sch.2 of the AIM Rules for Nominated Advisers. The Nomad is likely to seek supporting comfort from the company's directors, solicitors and reporting accountants.
3. Admission fees and ongoing charges will also be invoiced to the company at the time the three-day announcement is made.

7.17.3 Admission

Admission of the company's securities to trading on AIM will become effective on the publication of a dealing notice by the LSE.

7.18 Costs and timing

The costs involved in applying for admission will depend on a number of different factors, such as whether any new money is being raised on admission (and how much), the specific complexities which may arise during the process and the fees agreed by the company with its advisers.

An estimate of expenses will be compiled by the Nomad to cover all fees and commissions of advisers, printers and the LSE. The total will need to be approved by the board prior to the issue of the admission document (and will form the basis of the "net of expenses" figure in that document in relation to any fundraising). Regard must be had to VAT, some of which will be irrecoverable on a fundraising.

7.19 Conclusion

The whole of the admission process will generally take around three to four months, although if a prospectus is required then additional time to reflect the increased level of disclosure required and to obtain the UKLA's approval of the document should be factored into the timetable. Much will depend on the extent to which material issues arise out of the accounting and legal due diligence investigations into the company and its subsidiaries and their business. The admission process will generally involve a great deal of management time, in particular from the directors, and provision should be made for this at the outset so as to ensure that the process runs smoothly and without unnecessarily disrupting the company's business.

Chapter 8

Continuing Obligations and Transactions

Craig Lukins

Assistant Director, Deloitte LLP

8.1   Introduction

In contrast to most of the other Chapters of this Guide, which concentrate on pre-flotation issues, this Chapter deals exclusively with post-flotation matters. Once the applicant's shares have been admitted to AIM, there are numerous continuing obligations with which the company must comply. These include ongoing, day-to-day obligations such as disclosure of financial and price-sensitive information as well as rules governing transactions and further share issues.

8.2   Announcements

Information that is required to be disclosed by the AIM Rules for Companies must be notified to a Regulatory Information Service ("RIS") provider for release to the market. An AIM company must retain a RIS provider to ensure that information can be notified as and when required. In order to ensure that this obligation can be discharged at all times, an AIM company should consider enabling its Nomad and/or broker to notify information to a RIS on its behalf. Information must be released through the RIS without delay and no later than it is published elsewhere. A list of organisations authorised by the Financial Conduct Authority ("FCA") to provide regulatory disclosure services for listed companies and who have agreed to provide comparable services to AIM companies is shown in the AIM section of London Stock Exchange Plc's ("LSE") website, *www.londonstockexchange.com/companies-andadvisors/aim/ publications/forms/forms.htm.*

An AIM company must take reasonable care to ensure that any information it notifies to a RIS is not misleading, false or deceptive and does not omit anything likely to affect the import of such information.

It is presumed that information notified through a RIS is required by the AIM Rules for Companies or other legal or regulatory requirements. Any information that is notified to a RIS may be deemed to be price-sensitive. "Drip-feeding" of non-price-sensitive information into the marketplace via RIS announcements is actively discouraged by the LSE. Certain RIS providers, such as the LSE's RNS Reach service, offer AIM companies alternative information platforms on which to notify information that is not considered price-sensitive but might otherwise be of interest to the market.

Information which is notified to a RIS should be transmitted via electronic link. Advice on formatting regulatory announcements can be obtained on the LSE's website. Other than routine announcements, notifications should include the Nomad's name and a contact name.

When notifying information to a RIS, AIM companies should follow the Regulatory News Service Guidelines published by the LSE.

All notifications to a RIS made by an AIM company in the preceding 12 months must be available on its website. Any document provided by an AIM company to the holders of its AIM securities within the last 12 months must also be made available on its website and its provision notified to a RIS. An electronic copy of the document must be sent to the LSE.

All admission documents, documents sent to shareholders and any information required by the AIM Rules for Companies must be in English.

8.3 General disclosure obligations

8.3.1 *Price-sensitive information*

An AIM company must notify a RIS without delay of any new developments concerning a change in its financial condition, sphere of activity, business performance, expectation of performance or any other matter which are not public knowledge and, if made public, would be likely to lead to a significant movement in the price of its AIM securities.

An AIM company need not notify a RIS about impending developments or matters in the course of negotiation but must ensure it has effective procedures in place to ensure the confidentiality of unpublished price sensitive information and minimise the risk of a leak. It may give this information in confidence prior to any announcement to certain parties including its advisers, representatives of its employees or trade unions acting on their behalf and statutory or regulatory bodies or authorities.

However, in all cases, the AIM company must be satisfied that such confidants are aware that they must not trade in its AIM securities before the relevant information is announced.

If the AIM company has reason to believe that a breach of confidence has occurred or is likely to occur, it must notify a RIS with at least a warning announcement to the effect that it expects shortly to release information which may lead to a significant movement in the price of its AIM securities.

Where such information has been made public, the AIM company must notify that information to a RIS without delay, notwithstanding the fact that a RIS should be provided with all announcements before they are published elsewhere.

In relation to business performance, whether or not an announcement is required is not always clear. There are a number of factors to consider, but these may include significant differences between actual or expected business performance compared to market expectations.

An AIM company and its Nomad should ensure that they are aware of any research analysis published on the AIM company, whether by its retained broker or by any other party. For AIM companies where there is no published research, market expectations can be difficult to determine. Factors to consider in these cases include the impression conveyed in general press comment regarding the future trading results of the AIM company, as well as commentary included in interim and annual reports and trading statements issued by the AIM company.

Both the AIM company and its Nomad should regularly review the actual trading performance and financial condition of the AIM company against such market expectations. Regular discussions with management about business performance can help the Nomad to achieve this.

Similar disclosure obligations apply in relation to material changes against an AIM company's own profit forecasts, if any: see Section 8.3.2 below.

If an announcement is required, it should be released without delay. The LSE has expressly stated that negative trading updates should not be delayed in the belief that trading performance will improve in the short term or that an AIM company will shortly be in a position to announce other positive news at the same time. It is worth noting that many of the public censures issued by the LSE cite details of notifications that have been issued after an inappropriate delay, no notification issued when the situation required one, or notifications that were misleading or false.

Information that is required to be notified to a RIS must not be given to anyone else (except as set out above in relation to ongoing negotiations) before it has been so notified. Where potentially price-sensitive information is to be announced at a meeting of holders of the company's AIM securities, arrangements must be made for that information to be notified to a RIS no later than the announcement is made to the meeting. This is to ensure that equal information is available to all market participants and that all parties are made aware of this new information, even if they have not attended the relevant meeting.

If an AIM company makes progressive updates about a matter yet to be concluded, it should take care that a misleading impression of the status of the matter is not given. The sequence of events that needs to occur before conclusion of the matter should be set out. An AIM company should be mindful of information previously disclosed to the market, in particular any forthcoming deadlines or anticipated completion dates, and update the market accordingly.

Nomads are also expected to monitor their AIM clients' share prices and trading volumes, especially when there are forthcoming announcements to be made, and should have draft holding announcements prepared in advance. The LSE may contact the Nomad if an AIM company's share price moves significantly over a short period and the movement appears unusual in the context of general market or sector movements. In such cases, the LSE may ask the AIM company and its advisers to consider whether any announcement is necessary under the AIM Rules for Companies. The Panel on Takeovers and Mergers (the "Panel") also monitors share price movements of companies in takeover scenarios and may also ask the AIM company and its advisers to explain the likely reason for a share price movement or unusual trading volumes in the AIM company's securities and request that an appropriate announcement be made through a RIS.

8.3.2 Material change

A material change between an AIM company's actual trading performance or financial condition and any profit forecast, estimate or projection, which has been included in an admission document or otherwise made public on the company's behalf, should be notified to a RIS. As with the general obligations regarding announcements of changes in business performance set out above, one of the responsibilities of the Nomad is to regularly review the actual trading performance and financial condition against any such profit forecast, estimate or projection in order to help the AIM company to determine whether such an announcement is necessary.

In practice, it can be difficult to assess the likelihood of a material change since shortfalls in the short term may be rectified in the medium term, so the directors' assessment of future results may be as important as historical management information. As a general rule, a deviation of more than 10 per cent from previously published indications could be regarded as a material change for these purposes, but also see Section 8.3.1 above for a discussion of similar matters.

8.3.3 Significant share interests

Under the AIM Rules for Companies, an AIM company must notify a RIS without delay of any relevant changes to any significant shareholders, disclosing the information specified in Schedule 5 to the AIM Rules for Companies. For this purpose, relevant changes are changes to the holding of a significant shareholder of three per cent (excluding treasury shares) or more which increase or decrease such holding through any single percentage.

For UK registered AIM companies, certain provisions in the Disclosure and Transparency Rules (the "DTRs") of the FCA and the Companies Act 2006 ("CA 2006") also apply. AIM companies complying with the DTRs will usually also satisfy the significant shareholder disclosure obligations under the

AIM Rules for Companies. Two notable differences, however, are that the AIM Rules for Companies require the information to be "notified" (see Section 8.2 above) rather than "made public" and also require notification "without delay".

Chapter 5 of the DTRs requires that where a person knows that he has acquired or ceased to have a material interest of 3 per cent or more in the voting rights of the AIM company, or already has 3 per cent or more of the AIM company's voting rights and he increases or reduces his interest across one full percentage point, then he must inform the AIM company within two business days. The 3 per cent threshold relating to the voting rights of the AIM company excludes any votes attaching to treasury shares.

AIM companies not registered in the UK should use their reasonable endeavours to comply with the significant shareholder disclosure requirements of the AIM Rules for Companies. If local securities laws do not place equivalent requirements on shareholders to disclose to the company changes in their holdings, an AIM company should consider establishing suitable disclosure requirements in its constitutional documents.

If an AIM company, irrespective of the location of its registered office, becomes aware of a change in a significant interest which should have been disclosed to it under the DTRs or AIM Rules for Companies, details must be notified to a RIS as soon as possible. An AIM company should endeavour to ensure that an appropriate announcement is released without delay.

In order to enable shareholders to calculate whether they have a notification obligation, UK registered AIM companies are required under the DTRs to announce the number of voting rights attaching to each class of issued shares at the end of each month in which there has been a change. AIM companies must also announce acquisitions of their own shares, the number of shares they are holding in treasury and disposals of treasury shares.

8.3.4 Directors' dealings

Details of any changes to the interests that the directors of an AIM company and their families (as defined in the AIM Rules for Companies) have in the AIM securities must be notified to a RIS without delay, disclosing, insofar as it has such information, the information specified in Schedule 5 to the AIM Rules for Companies. In practice this disclosure must be made by the end of the business day following notification of the change.

The duty of disclosure extends to any dealing (including the grant, acceptance, acquisition, disposal, exercise or discharge) by a director and his family in any option or related financial product relating to the AIM company's securities, or any interest in such option or related financial product.

8.3.5 Board changes

An AIM company must notify a RIS of the resignation or dismissal of any director, or the appointment of any new director, giving the date of such occurrence. In the case of an appointment, the AIM company is required to disclose the information about the new director as set out in Schedule 2(g) to the AIM Rules for Companies. This information includes:

1. the director's full name and age, together with any previous names;
2   current and past (within five years) directorships and partnerships held;
3. details of any events such as receiverships or compulsory liquidations of any company or partnership where the director was a director or partner at the time or in the 12 months preceding such events;
4. details of any public criticisms, censures, unspent convictions and disqualifications from being a director. If, after a director's appointment, there is a change in the details disclosed in relation to unspent convictions, public criticisms, disqualifications or the disclosures required by point 3 above, these must be notified to a RIS; and
5. any shareholding in the AIM company.

8.3.6 *Change of Nomad or broker*

An AIM company must notify a RIS of the resignation, dismissal or appointment of its Nomad or broker. If an issuer ceases to have a Nomad the LSE will suspend trading in its securities. If an AIM company becomes aware that it is likely to cease to have a Nomad it should liaise with the LSE prior to notifying a RIS so that where no replacement has been appointed the necessary suspension may be put in place to coincide with the announcement. If a replacement Nomad is not appointed within one month of suspension, trading will be cancelled. It is therefore advisable for AIM companies to establish an appropriate period of notice on the engagement of a Nomad, for example at least one month, in order to allow sufficient time to find a replacement and thus avoid the potential suspension (or cancellation) of trading in its shares.

8.3.7 *Change in the number of securities in issue*

An AIM company must notify a RIS of the reason for the issue or cancellation of any of its AIM securities and consequent number of AIM securities in issue. The reason need only be brief, for example "exercise of options". Any changes in the number of shares in issue requires liaison with the AIM Admissions team at the LSE, so that they can arrange the appropriate dealing notice to be released. For new issues of shares, a copy of the AIM company's board minutes allocating such securities or confirmation from its Nomad will suffice as evidence that the securities have been unconditionally allotted.

The AIM Rules for Companies also cover treasury shares and require an AIM company to notify a RIS of the details of any movement of shares into or out of treasury, and the resultant change to the issued share capital of the AIM company (excluding any shares held in treasury) in accordance with Schedule 7.

8.3.8 Decision on dividend payment

An AIM company must notify a RIS of any decision to make any payment in respect of its AIM securities, specifying the net amount payable per security, the payment date and the record date. This information may be given in the preliminary statement of annual results, or the half-yearly report if appropriate. The payment dates should be agreed with the LSE in advance.

8.3.9 Admission to other exchanges

An AIM company must notify a RIS of any admission to trading (or cancellation from trading) of the AIM company's securities (or any other securities issued by the AIM company) on any other exchange or trading platform, where such admission or cancellation is at the application or agreement of the AIM company. This information must also be submitted separately to the LSE. This obligation does not arise when the AIM company's securities are admitted to trading on another exchange without its consent, as can be the case with some German exchanges.

8.3.10 Other general disclosure obligations

Notification to a RIS is required if an AIM company changes its legal name, accounting reference date, registered office address or its website address. Notification is also required if there is any subsequent change to the details or circumstances of directors required to be disclosed in Schedule 2(g) to the AIM Rules for Companies, whether such details were first published at admission or on subsequent appointment.

In addition, there is a general obligation that the LSE may require the AIM company to provide it with such information in such form and within such time limit as it considers appropriate. The LSE may also require the AIM company to publish such information.

The LSE may disclose any information in its possession:

1. to cooperate with any person responsible for supervision or regulation of financial services or for law enforcement;
2. to enable it to discharge its legal or regulatory functions, including instituting, carrying on or defending proceedings; and
3. for any other purpose where it has the consent of the person from whom the information was obtained and, if different, the person to whom it relates.

An AIM company should use all due skill and care to ensure that information provided to the LSE is correct, complete and not misleading, and should advise the LSE as soon as possible if it becomes aware that this is not the case.

8.4 Websites

In addition to its obligation to make public disclosure of certain information, an AIM company must, from admission, maintain a website which includes the following information free of charge:

1. a description of its business and, in the case of an investing company, its investing policy (as defined in the AIM Rules for Companies) and details of any investment manager and key personnel;
2. names and biographical details of its directors together with their responsibilities and any committees of the board of directors;
3. country of incorporation, main country of operation and, if not incorporated in the UK, a statement that rights of shareholders may differ from those of a shareholder in a UK incorporated company;
4. current constitutional documents (articles of association etc.);
5. details of any other exchanges or trading platforms on which the AIM company has applied or agreed to have any of its securities traded;
6. number of AIM securities in issue (noting any held as treasury shares), details of any restrictions on their

transfer, the percentage that are not in public hands and the identity and percentage holdings of significant shareholders. This information should be updated at least every six months and the website should include the date on which this information was last updated. For these purposes, shares not in public hands comprise securities held by:

(a) a related party;
(b) trustees of an employee share scheme or pension fund established for the benefit of any directors/ employees;
(c) any person with a right to nominate a person to the board of directors;
(d) any person subject to a lock-in;
(e) the AIM company as treasury shares;

7. the annual accounts for the last three years (or, if less, since admission), all half-yearly, quarterly or similar reports published since the last annual accounts, all announcements and circulars within the last 12 months and the most recent admission document;

8. details of the AIM company's Nomad and other key advisers;

9. details of the corporate governance code that the AIM company has decided to apply, how the AIM company complies with that code, or if no code has been adopted this should be stated together with its current corporate governance arrangements; and

10. whether the AIM company is subject to the Takeover Code, or any other similar such legislation or code in its country of incorporation or operation, or any other similar provisions it has voluntarily adopted.

The website must be kept up to date and include the last date on which it was updated. It should include a statement that the information is being disclosed for the purposes of r.26 of the AIM Rules for Companies and should be easily accessible from one part of the website.

An AIM company should seek appropriate legal advice on how to make available any prospectus, admission document, circular or similar shareholder publication on its website without infringing any securities laws that may apply to it.

8.5 Financial reporting

8.5.1 Publication of annual accounts

An AIM company must publish annual audited accounts. These must be sent to the holders of its AIM securities without delay (i.e. once they are finalised and reported on) and in any event no later than six months after the end of the financial period to which they relate. As UK registered AIM companies will need to hold their AGM no more than six months after their year end, in practice, where the annual accounts also include the notice of AGM, they will need to be dispatched to shareholders within five months of the year end. An AIM company incorporated in an EEA country must prepare and present these accounts in accordance with International Accounting Standards. Where, at the end of the relevant financial period, such company is not a parent company, it may prepare and present such accounts either in accordance with International Accounting Standards, or in accordance with the accounting and company legislation and regulations that are applicable to that company due to its country of incorporation.

AIM companies registered in non-EEA countries must prepare and present their accounts in accordance with one of the following:

1. International Accounting Standards;
2. US Generally Accepted Accounting Principles;
3. Canadian Generally Accepted Accounting Principles;
4. Australian International Financial Reporting Standards; or
5. Japanese Generally Accepted Accounting Principles.

The accounts must disclose any transaction with a related party, whether or not previously disclosed, where any of the class tests (see Section 8.6 below) exceed 0.25 per cent and must specify the identity of the related party and the consideration for the transaction. The accounts must also provide details of directors' remuneration received in respect of the period covered in their capacity as director of that AIM company.

AIM companies subject to the CA 2006 can send accounts to shareholders via electronic means. The LSE may suspend AIM companies that are late publishing their annual accounts (or late publishing their half-yearly report – see Section 8.5.2 below). A RIS must be notified of the publication of annual audited accounts and, as with any document sent to shareholders, the annual accounts must be available to the public at the same time for at least one month free of charge at an address notified to a RIS. The LSE will require that the Nomad confirms that the AIM company has discharged its duties under the AIM Rules for Companies r.18, 19 and 20 within the time periods described in this Section 8.5.1 and Section 8.5.2 below.

Although it is common practice for AIM companies to publish a preliminary statement of annual results, there is no requirement to do so. See also Section 8.9.4 below regarding preliminary results and close periods.

8.5.2 Publication of half-yearly report

An AIM company must prepare a half-yearly report within three months of the end of the relevant period and all reports must be notified to a RIS. The report need not be sent directly to shareholders, although AIM companies may choose to do so.

The information contained in a half-yearly report must include at least a balance sheet, an income statement and a cash flow statement and must contain comparative figures for the corresponding period in the preceding financial year (apart from the balance sheet which may contain comparative figures from the last balance sheet notified). Additionally, the half-yearly report must be presented and prepared in a form consistent with that which will be adopted in the AIM company's annual accounts having regard to the accounting standards applicable to such annual accounts. Where the half-yearly report has been audited, it must contain a statement to this effect.

The half-yearly report is expected to contain an explanatory statement covering the figures and an indication of the group's prospects for the current financial year. It is advisable to ensure that the indication of the group's prospects cannot be construed as a profit forecast, because that might give rise to an obligation to make further disclosures at a later date (both pursuant to the AIM Rules for Companies and other applicable regulation, such as the Takeover Code).

A profit forecast includes any form of words which expressly or by implication gives a floor or ceiling for the likely level of profits or losses for the current financial year, or which contains data from which a calculation of an approximate figure for future profits or losses may be made, even if no particular figure is mentioned and the word profit is not used.

8.6 Transactions

Certain transactions carried out by an AIM company or its subsidiaries are "classifiable" and may require disclosure and, in some cases, shareholder approval. A classifiable transaction is any transaction that is *not* either:

1. of a revenue nature in the ordinary course of business; or
2. carried out in order to raise finance which does not involve a change in the fixed assets of the AIM company or its subsidiaries.

Examples of classifiable transactions might include acquisitions and disposals of shares, businesses and assets, including agreed private deals and public takeovers, as well as the non pre-emptive issue of securities.

If a transaction is classifiable in nature (or any transaction whatsoever if with a related party), certain "class tests" must be applied to determine whether or not disclosure and/or shareholder approval is required. The implications for a substantial transaction (including a disposal resulting in a fundamental change of business), a related party transaction and a reverse takeover are set out in Sections 8.6.2, 8.6.3, 8.6.4 and 8.6.5 respectively below. The varying requirements for these types of transaction mean that an AIM company and its advisers are well advised to consider the class tests at an early stage in the planning of a proposed transaction.

8.6.1 Class tests

The class tests comprise the following ratios, expressed as a percentage, as set out in Schedule 3 to the AIM Rules for Companies (where detailed explanations of the calculations can be found):

1. *gross assets*: gross assets the subject of the transaction divided by the gross assets of the AIM company;
2. *profits*: profits attributable to the assets the subject of the transaction divided by profits of the AIM company;
3. *turnover*: turnover attributable to the assets the subject of the transaction divided by turnover of the AIM company;
4. *consideration*: consideration divided by aggregate market value of all of the ordinary shares of the AIM company (excluding treasury shares); and
5. *gross capital*: gross capital of the company or business being acquired divided by the gross capital of the AIM company.

In general, when calculating the class tests references to the balance sheet figures should be taken from the most recently notified consolidated balance sheet whilst references to the income statement are sourced from the last notified annual results although Schedule 3 should be consulted for the detailed application of these rules.

AIM companies and their advisers should bear in mind that class test results for the same transaction can change over time. If, for example, the AIM company or target publishes new financial information or the price of the AIM company's securities changes, the class test result at the time the transaction is executed might be different to that calculated when it was first envisaged.

In circumstances where the above tests produce anomalous results, or where the tests are inappropriate to the sphere of activity of the AIM company, the LSE may (except in the case of a transaction with a related party) disregard the calculation and substitute other relevant indicators of size, including industry-specific tests. Only the LSE can decide to disregard one or more of the class tests or substitute another test and the AIM company or its Nomad should contact the LSE at the earliest opportunity if such a dispensation is to be sought.

8.6.2 Substantial transactions

If any of the class tests results in a ratio of 10 per cent or more, the transaction is classified as a "substantial transaction" and the AIM company must notify a RIS without delay as soon as the terms of the transaction are agreed. The information to be disclosed is set out in Schedule 4 to the AIM Rules for Companies, which sets out detailed particulars on the transaction. AIM companies need only obtain shareholder approval where any of the class tests result in a ratio which exceeds 100 per cent (save for certain significant disposals as set out in Section 8.6.3). This is in contrast to companies listed on the Premium Segment of the Main Market where shareholder approval is required if any of the class tests exceed 25 per cent.

There is no general obligation for an AIM company to inform its shareholders directly of a substantial transaction. However, it may need to do so if shareholders are asked to vote on a related matter, for example, on the issue of further shares by the company either to be used as consideration for the particular transaction or to raise sufficient cash to pay for the transaction. It may also wish to do so for investor and public relations purposes.

8.6.3 Disposals resulting in a fundamental change of business

Any disposal by an AIM company which, when aggregated with any other disposal or disposals over the previous 12 months, results in a ratio that exceeds 75 per cent in any of the class tests (save for the Gross Capital test which is only relevant to acquisitions), is deemed to be a disposal resulting in a fundamental change of business. As such, the disposal must be conditional on the consent of its shareholders being given in a general meeting and notified without delay, disclosing the information specified by Schedule 4 to the AIM Rules for Companies and, insofar as it is with a related party, the additional information required by r.13. The required information should be published in a circular together with a notice convening the general meeting that is sent to the shareholders.

Shareholder consent may not be required where a substantial disposal is the result of insolvency proceedings.

Where the effect of the proposed disposal is to divest the AIM company of all or substantially all of its trading business activities, the AIM company will, upon disposal, be treated as an investing company and the notification and circular convening the general meeting must also state its investing strategy going forward.

The AIM company will then have to make an acquisition or acquisitions which constitute a reverse takeover under r.14 of the AIM Rules for Companies, or otherwise implement its investing policy, within 12 months of having received the consent of its shareholders.

8.6.4 Related party transactions

Where any transaction whatsoever with a related party results in a ratio which exceeds 5 per cent in any of the class tests, an AIM company must notify a RIS without delay. Such notification should disclose the information set out in Schedule 4 to the AIM Rules for Companies, the name of the related party concerned and the extent of its interest in the transaction. It should also contain a statement that its independent directors (i.e. those who are not involved in the relevant transaction as a related party) consider, having consulted with its Nomad, that the terms of the transaction are fair and reasonable insofar as the holders of its AIM securities are concerned. A related party is defined in the AIM Rules for Companies and includes, inter alia, the current directors of the AIM company, former directors of the AIM company who have resigned within the previous 12-month period, shareholders with more than 10 per cent holdings in the AIM company and associates of such persons. Where more than one director participates in the same transaction with an AIM company, it may be appropriate to aggregate their participation when calculating the class tests, as the directors could, or could be seen to be, acting in concert when setting the terms of the transaction.

Once again, this contrasts with the obligations imposed on a company listed on the Premium Segment of the Main Market which would require a circular to shareholders and shareholder approval for a related party transaction.

As detailed in Section 8.5 above, details of any transaction with a related party (including the identity of the related party, the consideration and all other relevant circumstances) where any class test results in a ratio which exceeds 0.25 per cent, must be included in the AIM company's next published accounts, whether or not notified to a RIS as described above. Thus, if all class tests result in ratios which are less than 5 per cent but at least one is greater than 0.25 per cent, this is the only disclosure which needs to be made.

8.6.5 *Reverse takeovers*

A reverse takeover is an acquisition or acquisitions in a 12-month period which for an AIM company would:

1. exceed 100 per cent in any of the class tests; or
2. result in a fundamental change in its business, board or voting control; or

3.   in the case of an investing company, depart materially from its stated and approved investing policy.

A reverse takeover requires shareholder consent and disclosure to a RIS, without delay, of the information set out in Schedule 4 to the AIM Rules for Companies and insofar as it is with a related party, the additional information required for related party transactions. Any agreement entered into must be conditional on the consent of shareholders and an admission document and notice convening a general meeting must be published at the same time as the announcement.

The LSE expects negotiations leading to a reverse takeover to be kept confidential until the point where a binding agreement can be notified and an admission document published. If this is not possible, the Nomad should contact the LSE at the earliest opportunity.

Where an AIM company is unable to publish its admission document at the same time as it agrees the terms of a reverse takeover, it will be suspended by the LSE until it has published such a document (unless the target is a listed company or another AIM company).

When shareholder approval for the reverse takeover is given, trading in the AIM company's securities will be cancelled. If the enlarged entity seeks re-admission, it must make an application in the same manner as any other applicant applying for admission of its securities for the first time. However, the enlarged entity may make an application in advance of the general meeting to approve the reverse takeover such that the securities are admitted on the day following the approval of the acquisition or as soon as possible thereafter. In addition to the 10-day announcement required by r.2 of the AIM Rules for Companies, the enlarged entity will need to submit a further fee, an electronic version of its admission document, a Nomad declaration and a company application form at least three business days prior to admission.

8.6.6 *Aggregation of transactions*

Transactions completed during the 12 months prior to the date of the latest transaction must be aggregated with the latest transaction for the purpose of classifying that transaction, where:

1. they are entered into by an AIM company with the same person or persons or their families;
2. they involve the acquisition or disposal of securities or an interest in one particular business; or
3. together they lead to the principal involvement in any business activity or activities which did not previously form a part of an AIM company's principal activities (the LSE will only consider this to apply where collectively any class test for such a 12-month period exceeds 100 per cent).

8.7 Further share issues

At least three business days before the expected date of admission of further AIM securities, the AIM company must submit an application form and, where required, an electronic version of any further admission document (see below). An AIM company must also inform the LSE in advance of any notification of the timetable for any proposed action affecting the rights of the holders of its AIM securities and update the LSE if this timetable changes.

The AIM Rules for Companies set out when a further admission document is required. This is only when the AIM company is:

1. required to issue a prospectus under the Prospectus Rules for a further issue of AIM securities; or
2. seeking admission for a new class of securities; or
3. undertaking a reverse takeover.

An AIM company is subject to the requirement in the Prospectus Rules for an issuer to produce a prospectus if it is to offer shares to the public in the United Kingdom. There are a number of exemptions available to this requirement concerning the type of recipient, number of recipients and value of shares sold. If no exemption is available, a prospectus is required.

The LSE may authorise the omission of information from a further admission document in the same circumstances as apply for first-time applicants under r.4 of the AIM Rules for Companies (unless it also constitutes a prospectus under the Prospectus Rules). In addition, an AIM company may omit certain historical financial information from any further admission document (other than a prospectus) provided that the AIM company has been complying with the AIM Rules for Companies. In such circumstances the Nomad must confirm to the LSE in writing that equivalent information is available publicly by reason of the AIM company's compliance with the AIM Rules for Companies.

Where the further admission document is also a prospectus, application for omission of information should be made to the United Kingdom Listing Authority. The LSE itself may not authorise exemptions from any requirement under the Prospectus Rules.

For non pre-emptive issues, the provisions in the AIM Rules for Companies governing substantial and related party transactions also apply (but the provisions relating to reverse takeovers will not apply if 100 per cent of more of the existing share capital is to be issued).

Where an AIM company intends to issue AIM securities on a regular basis, the LSE may permit admission of those securities under a block admission arrangement. Under a block admission arrangement an AIM company must notify the information required in Schedule 6 to the AIM Rules for Companies every six months. However, a block admission cannot be used where the securities to be issued under the block admission exceed 20 per cent of the existing class of AIM securities. The block admission can only be used pursuant to employee share schemes, personal equity plans, dividend reinvestment plans, warrant exercises and convertible securities.

8.8 The Takeover Code

If an AIM company is itself the subject of a takeover approach (or the directors are considering seeking a buyer for the company), it should be noted that the Takeover Code is likely to apply to the transaction. This will be the case for AIM companies that have their registered offices in the United Kingdom, the Channel Islands or the Isle of Man. An AIM company that is not registered in the UK, the Channel Islands or the Isle of Man that is subject to a takeover approach should consult the Panel immediately to ensure that it identifies the correct securities legislation to which it is subject.

8.9 Other eligibility requirements and restrictions

8.9.1 *Continuing eligibility*

Once admitted to AIM, an AIM company must continue to satisfy the initial eligibility criteria and have in place sufficient procedures, resources and controls to enable compliance with the AIM Rules for Companies. In particular, as described below, it must at all times retain a Nomad and a broker.

8.9.2 *Nomads*

An AIM company must continue at all times to retain a Nomad. It may only retain the services of one Nomad at any one time. If an AIM company ceases to have a Nomad, the LSE will suspend trading in its securities. As mentioned in Section 8.3.6 above, it is advisable, therefore, to establish a period of notice of at least one month on the engagement of a Nomad in order to allow time to avoid the potential suspension of shares.

An AIM company must seek advice from its Nomad regarding compliance with the AIM Rules for Companies and provide its

Nomad with any information it reasonably requests or requires to carry out its duties under the AIM Rules for Companies. This includes details of proposed board changes and draft announcements in advance.

8.9.3 Broker

An AIM company must retain a broker at all times and must ensure that appropriate settlement arrangements are in place, in particular (unless otherwise agreed with the LSE), AIM securities must be eligible for electronic settlement.

8.9.4 Directors' share dealing

In addition to the restrictions of the Criminal Justice Act 1993 to prevent insider dealing when a person is in possession of unpublished price-sensitive information, an AIM company must ensure that its directors and applicable employees (any employees who are aware of price-sensitive information) do not deal in any of its AIM securities during a "close period". In addition, the AIM company should not engage in share buy-back activities or early redemption of its securities or sale of any AIM securities held as treasury shares during a close period.

A close period is the period of two months immediately preceding the publication of the company's annual results (in compliance with the AIM Rules for Companies r.19), the two months preceding the notification of its half-yearly report, or when the company is in possession of unpublished price-sensitive information or any information that is required by the AIM Rules for Companies to be notified to a RIS. Note that the notification of preliminary annual results does not end a close period. If, however, the full annual results are uploaded to the company's website, and this is announced together with the key information, or specific approval from the LSE is sought, the close period may end before full compliance with r.19 has taken place (although note the requirement that accounts must be sent to shareholders "without delay").

This rule will not apply, however, where such persons have entered into a binding contract prior to the close period where it was not reasonably foreseeable at the time when such commitment was made that a close period was likely, and provided that the commitment was notified to a RIS at the time it was made.

The LSE may permit a director or applicable employee to sell his AIM securities during a close period to alleviate severe personal hardship, such as the need for a medical operation or to satisfy a court order, where no other funds are readily available.

Undertakings from directors/applicable employees to participate in fundraisings do not "dealings" if the close period arises solely due to the fundraising itself, the fundraising is the only unpublished price sensitive information and the director/ applicable employee's participation is on the same terms as all other investors in the fundraising. Note that if more than one director is participating it may be appropriate to aggregate their participation for the purpose of calculating the class tests for a related party transaction (see Section 8.6.4 above).

8.9.5 *Transferability of shares*

An AIM company must ensure that its AIM securities are freely transferable except where any jurisdiction, statute or regulation places restriction on transferability or the AIM company is seeking to ensure that it does not become subject to a statute or regulation if it has a particular number of shareholders domiciled in a particular country.

8.9.6 *Securities to be admitted*

Only securities which have been unconditionally (save as to admission) allotted can be admitted as AIM securities. An AIM company must ensure that application is made to admit all securities within a class of AIM securities. The LSE will require proof that securities have been allotted prior to admitting them to trading (such as a board minute or confirmation from the Nomad as noted in 8.3.7).

8.9.7 Precautionary suspension

The LSE may suspend the trading of AIM securities where:

1. trading in those securities is not being conducted in an orderly manner;
2. it considers that an AIM company has failed to comply with the AIM Rules for Companies;
3. the protection of investors so requires; or
4. the integrity and reputation of the market has been or may be impaired by dealings in those securities.

An AIM company should request a suspension in circum-stances where it is required to make a notification but is unable to do so (having used all reasonable endeavours). Any such suspension is at the discretion of the Exchange. The general principle applied by the Exchange when considering requests for a suspension is that interruptions to trading should be kept to a minimum.

Should an AIM company be suspended following such a request the AIM company must make a notification stating the reason for suspension to the fullest extent possible. An AIM company, while suspended, must continue to comply with the AIM Rules for Companies.

8.9.8 Cancellation of admission

The LSE will cancel the admission of a company's AIM securities where these have been suspended from trading for six months.

Where an AIM company voluntarily seeks cancellation, it will be conditional upon at least 20 business days' notice and the consent of not less than 75 per cent of votes cast by its shareholders in a general meeting, unless the LSE otherwise agrees. One circumstance in which the LSE will agree a cancellation is in the case of a takeover offer (or scheme of arrangement) where an offeror has received valid acceptances (or votes in favour of a scheme of arrangement and subsequent sanction by the court) in excess of 75 per cent of each class of AIM securities. In such cases, the 20 days' notice may be incorporated into the takeover documentation in advance of the offer becoming unconditional, in which case the wording should be agreed with the LSE.

8.9.9 Fees

An AIM company must pay the fees at the rates published by the LSE as soon as such payment becomes due. There are three types of fee payable by an AIM company to the LSE. The first fee is an admission fee payable by all companies following their initial admission to trading on AIM (and subsequent re-admissions following reverse takeovers). The admission fee is calculated based upon the market capitalisation of the AIM company upon admission and can range from £7,600 to £85,750 (excluding VAT).

In respect of further issues of securities a fee is due on any issues where capital of £5 million and above is raised and ranges from £3,800 to a maximum of £42,875 dependant on the market capitalisation of the new securities.

Finally, an annual fee amounting to £6,050 (excluding VAT) is payable by all AIM companies. They are billed in the first week of April for the 12 months commencing 1 April and the fee must be paid within 30 days of the invoice date. A pro-rata annual fee is payable by new applicants and an invoice will be raised at the time of admission to trading. No pro-rata annual fee is payable by the enlarged entity admitted to AIM following a reverse takeover, or by a company who has transferred to AIM from the Main Market.

The fees detailed above are correct for the year commencing 1 April 2014. The LSE publishes AIM fee updates in advance on its website.

8.9.10   *Directors' responsibility for compliance*

An AIM company must ensure that each of its directors:

1.   accepts full responsibility, collectively and individually, for its compliance with the AIM Rules for Companies;
2.   discloses without delay all information which it needs in order to comply with the disclosure requirements under r.17 of the AIM Rules for Companies, described at 8.3 above (insofar as that information is known to the director, or could with reasonable diligence be ascertained by the director); and
3.   seeks advice from its Nomad regarding its compliance with the AIM Rules for Companies whenever appropriate and takes that advice into account.

In practice these undertakings from the directors are usually dealt with either in the Nomad agreement (to which the AIM company and (on occasion) its directors are a party) and/or in comfort letters from the directors to the AIM company (and Nomad) given prior to admission.

Directors of AIM companies are required to comply with a host of other relevant regulations in addition to the AIM Rules for Companies. In particular, the LSE has given guidance around the applicability of the Bribery Act 2010. Each overseas company should consider whether it could fall within the scope of this legislation and Nomads may wish to ensure such a review has been undertaken.

8.10   Sanctions and appeals

If the LSE considers that an AIM company has contravened the AIM Rules for Companies it may issue a warning notice, a fine or a censure and publish the fact that it has been fined or censured and the reasons therefore, and/or cancel the admission of its AIM securities.

Where the LSE proposes to take any of the steps described in r.42 of the AIM Rules for Companies, the LSE will follow the procedures set out in the Disciplinary Procedures and Appeals Handbook, which is available from the LSE's website.

Any decision of the LSE in relation to the AIM Rules for Companies may be appealed to an appeals committee in accordance with the procedures set out in the Disciplinary Procedures and Appeals Handbook.

8.11 Modifications for certain types of AIM companies

Due to the characteristics of companies engaged in investment activity or within the natural resources sector, AIM companies which are deemed to be either "investing companies" or "resource companies" will be subject to specific interpretation and guidance in respect of certain of the AIM Rules for Companies.

8.11.1 *Specific guidance for resource companies*

AIM companies engaged in the mining and oil & gas sectors should take all care to ensure that any information notified to a RIS containing estimates in relation to that AIM company's reserves or resources are accurate and not false or misleading. Estimates must be prepared in accordance with an internationally recognised standard, a list of which may be found in the AIM Note for Mining and Oil & Gas Companies, and each resource update should state on which standard it is based. The estimates should be reviewed by a qualified person from the AIM company or an appointed adviser and the details of that individual (including their name, position and qualifications) must be included in the relevant notification. In addition, the LSE expects that an appropriate person from the Nomad will review the announcement. Such notifications must contain a glossary of key terms used and be in a format similar to that used for equivalent disclosures in the AIM company's admission document.

8.11.2 Specific guidance for investing companies

An AIM company which is an investing company must have a sufficiently precise investment policy setting out the criteria on which it can make investments. The investing policy should be regularly notified and at a minimum should be stated in the annual accounts. Any material change to this stated investment policy requires the approval of the AIM company's shareholders at a general meeting. Where an investing company has not substantially implemented its investment policy within 18 months of admission, it must seek the consent of its shareholders for its investment policy at its next annual general meeting (and on an annual basis thereafter) until such time as its investing policy has been substantially implemented. Note, however, that an AIM company that becomes an investing company as a result of a significant disposal (see Section 8.6.3 above) has only 12 months in which to execute a reverse takeover or implement its investing policy, or trading in its shares will be suspended by the LSE.

An investing company is also required to follow any procedure for regular periodic disclosures (such as net asset value or details of investments) set out in its admission document or subsequently.

For an investing company, that company's investment management company is considered to exert significant influence. As a consequence the investment manager, and any of its key employees, will be considered a director for the purposes of the AIM Rules for Companies governing related party transactions (see Section 8.6.4 above) and the disclosure of dealings by a director of an AIM company (see Section 8.3.4 above). In addition, the appointment, dismissal or resignation of any investment manager, or any key employee within such a manager, will generally be considered to be price-sensitive information requiring notification to a RIS without delay.

An investment made by an investing company that is in accordance with its investing policy and only exceeds 10 per cent of either the profits or turnover class tests will be considered as acting in the ordinary course of business and will not be deemed a substantial transaction as set out in Section 8.6.2 above. The AIM company should, however, consider whether such a transaction is price-sensitive and therefore requires notification to a RIS in any event.

Where an investment exceeds 100 per cent in any of the class tests it will ordinarily be considered a reverse takeover unless:

(a) it is in accordance with that AIM company's investing policy;
(b) it only exceeds either the profits or turnover class tests; and
(c) it does not result in a fundamental change of business.

If a substantial disposal is made, provided it is within the AIM company's investing policy, the transaction will not be subject to the separate requirements for a fundamental change of business as set out in Section 8.6.3 above, and the AIM company will not have to seek shareholder consent. In either of these circumstances the AIM company should still consider whether such a transaction is a substantial transaction or is otherwise price-sensitive.

8.12   Conclusion

The less onerous nature of the continuing obligations on AIM is often a key factor in influencing the decision of directors to seek admission of their company to AIM, as opposed to listing on the Premium Segment of the Main Market.

The reduced obligations in respect of share issues, acquisitions and disposals for AIM companies can mean that a company which is likely to engage in substantial fundraising and merger and acquisition activity can benefit from choosing admission to AIM. However, directors of AIM companies should also be conscious of actions required by law and by the company's constitutional documents in such situations. Compliance with the market abuse provisions of the Financial Services and Markets Act 2000 is also particularly important for directors of an AIM company.

A distinguishing feature of the AIM market is the Nomad requirement and role. Close interaction and regular dialogue between an AIM company and its Nomad is essential in ensuring ongoing compliance with the AIM Rules for Companies. It may be advisable to ensure that one or more executive directors are tasked with ensuring compliance with the continuing obligations of the AIM company and are always available as a primary contact for the company's Nomad.

Chapter 9

Directors' Dealings and Corporate Governance

Melanie Wadsworth

Partner, Faegre Baker Daniels LLP

9.1 Directors' dealings

9.1.1 Introduction

The directors and certain employees of an AIM company are subject to restrictions on dealing in shares of their company under statute, common law and also under the AIM Rules for Companies ("the AIM Rules"). The principle behind all regulation of dealings by directors is that no director should be able to take unfair advantage of his position as a director to deal in the company's securities.

Under the AIM Rules, the primary restriction on dealing in the AIM company's securities is set out in a single succinct sentence in r.21:

> "An AIM company must ensure that its directors and applicable employees do not deal in any of its AIM securities during a close period."

The rule itself is supplemented by the definitions that apply to the AIM Rules, which are found in the glossary to the Rules. These expand the scope of the restriction beyond what appears, at face value, to be a straightforward restriction.

The primary responsibility for ensuring compliance with the restriction on dealing that applies to the directors and employees of an AIM company lies with the AIM company itself. Under r.31, an AIM company is required to have in place sufficient procedures, resources and controls to enable it to comply with the AIM Rules and must ensure that each of its directors accepts full responsibility, collectively and individually, for the company's compliance with the AIM Rules.

9.1.2   To what securities does Rule 21 apply?

The restriction on dealing in securities of an AIM company applies only to securities that have been admitted to AIM. To the extent that a director or applicable employee holds securities issued by their AIM company, whether shares, loan stock, warrants or other securities, that have not been admitted to AIM, the restriction on dealing under the AIM Rules does not apply.

9.1.3   To whom does Rule 21 apply?

The restriction on dealing in r.21 applies to the directors of an AIM company and to any other person who acts as a director, whether or not officially appointed as a director of the company. Although the AIM Rules do not use the term "shadow director", they are clearly intended to apply also to persons who, under the Companies Act 2006 ("CA 2006"), would be shadow directors of a company.

The restriction on dealing applies also to "applicable employees", that is, any employee of the AIM company, or a subsidiary or parent undertaking of the AIM company, who is likely to be in possession of unpublished price-sensitive information in relation to the company as a result of their employment. The dealing restriction applies to applicable employees regardless of the size of their holding of, or the nature of their interest in, the AIM securities of the AIM company. Actual possession of unpublished price-sensitive information by the employee is not the test by which an employee is classified by the AIM Rules as an applicable employee and therefore subject to the dealing restriction. The nature of the employee's position and duties will determine

172

whether or not he or she is *likely to be* in possession of unpublished price-sensitive information and therefore subject to the dealing restriction under the AIM Rules. It is possible, depending upon the circumstances, that certain employees will be applicable employees from time to time and, as circumstances change, might cease to be applicable employees.

9.1.4   What are "deals"?

The scope of the restriction that applies to directors and applicable employees on dealings in securities under r.21 is expanded considerably by the definition of "deal" in the glossary to the AIM Rules. A "deal" includes both:

- "any change whatsoever to the holding of AIM securities of an AIM company in which the holder is a director of the AIM company or part of a director's family ... [or] an applicable employee";
  and
- "the acquisition, disposal or discharge (whether in whole or part) of a related financial product referenced to AIM securities of an AIM company in which the holder is a director or part of a director's family ... [or] an applicable employee".

A holding includes any legal or beneficial interest, whether direct or indirect. A director's family comprises his or her spouse or civil partner, any children under the age of 18 and other entities in which any of them is interested. A company of which a director or his or her spouse or civil partner or children under the age of 18 has control, or in which they together hold more than 20 per cent of the equity or voting rights in general meeting (excluding treasury shares), is part of a director's family. Any trust of which the director or his or her spouse or civil partner and children under the age of 18 are trustees or beneficiaries is also part of a director's family, except for any employee share scheme or pension scheme where the director or his or her spouse or civil partner and children under the age of 18 are beneficiaries and not trustees.

173

The following transactions are included in the definition of "deal" under the AIM Rules and are therefore subject to the restriction on dealing under r.21:

1. any sale or purchase, or any agreement for the sale or purchase, of AIM securities;
2. the grant or acceptance of any option relating to AIM securities or any other right or obligation, present or future, conditional or unconditional, to acquire or dispose of AIM securities;
3. the acquisition, disposal, exercise or discharge of, or any dealing with, any option, right or obligation in respect of AIM securities;
4. deals between directors and/or applicable employees;
5. off-market deals;
6. transfers for no consideration; and
7. any shares taken into or out of treasury.

Also included in the definition of "deal" are transactions for the acquisition, disposal or discharge (whether in whole or in part) of a related financial product referenced to AIM securities. A related financial product is any financial product whose value, in whole or in part, is determined directly or indirectly by reference to the price of AIM securities or securities which are the subject of an application for admission, including a contract for difference and a fixed odds bet. The widening of the restriction on dealing to include dealings in contracts for difference and similar financial products arose from an admission of a company to AIM where the underwriting of a placing of new shares effected in connection with the admission was effectively sub-underwritten by a director entering into a related financial product.

The following transactions are not deals for the purposes of the AIM Rules and therefore are not subject to the restriction on dealing by directors and applicable employees under r.21:

1. undertakings or elections to take up, and the actual taking up of, entitlements under a rights issue or other pre-emptive offer (including under a scrip dividend alternative);
2. allowing entitlements to lapse under a rights issue or other pre-emptive offer (including under a scrip dividend alternative);
3. the sale of sufficient entitlements nil-paid under a rights issue to allow the take up of the balance of the entitlement; and
4. undertakings to accept, and the acceptance of, a takeover offer.

9.1.5   What is a "close period"?

The restriction on dealing in AIM securities imposed by r.21 prohibits dealings by directors and applicable employees of an AIM company while the AIM company is in a "close period". A close period is:

1. the period of two months preceding the publication of annual accounts (or, if shorter, the period from a company's financial year end to the time of publication of annual results);
2. the period of two months immediately preceding the announcement of half-yearly results (or, if shorter, the period from the end of the relevant financial period up to and including the time of the announcement);
3. if the company reports on a quarterly basis, the period of one month immediately preceding the announcement of its quarterly results (or, if shorter, the period from the end of the relevant financial period up to and including the time of the announcement);
4. any other period when the AIM company is in possession of unpublished price-sensitive information; and
5. any time when it has become reasonably probable that the announcement of unpublished price-sensitive information will be required by the AIM Rules.

Determining whether or not an AIM company is in a close period by reference to the announcement of annual, half-yearly or quarterly results will not generally be problematic. Whether or not an AIM company is in possession of unpublished price-sensitive information raises two issues. What is unpublished price-sensitive information and when is an AIM company in possession of such information?

Unpublished price-sensitive information is defined in the glossary to the AIM Rules as information which:

1. relates to particular AIM securities or to a particular AIM company rather than to securities or issuers in general;
2. is specific or precise;
3. has not been made public; and
4. if it were made public would be likely to have a significant effect on the price or value of any AIM security.

As a close period includes any time when the AIM company is in possession of unpublished price-sensitive information, at any particular time *all* directors and applicable employees will either be prohibited from dealing or permitted to deal in the company's AIM securities. The AIM Rules do not admit the possibility that only certain directors, or only the directors but not applicable employees, will be prohibited from dealing or permitted to deal at any time.

As applied by the AIM team at the London Stock Exchange ("LSE"), the AIM Rules require an AIM company to demonstrate that the company was not in a close period at the relevant time when any question is raised as to whether or not a dealing by a director or applicable employee was made in compliance with the AIM Rules.

9.1.6 Exemptions from the restriction on dealing

The AIM Rules provide limited exemptions from the restriction on dealing in a close period. The dealing restriction does not apply where a binding commitment to deal was entered into prior to the AIM company entering a close period and where, at the time the commitment was made, it was not reasonably foreseeable that the company was likely to enter a close period. In order for a commitment to be "binding", its completion must be obligatory for all parties to the agreement, at a price agreed or which could be objectively determined. To rely on the exemption to permit a dealing that would otherwise be prohibited, the commitment must have been announced at the time the commitment was made. In effect, this exemption will only permit a dealing in a close period which is merely completing a deal that has already been made. Most obviously, a conditional contract entered into by a director or applicable employee to buy or sell AIM securities can be completed in a close period. Entering into the contract will be a dealing for the purposes of the AIM Rules which will require announcement. Without the exemption, the completion of the conditional contract during a close period would be a dealing for the purposes of the AIM Rules, as it gives rise to a change in the legal ownership of the securities which are the subject of the transaction.

The AIM Rules also provide for the LSE to permit a director or applicable employee of an AIM company to sell AIM securities during a close period to alleviate severe personal hardship. The Guidance Notes that accompany the AIM Rules explain that this exemption is limited to exceptional circumstances in which severe personal hardship would otherwise result to a director or applicable employee or their immediate relatives, such as the urgent need for a medical operation or the need to satisfy a court order where no other funds are reasonably available.

9.1.7 *Notification of dealings*

An AIM company is required by the AIM Rules (r.17) to announce without delay any dealing by a director in its AIM securities. The announcement must include:

1. the identity of the director;
2. the date on which the AIM company was notified of the dealing;
3. the date on which the dealing was made;

4. the price, number and class of the AIM securities which are the subject of the dealing;
5. the nature of the transaction; and
6. the nature and extent of the director's interest in the transaction.

Where the announcement concerns a related financial product it must include the detailed nature of the exposure under the related financial product. Where the dealing takes place when the AIM company is in a close period under r.21, the announcement must also include the date upon which any previous binding commitment was announced or the date on which the LSE granted permission to deal in order to mitigate severe personal hardship.

Compliance by an AIM company with the requirement to announce dealings by directors depends upon the notification of the dealing by the director to the company. As noted above, under the AIM Rules, the AIM company is responsible for ensuring its directors comply with the AIM Rules. In relation to dealings in AIM securities, the AIM Rules used to require the adoption of a model code for dealing in AIM securities. This requirement has been dispensed with. However, to ensure compliance with the dealing restriction and notification requirements under the AIM Rules, an AIM company must adopt some form of request and decision mechanism for the grant (or refusal) of permission for directors and applicable employees to deal in AIM securities. In addition, given the extension of the restriction on dealing to a director's family and entities connected with him or her, an AIM company must have guidance available to be issued to persons connected with a director. This guidance must explain when they can and cannot deal and what information will be required from them, and when, following a dealing in the securities of the AIM company.

9.1.8 Sanctions for breach of dealing restriction

As in any case where it considers that an AIM company has contravened the AIM Rules, in the case of a dealing in breach of the dealing restriction, the LSE may:

1. issue a warning notice;
2. fine the AIM company;
3. censure the AIM company;
4. publish the fact that the AIM company has been fined or censured and the reasons for the fine or censure; or
5. cancel the admission of the AIM company's securities to AIM.

If the LSE proposes to take any of these steps, it will follow the procedures set out in the *Disciplinary Procedures and Appeals Handbook*.

9.1.9 Lock-ins for new businesses

In the case of an applicant for admission to AIM whose main business activity has not been independent and earning revenue for at least two years, r.7 of the AIM Rules requires the AIM company to ensure that all related parties and applicable employees as at the date of admission to AIM agree not to dispose of any interest in its securities for one year from the date of admission to AIM. The rule also applies in the case of an AIM company effecting a reverse takeover and whose main business activity thereafter has not been independent and earning revenue for at least two years.

9.1.10 Who are related parties?

The related parties of an AIM company include the following:

1. the directors of the AIM company or any subsidiary or parent undertaking, or other subsidiary of its parent undertaking;
2. substantial shareholders, being any person who holds any legal or beneficial interest directly or indirectly in 10 per

cent or more of any class of AIM security of the company (excluding treasury shares) or 10 per cent or more of the voting rights (excluding treasury shares) of an AIM company, excluding any authorised person, or any company with securities quoted on the LSE's markets, unless the company is an investing company;

3. members of a director's family as noted above, and members of the family of any substantial shareholder, which includes a spouse, civil partner and children under the age of 18 and certain companies and trusts connected with any of them;

4. any company in whose equity shares any related party thus far mentioned (individually or taken together with his or her family and (in the case of a director of an AIM company) any other director of the AIM company and his or her family) has an interest, or has a conditional or contingent entitlement to become interested, in 30 per cent or more of the votes (excluding treasury shares) able to be cast at general meetings on all, or substantially all, matters or to appoint or remove directors of the company holding a majority of voting rights at board meetings on all, or substantially all, matters; and

5. any company which is a parent or subsidiary undertaking of a company mentioned in point (4) above and any other subsidiary undertaking of any parent undertaking of a company mentioned in point (4) above.

The definition of related party is extended further to include:

(a) any company whose directors are accustomed to acting in accordance with the instructions or directions of a director of the AIM company or any subsidiary or parent undertaking of the AIM company; and

(b) certain companies in which directors of an AIM company, and companies connected with them are able to exercise 30 per cent or more of the votes able to be cast at general meetings on all or substantially all matters.

Thus, the net is thrown far and wide and, in all but the most straightforward of situations, detailed analysis is required to determine whether or not a company with which a director of the AIM company is connected is a related party of the AIM company for the purposes of the AIM Rules. For the purposes of r.7, an applicable employee of an AIM company is any employee who together with his family has a holding or interest, directly or indirectly, in 0.5 per cent or more of a class of AIM securities (excluding treasury shares). An applicable employee's family for this purpose comprises his or her spouse or civil partner and any children under the age of 18 and also other entities in which any of them is interested. A company in which an employee or his or her spouse or civil partner and children under the age of 18 have control of more than 20 per cent of the equity or voting rights in general meeting is part of an employee's family, as is any trust of which the employee or his or her spouse or civil partner and children are trustees or beneficiaries, except for any employee share scheme or pension scheme where the employee or his or her spouse or civil partner and children under the age of 18 are beneficiaries and not trustees.

In contrast to the general restriction on dealing that applies to the directors and applicable employees of an AIM company, an AIM Rules lock-in applies to all securities of the AIM company, not just those that are admitted to AIM. In addition, r.7 does not apply just to securities in the AIM company that are held by related parties at the date of admission to AIM. Rather, r.7 is a prohibition on the disposal of any interest in the securities of an AIM company in the period of 12 months following admission. If a related party acquires securities following admission or, for example, were a director or employee to acquire shares on the exercise of an option, a lock-in given in compliance with r.7 would prohibit the sale of any of the shares acquired during such lock-in period.

The obligation to ensure compliance with the lock-ins rests with the AIM company. It is customary for lock-ins given in compliance with r.7 to be addressed by the related parties to both the company and its Nominated Adviser ("Nomad").

There are limited exemptions that apply to r.7 permitting the disposal by a related party of an interest in the securities of an AIM company in the period of 12 months following its admission to AIM. The exemptions permit a disposal of securities:

1. in the event of an intervening court order;
2. as a result of the death of the related party; or
3. by way of the acceptance of a takeover offer for the AIM company which is open to all shareholders.

A substantial shareholder who became so at the time of admission of the company to AIM and at a price more widely available (for example, an institutional investor subscribing at the placing price for shares in an initial public offering) need not be the subject of a lock-in under r.7.

9.2   Corporate governance

9.2.1   Introduction

Corporate governance has attracted increasing interest over the years and is now at the forefront of much discussion around corporate performance. In its report published in December 1992, the Cadbury Committee chaired by Adrian Cadbury on the Financial Aspects of Corporate Governance defined corporate governance, narrowly, as "the system by which companies are directed and controlled". Since that report was published, the concept has expanded to include matters as diverse as shareholder democracy, corporate transparency and even the way in which a company relates to society at large. According to the Quoted Companies Alliance Corporate Governance Code for Small and Mid-size Quoted Companies, which has become the benchmark for many AIM companies (see Section 9.2.3.1 below) ("QCA Code"), good corporate governance should inspire trust between a public company and its shareholders and reduce the risks that a company faces as it seeks to create growth in long-term shareholder value. This is a worthy goal, but does beg the question of whether an increasingly onerous corporate governance regime in the UK sits comfortably with the concept of entrepreneurial management and the perceived flexibility of the AIM market.

When considering the application of general principles of corporate governance to AIM companies, the first point of note is that there is no specific requirement under the AIM Rules to comply with any of the relevant guidelines. This contrasts with the position of companies with a premium listing on the main market of the LSE ("Main Market") which are required to state in their annual report and accounts whether or not they have complied, throughout the relevant period, with the main principles of the UK Corporate Governance Code (the "Code") published by the Financial Reporting Council ("FRC") and if not, why not (r.9.8.6(5) of the Listing Rules).

In May 2014, the AIM Rules were amended to require each AIM company to include on its website details of the corporate governance code that it has decided to apply and how the AIM company complies with that code or, if no such code has been adopted, to state that fact together with a description of its current corporate governance arrangements. Given that most corporate governance codes themselves require companies to describe and explain key areas of their governance structures, it is likely that quite detailed information will need to be disclosed. Stating that the AIM company complies with a certain corporate governance code insofar as appropriate for a company of its size and stage – as so often seen in the admission documents of AIM companies – is unlikely to discharge an AIM company's obligations in this regard.

In tough economic times shareholders inevitably demand greater accountability from the boards of the companies in which they invest. Increasingly, institutional investors are themselves under pressure to play a part in the efficient exercise of governance responsibilities, as evidenced by the publication by the FRC of the UK Stewardship Code in July 2010 (revised September 2012) which aims to enhance the quality of engagement between institutional investors and investee companies. As shareholder expectations in the area of corporate governance have risen, the pressure on AIM companies to address corporate governance issues, regardless of whether or not they are under a statutory or regulatory compulsion to do so, has increased and there is renewed focus on the way in which AIM companies are managed and how those in control are rewarded.

9.2.2 The corporate governance framework in the UK

Following a number of major corporate governance reviews in the 1990s, notably one chaired by Sir Ronald Hampel in 1998, and the publication of the principles of good governance and code of best practice then known as the Combined Code, by the end of that decade the UK had a well-established corporate governance model for Main Market companies. Nonetheless, the combination of a difficult trading climate and the very public criticism of the conduct of directors in relation to certain failed companies created an environment in which the call came for further scrutiny of corporate governance practices in the UK. Accordingly, the last decade has seen the instigation of many corporate governance initiatives and legislative changes which have had an impact on such practices.

9.2.2.1 The Large and Medium-sized Companies and Groups (Accounts and Reports) Regulations 2008

For financial years ending on or after 30 September 2013, the Large and Medium-sized Companies Regulations 2008, as amended by the Large and Medium-sized Companies and Groups (Accounts and Reports) (Amendment) Regulations 2013, ("Regulations") require companies whose shares are listed on certain Exchanges to publish a report on directors' remuneration which must be put to shareholders at the annual general meeting.

The remuneration report must include a directors' remuneration policy, which is subject to a binding vote by way of ordinary resolution at least once every three years. After the policy is approved, the company will only be able to make payments within the limits it allows and shareholder approval will be required if the directors wish to change the policy within the relevant three year period. If a remuneration policy is not approved, the company will have to continue operating in accordance with the last remuneration policy to have been approved by shareholders and seek separate shareholder approval for any specific remuneration or loss of office payments which are not consistent with the policy. Alternatively, the company may prefer to convene a general meeting and put forward a revised policy for approval by shareholders.

Amongst other things, the annual remuneration report must include:

1. a statement by the director who is the chair of the remuneration committee (or, if there is no such person, by a director nominated by the directors to make the statement) summarising:
    (i)   major decisions on directors' remuneration in that financial year;
    (ii) any substantial changes relating to directors' remuneration made during the year; and
    (iii) the context in which those changes occurred and decisions have been taken;
2. a single figure for total remuneration paid to each person who served as a director of the company during that financial year, including and broken down to show all taxable benefits and expenses, performance-related pay and bonuses, long-term incentive awards and pension-related benefits;
3. details of the link between company performance and the chief executive officer's pay and the percentage increase in his/her pay since the last financial year;
4. an explanation of how the company intends to implement the approved remuneration policy (see above) in the year ahead, including details and explanations of performance criteria for share options and long-term incentive schemes; and
5. a performance graph showing the company's total shareholder return compared with that of an appropriate

hypothetical comparator for between five and ten financial years of which the relevant financial year is the last.

The shareholder vote is advisory and, as such, does not require the directors to amend contractual entitlements, nor to amend their remuneration policy. A vote against a directors' remuneration report does, however, send a strong signal to directors about the level of support for the board's remuneration policy and will be expected to be taken into account in future remuneration decisions.

Although AIM companies are not required to comply with the Regulations, many do and, given renewed criticism of excessive executive remuneration in light of the banking crisis and resulting recession in the UK, this is likely to remain an area of concern to investors.

9.2.2.2   ABI Principles of Remuneration

Helpful guidance in the area of directors' remuneration is contained in the Principles of Remuneration published by the Association of British Insurers ("ABI principles"). A useful complement to the Code, the ABI principles advise that remuneration policy should seek to promote value creation through transparent alignment with agreed corporate strategy. The principles make practical suggestions to assist remuneration committees in establishing and implementing such policies, including the following advice:

1. Undeserved remuneration undermines the efficient operation of the company and so the fundamental principle of executive remuneration should be to pay no more than is necessary. Remuneration committees should seek specific points of reference against which the appropriateness of quantum can be judged and establish a relevant and fairly constructed peer universe;
2. Executive directors and senior executives should build up significant shareholdings in companies to align their interests with those of shareholders. Although it is not appropriate for chairmen and independent directors to

receive incentive rewards related to share price or corporate performance, non-executive directors should be
encouraged to own shares in the company;

3. A significant proportion of executive remuneration should
    be performance related and tied to the achievement of
    clear business targets and long-term value creation.
    Annual bonuses should be easily quantifiable and, follow-
    ing the payment of bonuses, companies should provide a
    full analysis in the remuneration report of the extent to
    which the relevant targets were actually met; and
4. Share-based incentives should align the interests of
    executive directors with those of shareholders and link
    reward to successful implementation of strategy over the
    longer term. Vesting should therefore be based on perfor-
    mance conditions measured over a period appropriate to
    the strategic objectives of the company, which should not
    be less than three years. All new incentive plans, and any
    substantive changes to existing schemes, should be subject
    to prior approval by shareholders.

9.2.2.3 *The UK Corporate Governance Code*

Much of today's Code is based on the findings of a review led
by Sir Derek Higgs in 2003 of the role and effectiveness of
non-executive directors. Following a period of speculation that
the UK might adopt a prescriptive regime to emulate the
unpopular US Sarbanes-Oxley law, the Higgs Report was
initially well received, with most quarters accepting that a
tightening up of the corporate governance regime was
required. As always, however, the devil was in the detail and
the view of many in the City remained that the regulatory
burden of the Code, particularly on smaller companies, was
too onerous and encouraged a level of bureaucracy which
risked stifling entrepreneurship. Mindful of such criticism, the
FRC has carried out periodic reviews of the implementation of
the Code, proposing changes where necessary.

Accordingly, the Code has evolved since it was first introduced, with an increased emphasis on the need for the whole
board to think deeply about the way in which it carries out its

role and the behaviours its members display, not just about the structures and processes that it puts in place. The current edition of the Code requires the board to consider carefully how it works together as a unit and to ensure that it has an appropriate mix of skills, experience, independence and knowledge. The Code also states that boards should disclose their policy on boardroom diversity, increasingly seen as an important measure of effectiveness, and report on any measurable objectives that have been set for implementing such policy and progress made in achieving them.

The Code is supplemented by useful FRC publications including the Guidance on Board Effectiveness ("Guidance") to assist companies in applying the principles of the Code. The Guidance relates primarily to the leadership and effectiveness of the board and supplements the FRC's separate guidance notes on audit committees and internal control. It emphasises the chairman's role in creating the conditions for overall board effectiveness and includes a list of key requirements for the role, such as demonstrating ethical leadership, ensuring a timely flow of information and making certain that there are no "no go" areas which prevent directors from operating effective oversight in relation to risk analysis. The Guidance also highlights the importance of investing time in the design of decision-making policies and processes in minimising the risk of poor decisions. It lists factors that can facilitate good decision-making capability (for example, high-quality documentation and allowing time for debate and challenge). It also lists factors that can limit effective decision making (for example, a dominant personality on the board; treating risk as a compliance issue, rather than part of the decision-making process), of which the board should be aware, and those that can distort judgement in decision making.

As previously noted, the Code does not apply directly to AIM companies, but it does form the benchmark for corporate governance in the UK and is the foundation of the QCA Code and the NAPF principles (see Section 9.2.3 below).

9.2.2.4 The Companies Act 2006

The CA 2006 was the result of an extensive overhaul of company law in the UK with the intention of addressing the perceived failures of a system based on years of case law and statutory amendment. It applies to companies incorporated in England and Wales.

From a corporate governance perspective, the most significant change brought in by the CA 2006 was the codification of the general duties owed by a director to his company. The key duty (contained in s.172 of the CA 2006) is that requiring a director to "act in the way he considers, in good faith, would be most likely to promote the success of the company for the benefit of its members as a whole". In discharging this duty, a director must have regard to factors as diverse as the interests of the company's employees, relationships with the company's customers and suppliers and the effect of the company's operations on the community and the environment.

Although there is no liability for overlooking, while acting in good faith, a factor which would have no impact on the final decision, one consequence of the CA 2006 has been an increased emphasis upon documentary records. Many boards have taken the view that discussions and decisions should be more carefully minuted to provide evidence that all relevant factors have been considered fully. Whilst this is not of itself a bad thing, concerns have been raised that directors could find themselves "going through the motions" on irrelevant factors simply to ensure that all boxes have been ticked and fail to focus sufficiently on those that really matter.

The CA 2006 also governs the requirement for all companies (other than certain small companies) to prepare a stand-alone strategic report, in addition to their directors' report, for financial years ending on or after 30 September 2013 (s.414A). The strategic report is intended to assist shareholders to assess how the board has performed its duty under s.172 to promote the success of the company. The report must contain a fair review of the company's business and a description of the principal risks and uncertainties facing the company. The review must be a balanced and comprehensive analysis of both the development and performance of the company's business during the relevant financial year, and the position of the company's business at the end of that year, consistent with the size and complexity of the business.

To the extent necessary for an understanding of the development, performance or position of the company's business, the fair review should include analysis using financial key performance indicators (KPIs) and, where appropriate, analysis using other KPIs, including information relating to environmental matters and employee matters.

9.2.3   *Corporate governance and AIM companies*

Whilst AIM companies are under no compulsion to comply with the Code, their shareholders do, of course, expect such companies to be governed properly and, in the absence of an alternative, have used the Code as their yardstick. To address this issue, each of the Quoted Companies Alliance ("QCA") and the National Association of Pension Funds ("NAPF") has published a set of guidelines for corporate governance of AIM companies.

9.2.3.1   *QCA Code*

Given that a light regulatory touch is one of AIM's great selling points, publication of the original QCA corporate governance guidelines in July 2005 gave rise to some concern that, even without the force of law, the guidelines risked codifying a standard for corporate governance which might not be appropriate for every AIM company. These guidelines were subsequently superseded in 2003 by the QCA Corporate Governance Code for Small and Mid-Size Companies ("QCA Code"). In fact, most such companies already fulfilled many of the Code's requirements relating to the constitution of the board and the role of non-executive directors, particularly in the context of the recommendations relating to an audit committee and a remuneration committee. Accordingly, much of the content of the QCA Code simply reflected the status quo. Although the QCA states that compliance with its code should represent a floor for standards of corporate governance, not a cap on them, and encourages AIM companies to aspire to compliance with the Code, the reality is that the QCA Code is increasingly viewed by Nomads as the corporate governance benchmark for AIM companies.

The QCA Code identifies 12 principles, grouped under two headings: (a) delivering growth in long-term shareholder value; and (b) maintaining a flexible, efficient and effective management framework within an entrepreneurial environment. Helpfully, it also provides some practical examples of governance structures and basic reporting requirements and takes an "outcome-oriented" approach, which is very user-friendly.

9.2.3.2 NAPF Policy and Voting Guidelines for AIM Companies

As the success of AIM grew, it attracted greater interest among institutional investors, including pension funds. This interest led NAPF, which plays an active role in monitoring corporate governance in the UK, to publish its AIM Corporate Governance Policy and Voting Guidelines in March 2007. Like the QCA, with which it consulted, NAPF took the code as its starting point and stated that companies at the top end of the AIM capitalisation range would be expected to comply with the Code or to explain non-compliance. It accepted, however, that very small AIM companies can best serve their shareholders by concentrating on growing their businesses without the burden of compliance with inappropriate guidelines. Between the two extremes, and for most AIM companies, it will be a case of applying the guidelines in a way that is consistent with the size and complexity of the company's business and the resources reasonably available to it.

9.2.3.3 Key compliance areas

Although AIM companies are under no legal obligation to comply with the corporate governance requirements in the

Code, in key areas, there is undoubtedly an expectation that AIM companies will, at least in part, adopt the principles of the Code. The Code contains main and supporting principles and provisions.

The following areas are some of those in which an AIM company should seek to comply, as far as possible, with the highest standards of corporate governance:

1. Roles of chairman and chief executive officer
    The Code states that companies must provide a clear explanation of the respective roles and responsibilities of the chairman and the chief executive officer ("CEO"). Main principle A.2 emphasises that no one individual should have unfettered powers of decision and, accordingly, the roles of chairman and CEO should be separated. The QCA Code states that these roles should only be exercised by the same individual in exceptional circumstances, where there is a clearly documented explanation of how other board procedures provide protection against the risks of concentration of power within the company. NAPF considers that the functions of chairman and CEO should be clearly distinguished and not confused or compromised by being combined. It accepts, however, that a pragmatic approach will be justified if a vote against a director combining these roles might be considered detrimental to the company.
2. Independent non-executive directors
    The first principle of the Code (Code main principle A.1) is that every company should be headed by an effective board, which is collectively responsible for the success of the company. The supporting principles to main principle B.1, state that the board should include an appropriate balance of executive and non-executive directors – in particular, independent non-executive directors – such that no individual or small group of individuals can dominate the board's decision making.
    The old Combined Code offered no guidance on the role of the non-executive director, and the lack of clarity surrounding the role was a central concern of the Higgs

review (see Section 9.2.2.3 above). The FRC now gives extensive guidance to non-executive directors, both in the Code's supporting principles and in the supplementary Guidance (see Section 9.2.2.3 above). The Code states in main principle A.4 that, as part of their role as members of a unitary board, non-executive directors should constructively challenge and help develop proposals on strategy. Increasingly, the role of the non-executive director is a proactive one: he or she must be well informed about the company, its policies and procedures and the external environment in which it operates with a view to scrutinising and, where necessary, challenging the performance of executive management. It certainly should not be seen as a job which offers the retired executive, seeking a large portfolio of non-executive directorships, the opportunity for a quiet life.

The Code provides that a company outside the FTSE 350 should have at least two non-executive directors determined by the board to be independent (Code provision B.1.2). This requirement is echoed by the QCA Code and the NAPF AIM Policy. Whether a director is or is not independent must be determined by reference to any relationships or circumstances which are likely to affect, or could appear to affect, the director's judgment. The board should state its reasons for deciding that a director is independent, notwithstanding the existence of relationships or circumstances which may appear relevant, for example, if the director has been an employee of the company within the last five years, has had, directly or indirectly, a material business relationship with the company within the last three years, if he or she has close family ties with any of the company's advisers, directors or senior employees or represents a significant shareholder (Code provision B.1.1).

The Code provides that the board should appoint one of the independent non-executive directors to be the senior independent director or SID (Code provision A.4.1) to be a sounding board for the chairman and to serve as an intermediary for the other directors, when necessary. The QCA Code also highlights the important role of the SID and encourages even smaller companies to consider carefully whether they should have one. The SID should be available to shareholders if they have concerns which they have failed to resolve through the usual channels of chairman, CEO or finance director, or for which such contact is inappropriate. Given the current move towards increased shareholder activism, and the issue of the Stewardship Code by the FRC, it is reasonable to expect that shareholders would take advantage of this new line of communication. The NAPF AIM Policy requires the appointment of an SID where a company has a combined chairman and CEO and encourages such an appointment in other circumstances. Nonetheless, it remains unusual for an AIM company to nominate a non-executive director for the SID role.

3.   Audit committee

Main principle C.3 of the Code states that the board should establish formal and transparent arrangements for considering how it should apply the corporate reporting and risk management and internal control principles of the company and for maintaining an appropriate relationship with the company's auditors. Most AIM companies appoint an audit committee and will look to the Code when drawing up its terms of reference.

The constitution of the audit committee

Provision C.3.1 of the Code provides that the board should establish an audit committee of at least three or, in the case of a company below the FTSE 350, two, members, who should all be independent non-executive directors. At least one member of the committee should have recent and relevant financial experience.

The role of the audit committee

Whilst every director has a duty to act in the interests of the company and, following the principle of the unitary board, remains equally responsible for the company's affairs as a matter of law, the audit committee has a particular role to ensure that the interests of shareholders are properly protected in relation to financial reporting and internal control. Provision C.3.8 of the Code provides that the work of the committee in discharging its responsibilities should be the subject of a separate section in the company's annual report, with a view to giving the audit committee a prominence and authority it might otherwise lack.

The main role and responsibilities of the audit committee should be set out in writing and made available on request and included on the company's website, if it has one. These should be reviewed by the audit committee annually and should include:

(a) monitoring the integrity of the financial statements of the company and any formal announcements relating to the company's financial performance, including reviewing any significant financial reporting judgments contained in them;

(b) reviewing the company's internal financial controls (i.e. the systems established to identify, assess, manage and monitor financial risks) and, unless expressly addressed by a separate risk committee composed of independent directors, or by the board itself, reviewing the company's internal control and risk management systems;

(c) monitoring and reviewing the effectiveness of the company's internal audit function and. where there is no internal audit function, the audit committee should consider annually whether there is a need for such a function and the reasons for its absence should be explained in the relevant section of the annual report;

(d) making recommendations to the board, for it to put to the shareholders for their approval in general meetings, in relation to the appointment, reappointment and removal of the external auditor and approving the remuneration and terms of engagement of the external auditor. If the external auditor resigns, the audit committee should investigate the issues giving rise to such resignation and consider whether any action is required;

(e) reviewing and monitoring the external auditor's independence and objectivity and the effectiveness of the audit process, taking into consideration relevant UK professional and regulatory requirements; and

(f) developing and implementing policy on the engagement of the external auditor to supply non-audit services, taking into account relevant ethical guidance regarding the provision of non-audit services by the external audit firm. If the external auditor provides non-audit services, the annual report should explain to shareholders how auditor independence and objectivity are safeguarded.

Ultimately, the effectiveness of the audit committee will depend upon an open relationship with management and a high level of mutual respect between the committee and the executive. It will also require the audit committee to be properly and promptly informed of all relevant developments and decisions. The audit committee should not hesitate to request additional information and ask difficult questions where it is not satisfied with the explanations of management and the auditors about a particular financial policy procedure. Equally, the executive directors must ensure that they are quick to canvass, and willing to listen to, the audit committee's views and should take the initiative in supplying all information which the committee may need to discharge its obligations effectively.

4. Remuneration committee

One of the most controversial and highly publicised areas of corporate governance is the determination of directors' remuneration. Whilst most shareholders accept that levels of remuneration must be sufficient to recruit, retain and motivate directors of the calibre required to run a company successfully, and so increase shareholder value, there has been much criticism of perceived failure to link rewards to corporate and individual performance.

It is a main principle of the Code (Code main principle D.2) that there should be a formal and transparent procedure for developing policy on executive remuneration and for fixing the remuneration packages of individual directors. No director should be involved in deciding his or her own remuneration. The appointment of a remuneration committee is standard for most AIM companies and, as when appointing an audit committee, such companies will usually base the terms of reference of the remuneration committee on the standards set out in the Code.

The constitution of the remuneration committee

The Code provides (in Code provision D.2.1) that the remuneration committee should consist exclusively of independent non-executive directors and should comprise at least two such directors in the case of a company outside the FTSE 350. The remuneration committee should make available on request and on the company's website its terms of reference, explaining its role and the authority delegated to it by the board. These terms should be reviewed and, where necessary, updated annually by the committee.

The role of the remuneration committee

The main duties of the remuneration committee should include:

(a) Determining and agreeing with the board the framework or broad policy for the remuneration of the chief executive, the chairman of the company and such other members of the executive as it is designated to consider. As a minimum, the Code provides that the committee should have delegated responsibility for setting remuneration for all executive directors and the chairman, including pension rights;

(b) Considering whether the directors should be eligible for annual bonuses. If so, it is recommended that the performance conditions should be relevant, challenging and designed to promote the long-term success of the Company;

(c) Ensuring that contractual terms on termination, and any payments made, including pension contributions, are fair to the individual and the company and that a departing director's duty to mitigate his loss is fully recognised. The aim should be to avoid rewarding poor performance, and to set notice periods at one year or less;

(d) Ensuring that applicable provisions regarding the disclosure of remuneration, including pensions are fulfilled; and

(e) Being exclusively responsible for establishing the selection criteria for selecting, appointing and setting the terms of reference for any remuneration consultants who advise the committee. If such consultants are appointed, a statement should be made available on request and on the company's website as to whether they have any other connection with the company.

The remuneration of non-executive directors should be a matter for the board or, where required by the company's articles of association, the shareholders. If remuneration consultants are appointed, they should be identified in the company's annual report and a statement made as to whether they have any other connection with the company. Non-executive remuneration should reflect the time commitment and responsibilities of the role and should only exceptionally include share options or other performance-related elements. If such options are granted, shareholder approval should be sought in advance. Any shares acquired by a non-executive director by exercise of share options should be held until at least one year after the non-executive director leaves the board.

5. Nomination committee

The Code provides (in Code provision B.2.1) that there should be a nomination committee which leads the process for board appointments and making recommendations to the board. The QCA Code and the NAPF AIM Policy support this provision. Although Nomads are increasingly keen on seeing nomination committees being constituted, it still remains somewhat unusual for an AIM company, particularly at the lower end of the capitalisation range, to have a separate nomination committee. Typically, new appointments are dealt with by the whole board or, in some cases, by the remuneration committee as an extension of its role.

The QCA Code and NAPF AIM Policy are broadly aligned with the Code in relation to the composition of committees, while recognising that some AIM companies will not have sufficient independent non-executive directors to achieve full compliance. Although the audit, remuneration and (if there is one) nomination committees ideally should be comprised of solely independent non-executive directors, it is sometimes the case that an AIM company will succeed only in having a majority of independent directors on its committees.

9.3. Conclusion

In positioning AIM, much is made of its lighter regulatory touch, including the ability of AIM companies to take a more pragmatic view in the area of corporate governance without having to explain publicly any deviation from the requirements of the Code. There is, however, a continuing trend among companies whose shares are publicly traded towards greater accountability to shareholders, not least in relation to directors' remuneration. Inevitably, these pressures have made themselves felt in the boardrooms of AIM companies, regardless of whether or not the directors of such companies are under a statutory or regulatory obligation to comply with the increasing volume of guidelines on corporate governance. Recent changes to the AIM Rules have made it essential that directors of AIM companies exhibit a good understanding of the relevant issues and can explain clearly their company's stance on them. Where an AIM company does not comply with the key governance standards outlined above, it is increasingly likely to have to justify such non-compliance to aggrieved investors.

Chapter 10

Investing Companies

John Reed
Partner, Wragge Lawrence Graham & Co LLP

Kristian Rogers
Partner, Wragge Lawrence Graham & Co LLP

10.1   Introduction

In April 2005 the AIM Team introduced new AIM rules for investing companies in order to regulate the increasing number of companies that were coming to market as "cash shells". The next few years saw a large number of companies (especially closed-ended investment companies) admitted to AIM using the investing company rules.

This led the AIM Team, in December 2008, to propose changes to the rules relating to investing companies. The aim was to introduce tailored rules for investing companies. After a six month consultation, the AIM Team amended the AIM rules dealing with investing companies and also published a new AIM Note for Investing Companies.

This chapter: (a) explains what an investing company is and how it differs from AIM trading companies; (b) provides a description of the other specific advisers an investing company may appoint when compared to AIM trading companies; (c) explains the additional requirements for an investing company to be admitted to AIM (including a brief summary of Directive 2011/61/EU of the European Parliament and of the Council of 8 June 2011 on Alternative Investment Fund Managers (a detailed description of which is outside the scope of this

Guide); and (d) sets out how an investing company's continuing obligations differ to those of AIM trading companies.

10.2 What is an investing company?

10.2.1 The AIM Rules for Companies

The AIM Rules for Companies define an investing company as:

> "Any AIM company which has, as its primary business or objective, the investing of its funds in securities, businesses or assets of any description."

Broadly, there are two types of investing companies: closed-ended investment companies (see Section 10.2.2 below) and cash shells (see Section 10.2.3 below), although the definition can also apply to special purpose acquisition companies (known as "SPACs"). Although the definition is broad, it should be noted that an AIM company which is the holding company for a trading business is not considered an investing company under the AIM Rules for Companies.

Investing companies seeking admission to AIM should generally be straightforward in their structure and investing policy. Promoters and/or advisers of complex investing entities which are primarily designed for sophisticated investors (e.g. open-ended investment companies or limited partnerships) should consider whether an alternative market, such as the London Stock Exchange's ("LSE's") Main Market or Specialist Fund Market would be more appropriate.

Nominated Advisers ("Nomads") should consult the AIM Team if there is any doubt if an applicant or, following a significant disposal (see Section 10.2.3 below), an existing AIM company, should be treated as an investing company.

10.2.2 *Closed-ended investment companies*

A closed-ended investment company is a pooled investment entity incorporated as a company typically managed by an external investment manager (see Section 10.3.1 below). As a body corporate, a closed-ended investment fund company will not fall to be categorised as a "Collective Investment Scheme" for the purposes of s.235 of the Financial Services and Markets Act 2000 and can therefore be marketed in the UK in the same way as other corporate vehicles pursuant to normal UK financial promotions rules.

An investing company that is a closed-ended investment company will usually be a newly incorporated limited liability company and will typically have the following characteristics:

- incorporated in a tax efficient jurisdiction such as Guernsey, Jersey or the Isle of Man;
- shares that are not redeemable at the option of shareholders (although the shares may be redeemable at the option of the investing company); and
- investors buy and sell shares in the secondary market.

10.2.3 *Cash shell*

If an existing AIM company divests all, or substantially all, of its trading business, activities or assets, that AIM company will, upon completion of the disposal, be treated as an investing company. Such a disposal must be conditional on shareholder approval and be announced to the market (such announcement containing the information specified by Sch.4 to the AIM Rules for Companies). Furthermore, any notification and shareholder circular must state the AIM company's new investing policy (see Section 10.4.1.1 below). The new investing policy must also be approved by shareholders and the Nomad must inform the AIM Team as soon as an existing AIM company becomes an investing company.

10.3 Advisers to the investing company

In addition to the typical advisers appointed by an AIM company (e.g. Nomad, broker, auditors, etc.), an investing company will also usually appoint an investment manager and an administrator and, in certain circumstances, a custodian and/or a prime broker.

10.3.1 Investment manager

An investment manager is a professional adviser who manages an investment company in order to meet specified investment goals for the benefit of investors.

An investment manager is defined in the AIM Rules for Companies as:

> "Any person external to the investing company, who, on behalf of that investing company, manages their investments. This may include an external adviser who provides material advice to the investment manager or the investing company."

Nomads should ensure that, before its proposed appointment, it is satisfied that an investment manager has sufficient experience to manage the investing company's investments.

When considering the proposed terms of an investment manager's appointment, advisers should pay particular attention to the terms of the investment management agreement relating to, amongst other things, any initial length of appointment, the scope of services (including the ability to delegate), the amount of fees (typically a management fee and, sometimes, a performance fee), the right of the investing company to terminate the investment manager's appointment, the notice period on termination and whether any accrued but unpaid fees become due on termination.

10.3.2 *Administrator*

More often than not, neither an investing company nor its investment manager (should one be appointed) will have the resources, facilities or personnel to carry out the investing company's day-to-day administrative operations. Typically, an investing company will appoint a professional services firm as their "administrator" who will carry out, inter alia, some or all of the following activities: (a) calculation of the investing company's net asset value ("NAV") and the NAV per share (see Section 10.4.3.2 below); (b) preparation of annual accounts and half-yearly accounts; (c) payment of expenses; (d) maintenance of the financial books and records; and (e) company secretarial duties such as calling and holding general meetings and taking minutes of any board meetings.

An administrator should be involved with the preparation of an investing company's admission document from an early stage in order to make sure that any description of the investment company's administrative functions (e.g. the preparation of accounts, how the investing company will value its investments etc.) is consistent with how the administrator will operate on a day-to-day basis following the investing company's admission to AIM.

10.3.3 *Custodian*

A custodian is responsible for safeguarding an investing company's investments and is typically appointed when it is not cost effective for an investing company to hold its investments directly (for example, holding shares directly in an overseas market could require an investing company to open a branch and/or be authorised in the relevant jurisdiction). A custodian, inter alia, would: (a) hold and arrange settlement of assets/securities; (b) collect information on, and income from, such assets; (c) administer voluntary and involuntary corporate actions on securities; (d) provide information on the securities and their issuers, such as annual general meetings and related proxies; and (e) maintain currency/cash bank accounts.

Custodians may have a worldwide network of branches and/or local sub-custodians (who may or may not be part of the custodian's group). This allows the custodian to hold assets for an investing company in multiple jurisdictions.

When considering a custodian's proposed appointment, advisers should be aware of the effect on the investing company's assets of an insolvency of the custodian and/or any sub-custodian.

10.3.4 *Prime broker*

Prime brokerage is the generic name for a bundled package of services offered by investment banks and securities firms to investing companies and other professional investors who need the ability to borrow securities and cash to be able to invest on a netted basis. A prime broker frequently offers some or all of the following services: (a) securities lending; (b) margin financing; (c) trade processing; and (d) cash processing. It will also typically offer traditional custodian services.

Advisers should consider the proposed appointment of a prime broker in the same way as they would a custodian, as the same risks regarding ownership of assets and insolvency are applicable.

10.4 Admission requirements

On its admission to AIM, an investing company (like any other applicant) must produce an admission document. However, as it is an investing company, Sch.2 to the AIM Rules for Companies, inter alia, requires an admission document to include:

- details of its investing policy (see Section 10.4.1.1 below); and
- the information required by the AIM Note for Investing Companies (see Section 10.4.2 below).

Section 10.4.1 sets out the specific requirements relating to an investing company's admission document which are contained in the AIM Rules for Companies and Section 10.4.2 sets out the requirements of the AIM Note for Investing Companies. There are also a number of other considerations specific to investing companies that advisers should bear in mind when drafting an admission document and these are set out at Section 10.4.3.

10.4.1   The AIM Rules for Companies

10.4.1.1   Investing policy

An investing policy is the policy the investing company will follow in relation to asset allocation and risk diversification.

Schedule 2 to the AIM Rules for Companies requires an investing company to prominently set out details of its investing policy in its admission document. The investing policy must be sufficiently precise and detailed so that it is clear, specific and definitive. The investing policy must contain, as a minimum, a description of:

- the assets or companies in which the investing company can invest;
- the means or strategy by which the investing policy will be achieved;
- whether such investments will be active or passive and, if applicable, the length of time that investments are likely to be held for;
- how widely the investing company will spread its investments and its maximum exposure limits (if applicable);
- the investing company's policy in relation to gearing and cross-holdings (if applicable);
- details of any investing restrictions (e.g. gearing limits, geographical or industry sector restrictions); and
- the nature of returns the investing company will seek to deliver to shareholders (e.g. capital growth or regular distributions of income) and, if applicable, how long the

investing company can exist before making an investment and/or having to return funds to shareholders.

An investing company's investing policy should state the nature of returns the investing company will seek to deliver to shareholders (e.g. capital growth or regular distributions of income). The description of an investing company's dividend policy should be consistent with its investing policy regarding distributions of income. It should also be considered whether it would be more tax efficient for investors to structure distributions as a dividend or, for example, a tender offer.

10.4.1.2 *Schedule 2 to the AIM Rules for Companies*

The AIM Note for Investing Companies states that in interpreting Sch.2 to the AIM Rules for Companies, investing companies should include the following information within the front part of their admission documents:

- the expertise its directors have, as a board, in respect of the investing policy;
- where there is an investment manager (see Section 10.3.1 above):
  - the name of the investment manager;
  - the experience of the investment manager and its expertise in respect of the investing policy;
  - a description of the investment manager's regulatory status including the name of the regulatory authority by which it is regulated, if applicable;
  - a summary of the key terms of the agreement(s) with the investment manager, including fees, length of agreement and its termination provisions; and
  - if applicable, the investing company's policy in relation to regular updates such as the frequency with which it will update shareholders as to the performance of the portfolio. The performance of liquid portfolios (e.g. shares in listed companies) might be updated daily or weekly whereas illiquid portfolios (e.g. real estate or unlisted private equity investments)

might be updated on a less regular basis such as quarterly or semi-annually.

The admission document should also include information about the investing company's taxation status and any policy or strategy it has in relation to taxation if applicable.

10.4.1.3 Minimum fund raise

An investing company is expected to raise a minimum of £3 million in cash via an equity fundraising on, or immediately before, admission. This requirement is typically satisfied by an independent fundraising and not from related party funds (unless the related party in question is a substantial shareholder only and authorised by the FCA or another EU regulator). The AIM Team should be consulted at an early stage if this is not the case.

10.4.1.4 Lock-ins

For the majority of investing companies, their main business activity will not have been independent and earning revenue for two years. This means that, in accordance with the AIM Rules for Companies r.7, all the investing company's related parties and applicable employees must agree not to dispose of any interest in the investing company's securities for one year from admission (subject to certain limited exceptions).

The AIM Note for Investing Companies states that an investing company's investment manager (or any company in the same group) and the investment manager's key employees (i.e. those who are responsible for making investment decisions) should also be subject to the restrictions set out in the AIM Rules for Companies r.7. Accordingly, in such circumstances, investment managers and their key employees should sign lock-in deeds in addition to the investing company's directors.

10.4.2 The AIM Note for Investing Companies

10.4.2.1 Suitability

As part of the AIM admission process, Nomads are required to assess whether an investing company is appropriate for AIM. Unless the AIM Team can be persuaded otherwise, this means the investing company will be a closed-ended company that does not require a restricted investor base and is straightforward in terms of structure and investing policy (see Section 10.2.2 above). The investing company should also predominantly issue ordinary or common shares.

10.4.2.2 Feeder funds

An investing company may be structured as a "feeder fund". A feeder fund principally invests its funds in an unquoted fund vehicle (known as the "master fund"). In such circumstances, Nomads should consider the impact of the master fund on the investing company's investing policy (e.g. should the investing policy mirror that of the master fund?). Careful consideration should also be given to any additional master fund disclosures in the admission document required under Annex XV of the Prospectus Rules (see Section 10.4.2.7 below).

10.4.2.3 Controlling stakes

An investing company could take a controlling stake (i.e. over 50 per cent) in one or more of its investments. When that happens, the Nomad should make sure there is sufficient separation between the investing company and its investment(s) in order to make sure the investing company does not become a trading company. A Nomad should also make sure any overlap between an investing company's investments (e.g. cross-financing or sharing of operations) is limited.

10.4.2.4 Experience of directors and investment managers

A Nomad must satisfy itself that an investing company's board of directors and any investment manager are in each case, appropriate and have sufficient experience for the investing company and its investing policy. There should also be appropriate agreements in place between an investing company and any investment manager covering key matters (see Section 10.3.1 above).

Where there is an investment manager, an investing company should have in place sufficient safeguards and procedures to ensure that its board of directors retains sufficient control over its business (e.g. the board of directors having the right to veto investment decisions, regular reviews of the investment manager's performance etc.).

10.4.2.5   Independence of the board

The AIM Team expects the board of directors of an investing company (as a whole), and its Nomad, to be independent from any investment manager unless there are extenuating circumstances. The investing company's admission document should disclose whether or not its board of directors and/or Nomad are independent from its investment manager. Any subsequent changes to this position should be announced.

The AIM Team also usually expects the Nomad and the board of directors (as a whole), to be independent of any substantial shareholders or investments (and any associated investment manager) which comprise over 20 per cent of the gross assets of the investing company. Again, this should be adequately disclosed in the admission document and/or announced. The principles set out in r.21 (Independence on a continuing basis) and r.22 (Conflicts of Interest) of the AIM Rules for Nominated Advisers should be consulted when considering if any relevant party is independent.

10.4.2.6   Periodic disclosures

The Nomad, together with the investing company, should consider whether regular periodic disclosures (such as a regular NAV statement or details of principal investments) should be released to the market in order to update market participants, having due regard to market practice and the activities of the investing company. As mentioned in Section 10.3.2 above, it is sensible to consider the views of the investing company's administrator from an early stage.

The approach to making regular updates should be included in the admission document and any changes to this should be announced. Such periodic disclosures do not negate the need for any other notification which would otherwise be required under the AIM Rules for Companies (e.g. r.11).

10.4.2.7 Annex XV

An admission document in relation to an investing company, should disclose the information required by Annex XV of the Prospectus Rules in addition to the requirements of Sch.2 to the AIM Rules for Companies. An investing company will be required, inter alia, to include the following additional disclosures in its admission document in accordance with Annex XV:

- borrowing and/or leverage limits;
- the profile of a typical investor;
- an indication of how investors will be informed of the actions the investment manager will take in the event of a breach of the investing company's investment policy;
- how investments will be held and by whom and any fiduciary or similar relationship between the investing company and any third party in relation to custody; and
- a description of how often, and the valuation principles and the method by which, the NAV of the investing company will be determined.

It should also be noted that if an investing company invests 20 per cent or more of its gross assets in a single underlying issuer (for example, if it is a feeder fund that invests in an underlying master fund (see Section 10.4.2.2 above)), then Annex XV requires the investing company's admission document to include the same disclosures about the underlying issuer as the investing company. This additional disclosure can be time-consuming and it is recommended that advisers establish at an early stage if such additional disclosures are likely.

10.4.2.8   *Financial information*

If the Nomad considers it is appropriate, a newly incorporated investing company that has not traded, made any investments or taken on any liabilities does not need to include financial statements in its admission document. Instead the investing company must include a statement in its admission document that since the date of its incorporation the investing company has not yet commenced operations and that it has no material assets or liabilities, and therefore that no financial statements have been prepared as at the date of the admission document.

10.4.3   **Other considerations**

10.4.3.1   *The Alternative Investment Fund Managers Directive (2011/61/EU) ("AIFMD")*

The AIFMD was published in the Official Journal of the European Union on 1 July 2011 and entered into force in the UK on 22 July 2011. A detailed description of the AIFMD is outside the scope of this Guide but its impact on investing companies and their investment managers should not be underestimated and should be dealt with at an early stage in the AIM admission process.

The AIFMD introduced a regulatory framework across the EEA for the regulation of EEA-established alternative investment fund managers ("AIFMs"). An AIFM includes any legal or natural person whose regular business is to manage one or more alternative investment funds ("AIFs"). An AIF may be its own AIFM. AIM investing companies will generally be considered AIFs. Certain provisions of the AIFMD relating to marketing also apply to a non-EEA AIFMs (e.g. an offshore investment manager marketing an investing company in the EEA).

Some of the principal ways the AIFMD impacts an investing company (and its investment manager) are:

•Subject to certain partial exemptions, an EEA AIFM must be authorised and subject to supervision by the regulator in its home member state.

•AIFMs are subject to governance and conduct of business standards and must have robust systems in place to manage risks, liquidity and conflicts of interest.

•There are increased disclosure requirements and reporting obligations.

•AIFMs are subject to certain capital requirements as well as requirements to cover professional negligence risks.

•Many of the AIF's key service providers (e.g. in particular, depositaries) are subject to regulatory standards.

•There are restrictions on the delegation of AIFM functions.

•A European "passport" has been introduced under which authorised AIFMs can manage and market EEA AIFs to professional investors throughout the EEA, subject to compliance with certain regulatory standards.

When bringing a new investing company to market, the Nomad should speak to the investing company's solicitors as early as possible about the AIFMD's impact on the investing company's structure and any impact on the proposed timetable.

10.4.3.2   Net asset value

The value of an AIM trading company is typically derived from, inter alia, a combination of the profit generated by its business and the value of its assets, whereas the value of an investing company is principally derived from the value of its investments. Accordingly, the value of an investing company is typically assessed by reference to its "NAV" (i.e. the total value of its assets less the total value of its liabilities) and the intrinsic value of the shares of an investing company is usually assessed by reference to its "NAV per share" (i.e. its net asset value divided by the number of shares in issue from time to time).

An investing company's admission document should contain, as a minimum, details of the basis on which the investing company's assets will be valued (e.g. at the prevailing market price or at book value or some other method of valuation), how often the net asset value and NAV per share will be published (e.g. daily, weekly, monthly or quarterly) and how investors will be notified (usually by way of RIS announcements).

10.4.3.3   *Premiums and discounts to NAV*

An investing company's shares trade at a "premium to NAV" when the prevailing market price of a share is greater than the prevailing NAV per share. Similarly, an investing company's shares trade at a "discount to NAV" when the prevailing market price of a share is less than the prevailing NAV per share.

Shares trade at a premium or a discount to NAV for a number of reasons including: (a) past performance or expected future performance of the investing company; (b) concern by investors that the valuations used in calculating the net asset value and NAV per share do not reflect the true value of some or all of the investing company's portfolio; (c) market sentiment towards a particular geographic region or type of asset; or (d) belief that an investing company that invests in illiquid assets will have difficulty realising its assets or face greater costs in doing so.

Advisers should consider whether an investing company's admission document should contain details of any mechanisms (e.g. share buy-back programmes, regular tender offers etc.) which could be used to attempt to narrow any discount to NAV, if and when, it arises.

10.4.3.4   Further issue of shares

It is usual for an investing company's admission document to provide that the investing company will not issue any further shares for cash at a price below the prevailing NAV per share unless: (a) such shares are first offered pro rata to existing shareholders; or (b) the proposed issue is authorised by shareholders. This is an additional shareholder protection to those typically available to shareholders of an AIM trading company and mirrors certain requirements for a closed-ended investment company admitted to trading on the Main Market of the LSE.

10.4.3.5   Life of the investing company and continuation votes

In some instances an investing company may have a fixed life and, if this is the case, it will be set out in its constitutional documents and disclosed in its admission document. In such circumstances the constitutional documents will usually require the investing company to convene a shareholder meeting to propose a resolution to wind-up the investing company voluntarily on a certain date.

Alternatively an investing company may be structured as an "evergreen" vehicle with no defined fixed life. In this instance investors will typically be given an opportunity to assess the continued operations of the investing company through a periodic "continuation vote". A continuation vote could, as an example, be proposed once every three years with investors being asked to vote on whether the investing company should continue as currently constituted. In the event that the resolution is rejected by shareholders, the board of directors generally will be mandated to put forward proposals to shareholders within a defined timeframe to reconstruct or wind-up the investing company.

10.4.3.6   Corporate governance

AIM companies (trading and investing) do not have to comply with the UK Corporate Governance Code. However, admission documents typically contain a statement that they will do so to the extent it is practicable and appropriate in the circumstances.

A number of provisions of the UK Corporate Governance Code (for example, the requirement to separate the role of chairman and chief executive) are not applicable to investing companies as the majority of their activities are outsourced (see Section 10.3 above). This led the Association of Investment Companies (commonly known as the AIC) to produce its own corporate governance code designed specifically for investment companies (which include investing companies), called the AIC Code of Corporate Governance, and advisers should consider whether it would be appropriate for an investing company to follow the AIC Code of Corporate Governance rather than the UK Corporate Governance Code.

It should be noted that an investing company must become a corporate member of the AIC before it can publicly state that it will comply with the AIC Code of Corporate Governance.

10.5 Continuing obligations

Before publication of the AIM Note for Investing Companies, the application of the AIM Rules for Companies' continuing obligations to investing companies could generate anomalous results. For example, it was not uncommon for an investing company that had made a large investment in accordance with its investing policy prima facie to be required to publish a new admission document under the AIM Rules for Companies r.14 (Reverse takeovers). Whilst, in practice, the investing company's Nomad would request a derogation from the AIM Team, the introduction of the AIM Note for Investing Companies has clarified the AIM Rules for Companies' continuing obligations (e.g. a large investment by an investing company will now only trigger the requirements under the AIM Rules for Companies r.14 in limited circumstances) and made them much more relevant to investing companies.

Section 10.5.1 below sets out how the continuing obligations in the AIM Rules for Companies should be interpreted for investing companies and Section 10.5.2 sets out specific ongoing obligations relating to an investing company's investing policy.

10.5.1 Interpretation of the AIM Rules for Companies

10.5.1.1 Related party transactions, disclosure of miscellaneous information, restriction on deals

An investment manager (or any company in the same group) and any of its key employees (i.e. those responsible for making investment decisions in relation to the investing company) will be considered a director for the purposes of: (a) the application of the AIM Rules for Companies rr.13 and 21; and (b) the disclosure of any deals by directors under the AIM Rules for Companies r.17. Accordingly, Nomads should always consider whether any proposed transaction by an investing company with its investment manager or any of its key employees will require the director to give a fair and reasonable statement (i.e. is it greater than 5 per cent on any of the class tests?). Similarly, advisers should make sure an investing company is not in a close period before an investment manager or any of an investment manager's key employees are permitted to deal in any of the investing company's shares.

10.5.1.2 General disclosure of price-sensitive information

Change of investment manager

The appointment, dismissal or resignation of any investment manager (or any key personnel within the investing company, or investment manager, which might impact achievement or progression of the investing policy) would generally be considered price-sensitive information requiring an announcement without delay. Any such announcement should include information on the consequences of the appointment, dismissal or resignation.

218

Cumulative effect of investment changes

Investing companies and Nomads should, when making an assessment as to whether notification of an investment or a disposal of an investment is required, consider the cumulative impact of a series of investments or disposals.

Change of information previously disclosed

Any changes to the information set out at Section 10.4.1.2 above which have been included should be considered and assessed with the investing company to determine whether such change should be announced.

10.5.1.3   Substantial transactions

Any investment made by an investing company that: (a) is in accordance with its investing policy; and (b) only breaches the profits and turnover tests contained in the class tests, would be considered as being one of a "revenue nature in the ordinary course of business" and would not require disclosure as a substantial transaction in accordance with the AIM Rules for Companies r.12. However, a disclosure may still be required under the AIM Rules for Companies r.11 if the transaction in question is price sensitive in nature. If a disclosure is required, the information required by Sch.4 to the AIM Rules for Companies is a useful guide to establish the content of such announcement.

10.5.1.4   Reverse take-overs

Pursuant to the AIM Rules for Companies r.14, an acquisition by an investing company (which should be interpreted broadly and includes, for example, an investment in a company or assets) which exceeds 100 per cent in any of the class tests may be considered a reverse take-over, even if such an acquisition is made in accordance with its stated investing policy.

However an acquisition made by an investing company that: (a) is in accordance with its investing policy; (b) only breaches the profits and turnover tests contained in the class tests; and (c) does not result in a fundamental change in its business, board or voting control, would not be considered a reverse take-over under the AIM Rules for Companies r.14. In all other instances, a Nomad should approach the AIM Team if it considers that an acquisition falling within the AIM Rules for Companies r.14 should not be treated as a reverse take-over. However, this does not mean that the AIM Rules for Companies rr.11 and 12 will not require notification of such an investment.

If an investing company is intending to undertake an acquisition that might result in it not being an investing company (for example, it will become an operating business following the acquisition), the application of the AIM Rules for Companies r.14 should be considered.

10.5.1.5 *Fundamental change of business*

A disposal by an investing company which is within its investing policy will not be subject to the requirement under the AIM Rules for Companies r.15 to obtain shareholder consent. However, a disclosure in accordance with Sch.4 to the AIM Rules for Companies should still be made.

Where an investing company disposes of all, or substantially all, of its assets the investing company will have 12 months from the date of that disposal to implement its current investing policy. If this is not fulfilled, the investing company will be suspended from trading on AIM. Any material change to its investing policy will require shareholder approval, but the twelve month period will continue to apply.

10.5.2 *Investing policy*

10.5.2.1 *Substantial implementation of investing policy*

Where an investing company has not substantially implemented its investing policy within eighteen months of admission, it should seek the consent of its shareholders for its investing policy at its next annual general meeting and on an annual basis thereafter, until such time that its investing policy has been substantially implemented.

In making the assessment of whether or not an investing company has substantially implemented its investing policy, the AIM Team usually considers this to mean that the investing company has invested a substantial portion (usually at least in excess of 50 per cent) of all funds available to it (including funds available through agreed debt facilities) in a range of investments; and in accordance with its investing policy.

10.5.2.2 Change to investing policy

An investing company must seek the prior consent of its shareholders in a general meeting for any material change to its investing policy. In making the assessment of what constitutes a material change to the published investing policy, Nomads should consider the cumulative effect of all the changes made since shareholder approval was last obtained for the investing policy or, if no such approval has been given, since the date of admission. The Guidance Notes to the AIM Rules for Investing Companies state that any material change to the specific points set out in the definition of investing policy is likely to constitute a material change requiring shareholder consent.

Any circular convening a meeting of shareholders for the purpose of obtaining consent for a change in investing policy should contain adequate information about the current and proposed investing policy and the reasons for and expected consequences of any proposed change. A resolving action, such as the return of funds to shareholders, may need to be considered if consent is not obtained and the Nomad must keep the AIM Team informed if such a situation occurs. If shareholder approval for the change to investing policy is not obtained, the investing company's existing investing policy will continue to be effective.

10.5.2.3   *Regular notice of investing policy*

An investing company's investing policy should be regularly notified and at a minimum should be stated in the investing company's annual accounts.

10.5.3   *AIM Rule 26 website*

If an AIM company is also an investing company, the website it is required to maintain, pursuant to the AIM Rules for Companies r.26, should contain details of the investing company's investing policy as well as details of any investment manager and the investment manager's key personnel.

10.6   Conclusion

The introduction of the AIM Note for Investing Companies was almost inevitable following the large number of companies (especially closed-ended investment companies) admitted to AIM using the previous investing company rules. It is a useful addition to the AIM Rules for Companies and helps clarify how the rules should operate when applied to investing companies.

Chapter 11

The Tax Regime

Chilton Taylor

Partner, Head of Capital Markets, Baker Tilly

11.1 Introduction

The UK tax regime has historically offered certain advantages to investments in unquoted trading companies. These advantages extend, somewhat counter-intuitively, to companies whose shares are traded on AIM, for the simple reason that AIM is not, for tax purposes, a "recognised stock exchange" and for tax purposes shares in AIM companies are therefore regarded as "unquoted". A list of recognised stock exchanges is maintained by HM Revenue & Customs at *www.hmrc.gov.uk/fid/rse.htm*.

Key reliefs include:

1. those in the venture capital schemes (i.e. the Seed Enterprise Investment Scheme ("SEIS"), the Enterprise Investment Scheme ("EIS") and Venture Capital Trust scheme ("VCT"));
2. loss relief for share disposals;
3. capital gains tax business asset gift relief; and
4. inheritance tax business property relief.

This chapter provides a brief synopsis of these reliefs and some of the more common problems and issues that practitioners face. It is, however, no substitute for specialist advice, which is always recommended. This is particularly true in relation to the venture capital schemes as the legislation governing these has a deserved reputation for complexity, not assisted by the inclusion of widespread anti-avoidance provisions. Advice should only be provided by (and accepted from) experienced practitioners who are familiar with the entirety of the legislation and regularly advise on it.

The venture capital tax schemes have undergone a number of changes in recent years and this state of flux means that the usual warning that the reader should remember that tax law is prone to change is thus more than usually apt.

The commentary provided in this chapter is based on legislation up to and including Finance Act 2014.

Other important recent changes affecting AIM shares

Finance Act 2013 and The Individual Savings Account (Amendment No 3) Regulations 2013 update

From 5 August 2013, individuals are able to invest in AIM companies through their stocks and shares Individual Savings Accounts (ISAs). ISAs are generally seen as tax efficient as an individual pays no tax on the income received from ISA savings and investments (including dividends), nor does the individual pay tax on capital gains arising on ISA investments (losses are not allowable). The annual limit which an individual can pay into a stocks and shares ISA for the period 6 April 2014 to 5 April 2015 is £15,000 (£11,520 for 2013/14).

Finance Bill 2014 and stamp duty tax exemption for eligible securities on a recognised growth market

From 28 April 2014, stamp duty and the stamp duty reserve tax will no longer be chargeable on transactions in securities admitted to a recognised growth market provided that they are not also listed on a recognised stock exchange (as defined in Section 1005 (3) – (5) of the Income Tax 2007).

AIM has been approved as a recognised growth market under the criteria set out in Clause 108 and Schedule 20 of the Finance Bill 2014. On this basis, securities on AIM that are not listed on a recognised stock exchange will not be subject to the tax. AIM issuers must ensure they inform Euroclear UK & Ireland Limited of their stamp duty exemption status by way of a Stamp Duty Exemption self-certification form.

11.2 The Venture Capital Schemes

11.2.1 Background

The venture capital schemes exist to encourage investment in small, unquoted trading companies, which, as noted above, potentially include AIM companies. The schemes, although possessing some key differences, do also display considerable overlap – particularly in the qualifying conditions for investee companies – and it is therefore useful to consider them together. The three schemes are:

1.   the Seed Enterprise Investment Scheme;
2.   the Enterprise Investment Scheme; and
3.   the Venture Capital Trust scheme.

The EIS benefits individual investors who can claim generous tax reliefs as an encouragement to invest in qualifying companies. AIM companies which qualify can therefore attract a wider spread of investors, friends and certain family members and (subject to certain conditions) new directors who are able to invest under the EIS.

VCTs are fully listed companies, similar to quoted investment trusts, whose investors are private individuals. As with the EIS, individual investors are able to obtain certain tax reliefs but by investing via a VCT can gain access indirectly to a professionally managed portfolio of unquoted investments – which for this purpose can include shares in qualifying AIM companies. A VCT must invest 70 per cent of its funds in qualifying unquoted companies (which can include those on AIM), broadly within three years of obtaining its quotation; accordingly VCTs have become an important source of AIM funding, particularly in difficult market conditions when other investors are reluctant to invest. SEIS was introduced for investments from 6 April 2012 and intended to encourage investment in start-up and early stage companies. There a number of conditions similar to the EIS which need to be met in order to qualify for the generous tax reliefs. The amount that a company can receive is currently limited to total investments under SEIS of £150,000.

Under SEIS a single company or group must have gross assets of less than £200,000 immediately before investment, fewer than 25 full time equivalent employees and must be carrying on a new qualifying trade i.e. one within two years of trade prior to investment. It is therefore unlikely that SEIS will apply to AIM companies, if you consider SEIS to be available then we recommend specialist advice is sought.

The EIS and VCT schemes together with any EU Equity based State Aid (see para.11.2.7.11) allow qualifying companies to raise up to £5 million from these sources annually.

11.2.2   EIS: investor benefits

There are four main reliefs available to individuals investing under the EIS.

11.2.2.1   EIS income tax relief

An individual is entitled to an income tax reduction equal to 30 per cent of the amount subscribed by him for new ordinary shares in the investee company such that investments have an effective initial cost of only 70 per cent of cost.

The total amount subscribed in a single tax year which is eligible for relief is currently capped at £1,000,000 . Spouses or civil partners may each invest up to this limit, so couples may potentially make qualifying investments in the course of a tax year of up to £2 million. In this context it is worth noting that where subscriptions by a couple are made jointly, HM Revenue & Customs will regard each of the individuals as having invested half the total amount subscribed, regardless of which individual provided the funds. Thus if Mr and Mrs Jones jointly subscribe £2 million for 100,000 shares, with the funds being provided by Mrs Jones, they will for the purposes of the relief each be regarded as investing £1,000,000.

The tax reduction cannot reduce an individual's income tax liability below £nil. Following a relaxation of the rules in Finance Act 2009, however, it is possible to elect that all or part of the subscription be treated as made in the previous tax year so as, for example, to avoid any available relief being wasted.

The EIS includes certain conditions that must be met throughout the period commencing with the issue of shares and running for three years (or, if longer, to the third anniversary of the investee company starting to trade). Upfront relief will be entirely or partially withdrawn if the investor disposes of the shares within this period or if the relevant qualifying conditions are not in fact complied with throughout the period.

An investor may have EIS relief withdrawn if he or she "receives value" from the investee company or the investee company repays, redeems or repurchases any of its share capital held by any investor (not necessarily themselves as an EIS investor). These rules bite in relation not only to transactions in the period following the investment referred to above, but also to transactions in the year preceding the investment. Thus a company which had, for example, redeemed a number of redeemable preference shares a few months before seeking to raise new investment might find its ability to raise funds under the EIS restricted, as potential investors would face an immediate reduction in the relief that would otherwise be available to them.

The rules governing when an investor is deemed to "receive value" from an investee company are highly complicated. Where, as will be the case for many AIM companies, the only relationship between the company and the investor is the investment made under the EIS, the company makes no payment to the investor other than a "dividend or distribution which does not exceed a normal commercial return on the investment" and the company provides no benefits to the

227

investor, these provisions will not usually give rise to any concerns. In all other cases specialist advice is imperative to avoid any inadvertent breach of the rules.

It should be noted that any withdrawal of income tax relief may impact on the availability of the other EIS reliefs outlined below and that accordingly this will need to be factored in when considering undertaking a transaction which may impact EIS relief claimed by a company's investors; for example, a takeover or offer for the company's shares.

11.2.2.2 EIS capital gains tax disposal relief

A gain arising on the disposal of shares in relation to which income tax relief has been given (and which has not been withdrawn) is exempt from capital gains tax ("CGT"). This is a valuable relief which recent changes in the law, such as the abolition of business asset taper relief in favour of a flat rate of CGT of 18 per cent and the subsequent increase in this rate to 28 per cent for (broadly) higher rate taxpayers, have made increasingly important.

The requirement for income tax relief to have been given in respect of the shares means that where over £1,000,000 has been subscribed by an individual in a particular tax year any gain on a future disposal of those shares will only be partially exempt. Similarly if income tax relief has been partially withdrawn (for example, following a "receipt of value") any gain will be only partially exempt.

The requirement that the income tax relief not be withdrawn means that, in particular, the shares must be held for at least three years if a gain on their disposal is to be exempt.

It is important to note that the exemption only applies to a capital gain arising on a disposal of the shares. This can cause problems in the case of a share buyback by the company, as by default such a transaction falls to be treated as a distribution for tax purposes. An exception to this treatment is available for buybacks by unquoted trading companies (which would include AIM companies), but the criteria for this exception to apply are stringent and, in particular, include a requirement that the shares be held for at least five years. This means that where an investor disposes of their shares as a result of a direct share buyback by the issuing company within five years of issue, they will typically be unable to benefit from the capital gains exemption even if the shares have been held for the three-year qualifying period. An EIS investor who has passed the three years' ownership test but has not held the shares for the five years necessary to obtain CGT treatment may be able instead to obtain the benefit of the exemption by selling those shares to a third party in anticipation of the buyback but this course of action should only be considered under suitable professional guidance. This procedure is sometimes called an "on-market buyback".

Usually if gains arising on the disposal of an asset would be exempt, no relief is given for a loss arising on that disposal. Shares qualifying for EIS relief are an important exception to this, however, and even if a gain on the disposal of the shares would fall to be treated as exempt, relief is still allowed for a loss. The amount of the loss is reduced, however, by the amount of any income tax relief given (and not withdrawn).

11.2.2.3   EIS loss relief

Clearly investors will be hoping ultimately to dispose of shares acquired under the EIS at a gain, focussing attention on the EIS capital gains exemption described above. Equally clearly such hopes will not always be fulfilled, and investors will on occasion dispose of their shares at a loss.

When this happens a capital loss will arise. Typically capital losses may only be offset against capital gains; however, where EIS income tax relief has been given in respect of the shares, an individual may elect to offset the loss against their general income. The ability to make such claims both increases the likelihood that relief can be obtained for the loss and, with the top rate of income tax remaining significantly higher than the top rate of CGT, offers the prospect of relief at an increased rate.

A very similar relief (discussed further at Section 11.3 below) exists for investments meeting many of the criteria for EIS income tax relief, but on which no income tax relief has been given. Investments in excess of the £1,000,000 limit referred to above, or in respect of which income tax relief has been withdrawn, may therefore still sometimes qualify for loss relief.

11.2.2.4   *EIS capital gains tax deferral relief*

If a capital gain accrues to an individual and, in the period running from one year before to three years after the date the gain arises, that individual also subscribes for shares under the EIS, they may then elect to defer an amount of the gain equal to the amount subscribed (or the amount of the gain if less). It should be noted, however, that a recent change to the rules prevents the deferral of a gain in respect of which Entrepreneur's Relief has been claimed.

The gain will be brought back into charge on the occurrence of a "chargeable event", most typically a disposal of the EIS shares.

As with the EIS income tax relief described above, there are certain qualifying conditions that must be met throughout the period commencing with the issue of shares and running for three years (or if longer to the third anniversary of the investee company starting to trade). A breach of these conditions will either cause the deferred gain to be brought back into charge or in certain situations simply render the original claim to defer the gain ineffective.

Again paralleling the EIS income tax relief provisions, the deferred gain will be brought back into charge where an EIS investor "receives value" from the investee company or where the investee company repays, redeems or repurchases any of its share capital held by any investor (not necessarily themselves an EIS investor).

A key difference from the EIS income tax relief provisions is that there is no cap on the investment in respect of which deferral relief may be claimed. It should be noted, however, that whilst there is no limit on the amount an individual investor may invest under the EIS, there is a limit on the amount an individual company may raise (see Section 11.2.6.11 below). An investor seeking to shelter a gain in excess of this amount may therefore be obliged to spread his or her investment across a number of companies.

As with the EIS capital gains exemption discussed above, the recent trend of increasing effective rates of CGT has made the availability of this relief correspondingly more attractive to potential investors.

11.2.3   EIS: Qualifying investors

11.2.3.1   Overview

Relief under the EIS is only available to individuals (not companies or partnerships) who subscribe for new ordinary shares in a qualifying company. Most individual investors should be eligible, subject to meeting the conditions set out below.

11.2.3.2   EIS income tax relief, capital gains tax exemption and loss relief

Eligibility for the capital gains exemption (see Section 11.2.2.2 above) and loss relief (see Section 11.2.2.3 above) is contingent on the investor having obtained EIS income tax relief in respect of the investment and such relief not having been withdrawn. Thus whilst there is no requirement that the individual be a UK resident they must have a UK tax liability in the year the investment is made against which to claim relief.

To qualify for relief an investor must not be "connected" with the investee company at any point in the period running from two years to the issue to three years after (or, if later, three years after the company commenced trading). An individual will be connected with a company for these purposes if they or an associate (which includes, in particular, a spouse or civil partner, ancestor or lineal descendant):

1. are an employee, partner or director of the issuing company or any of its subsidiaries (but see below in relation to directors);
2. directly or indirectly possess or are entitled to acquire more than 30 per cent of:
    (a) the ordinary share capital of the issuing company or any of its subsidiaries;
    (b) the loan capital and issued share capital of the issuing company or any of its subsidiaries; or
    (c) the voting power in the issuing company or any of its subsidiaries;
3. directly or indirectly possess or are entitled to enquire such rights as would, in the event of the winding up of the issuing company or any of its subsidiaries, entitle the individual to receive more than 30 per cent of the assets of the company concerned which would then be available for distribution to equity holders;
4. have control of the issuing company or any of its subsidiaries; or
5. subscribe for shares under arrangements that provide for another person to invest in a company with which the individual is connected under (1)–(4) above.

For the purposes of the tests of connection outlined in (2)–(4) above, there are attributed to the individual the rights and powers of their associates; in particular any spouse or civil partner, ancestor or lineal descendant.

As noted above, directors of a company are generally regarded as connected to it. There are, however, two key exceptions to this rule. Firstly, a director will not be regarded as connected to a company if, broadly, they are not remunerated. Secondly, by virtue of the so-called "Business Angel exemption", a director receiving only reasonable remuneration will not be regarded as connected to the company if, broadly, they became a share-holder of the company prior to becoming a paid director.

11.2.3.3   EIS capital gains tax deferral relief

To qualify for the EIS CGT deferral relief an individual must be either resident or ordinarily resident in the UK at both the time the gain they are seeking to defer arose and the time they make the investment under the EIS. If the individual ceases to be either resident or ordinarily resident at a point less than three years after the issue of the shares (or, if later, the investee company commencing to trade) the deferred gain will be brought back into charge.

Unlike the other EIS reliefs described above there is no requirement that the investor not be connected with the investee company. This relief is therefore potentially available to directors, significant shareholders, etc.

11.2.4   VCTs: investor benefits

Following the abolition of VCT deferral relief in the Finance Act 2004 there are three main reliefs available to individuals investing in a VCT.

11.2.4.1   VCT income tax relief

An individual is entitled to an income tax reduction equal to 30 per cent of the amount subscribed by them for new ordinary shares of a VCT such that investments have an effective initial cost of only 70 per cent of cost.

The total amount subscribed in a tax year which is eligible for relief is currently capped at £200,000 (i.e. the maximum tax reduction is £60,000). As with the EIS this limit is not divided between spouses or civil partners.

Relief may be all or partly clawed back if the investor disposes of the shares within five years of issue, although this does not apply to transfers between spouses or civil partners made at a time when the individuals concerned are living together.

11.2.4.2   VCT dividend exemption

An individual is exempt from income tax in relation to dividends paid in respect of shares in a VCT, provided that the company concerned was a VCT both when the individual acquired the shares and at the end of the accounting period in which the profits distributed were accrued.

There is no requirement that the investor has originally subscribed for the shares, but the exemption only applies to the extent that the aggregate market value at acquisition of all VCT shares acquired by the individual in the course of the tax year in which they acquired the shares concerned does not exceed £200,000.

11.2.4.3   VCT capital gains tax exemption

An individual is exempt from CGT in relation to a disposal of shares in a VCT, provided that the company concerned was a VCT both when the individual acquired the shares and at the time of the disposal.

As with the dividend exemption, there is no requirement that the investor had originally subscribed for the shares, but the exemption only applies to the extent that the aggregate market value at acquisition of all VCT shares acquired by the individual in the course of the tax year in which they acquired the shares concerned does not exceed £200,000.

Unlike the corresponding relief for EIS shares (see Section 11.2.2.2 above) the exemption also applies to losses arising on a disposal of VCT shares and accordingly no relief is given for such losses.

11.2.5   *VCTs: qualifying investors*

As with the EIS, relief is only available to individuals. Moreover, the various VCT reliefs are further restricted to individuals who are at least 18 years of age at: the date the shares are issued for the income tax relief; the date the dividend would otherwise be taxable for the dividend exemption; and the date the shares are disposed of for the CGT exemption.

The three reliefs also contain a requirement that the individual has acquired the shares (and for the income tax relief the shares have been issued) for genuine commercial reasons and not as part of a scheme or arrangement the main purpose of which, or one of the main purposes of which, was the avoidance of tax.

11.2.6   *EIS and VCTs: qualifying investments*

11.2.6.1   *Overview*

For an investment to qualify under the EIS or form part of a VCT's qualifying holdings there are a number of conditions to be met in relation both to the company invested in and the form, etc. of the investment. The conditions to be met by the investee company are virtually identical for both EIS and VCT purposes and are discussed in Section 11.2.6 below.

The conditions relating to the form, etc. of the investment do however vary slightly between the schemes, as follows.

11.2.6.2   *Investments under the EIS*

To qualify for the purposes of the EIS any investment must be in the form of new ordinary shares which at no time in the period running from the issue of the shares until the third anniversary of the issue (or, if later, the third anniversary of the company commencing trade) carry:

1. any present or future preferential right to dividends or to a company's assets on its winding up; or

2.   any present or future right to be redeemed.

The definition of eligible shares has been extended to allow a preferential right to dividends, provided that, broadly, the right is not cumulative and does not include scope for the amount of the dividend to be varied on the basis of a decision by the company, the shareholder, or any other person.

In assessing whether a right is preferential the practice adopted by HM Revenue & Customs is to compare the rights of the shares to those of the investee company's other classes of issued shares. A common pitfall is for a company to issue an additional class of shares or deferred shares which (unless they only have only a theoretical right to any distribution) rank behind the ordinary shares on a winding up, thus making the ordinary shares preferential. The shares held by the investor must meet the criteria throughout the period described above and it is unfortunately not unknown for companies to create such an additional class of shares a couple of years after the EIS investment was received, inadvertently triggering a claw back of relief for investors. Such occurrences underline the importance of obtaining appropriate specialist advice before undertaking significant transactions, including those impacting a company's capital structure.

It is important to understand that "preferential" is not synonymous with "better". For example, consider a company which has issued equal numbers of "A" and "B" £1 ordinary shares, with the only key difference between the classes being that on a winding up the right to assets of "A" shares is capped at the nominal value of the shares. It does not follow that the right of the "B" shares is preferential simply because it is a better right. Indeed, if the "A" shareholders were entitled to receive payment out of the company's assets up to the amount of the cap first i.e. in priority, this would make the "A" shares preferential – even if the likelihood was that the "B" shareholders would still receive the majority of the available assets.

Other than in the case of bonus shares issued to the investor, there is a further requirement that the shares are subscribed for wholly in cash and are fully paid up at the time of issue.

Finally, there is a widely drawn anti-avoidance provision, which prohibits relief in cases where the issuing arrangements for the relevant shares include:

1. arrangements with a view to the subsequent repurchase, exchange or other disposal of those shares or of other shares in or securities of the issuing company;
2. arrangements for or with a view to the cessation of any trade which is being or is to be or may be carried on by the issuing company or of a person connected with that company;
3. arrangements for the disposal of, or of a substantial amount of, the assets of the issuing company or of a person connected with that company; or
4. arrangements the main purpose or one of the main purposes of which is to provide partial or complete protection for the persons investing in shares in the issuing company against what would otherwise be the risks attached to making the investment.

Problems most frequently arise in relation to the first of these points as investors will usually wish to understand the available exit routes; it is important that discussions around this do not progress to the point where they may constitute "arrangements" of the type described above. Clearly for most AIM companies investors will already have a straightforward exit route and it should therefore be possible to avoid this type of difficulty.

11.2.6.3 *Investments by VCTs*

Investments by VCTs are not restricted to ordinary shares, but may consist of any shares and securities of the investee company that were first issued by the investee company to the VCT and have been held by the VCT ever since. It is therefore common for VCTs to look to make an investment by way of a combination of different classes of share and loan stock. There is, however, a requirement that at least 10 per cent by value of the totality of the shares and securities of the investee company held by a given VCT be represented by "eligible shares".

For VCTs investing funds raised (or deemed to have been raised) prior to 6 April 2011, the definition of "eligible shares" is essentially identical to the basic requirement for shares issued under the EIS, being shares which do not carry:

1. any present or future preferential right to dividends or to a company's assets on its winding up; or
2. any present or future right to be redeemed.

Where a VCT invests funds raised on or after 6 April 2011 a slightly broader definition of "eligible shares" applies. This allows eligible shares to carry a preferential right to dividends, provided that, broadly, the right is not cumulative and does not include scope for the amount of the dividend to be varied on the basis of a decision by the company, the shareholder, or any other person.

The term "securities" encompasses any liability of the company in respect of a loan (whether or not the loan itself is secured), but exclude such liabilities where the loan is on terms that would allow any person to require the loan to be repaid (or any stock or security relating to the loan to be repurchased or redeemed) within five years. This restriction effectively prevents short-term loan stock being included within a VCT's qualifying holdings.

Interestingly there does not appear to be an equivalent restriction that would prevent part of the investment being made by way of redeemable preference shares with an expected redemption date of less than five years, although the redemption of such shares within three years may trigger a claw back of relief for any EIS investors in the company under the value received rules.

If any security held by the VCT relates to a guaranteed loan (broadly where there are arrangements for the VCT to receive something from a third party in the case of a breach by the investee company of any terms of the security or underlying loan) then the VCT's investment in the company will not form part of its qualifying holdings.

Subject to a company exceeding the annual investment limit of £5 million from risk capital schemes (which include in aggregate from the SEIS, EIS, VCTs and any other EU equity state aid) there is no limit a single VCT can invest in any company except where the company is party to a partnership or joint venture. In such a case there is a limit on the amount a single VCT may invest in a company in the 6 months up to the date of investment or the beginning of the tax year if earlier. This limit is calculated by dividing £1 million by the number of companies who are parties to the joint venture or partnership.

The Finance Act 2014 introduced a restriction on enhanced buy-back transactions for VCTs. This is anti-avoidance legislation which looks to exclude investments in VCTs that are conditionally linked in any way to a share buy-back.

11.2.7 *EIS and VCTs: qualifying companies*

11.2.7.1 *Overview*

This list of conditions to be met by qualifying companies is lengthy and can be daunting to companies seeking investment. In practice, whilst the rules are certainly complex, many companies will fall within them. Companies that do not obviously meet the requirements may, with some restructuring or other planning, be enabled to do so. AIM companies looking to raise new investment, especially in a difficult market where the tax incentives for qualifying investments are increasingly important, will often be well advised to ensure that appropriate consideration is given to whether they have, or could achieve, qualifying status.

The requirements fall broadly into two categories. Some, such as the gross assets requirements and employee limits, apply only at the time the investment is made. Careful structuring of the investment may mitigate these requirements, which at present are otherwise highly restrictive. Such structuring is considered at Section 11.3 below.

Other requirements, for example the qualifying subsidiaries requirement, are ongoing. For EIS purposes such requirements must typically continue to be met from the time the investment is made through to the third anniversary of the investment, or, if later, the third anniversary of the company starting to trade. Breaching the requirements during this period will usually cause relief to be forfeited; breaching the requirements after the end of the period will usually have no consequence at all. This is a significant contrast to the way these requirements are applied for VCT purposes. A VCT is required to maintain a certain proportion of its investments in "qualifying holdings" and in most cases investments will be included within its qualifying holdings when they meet the requirements and excluded when they do not. On the one hand this means that the investee company must continue to meet the requirements indefinitely. On the other hand a breach of the conditions may well not be fatal – if it is possible to take steps to rectify the breach the investment will only be temporarily excluded from the VCT's portfolio of qualifying holdings.

Whether the investment is under the EIS or from VCTs it is important that investee companies understand the ongoing compliance obligations and that they seek appropriate advice before undertaking any action which might lead to a breach.

11.2.7.2 The trading requirement

If a standalone company, the investee company must, ignoring any incidental purposes, exist wholly for the purpose of carrying on one or more qualifying trades. If a parent company, the requirement is instead that the business of the group should not consist wholly or as to a substantial part in the carrying on of non-qualifying activities. This requirement applies for EIS purposes from the date the shares are issued through to the third anniversary of the issue (or, if later, to the third anniversary of the company commencing to trade). For VCT purposes the requirement must be met at any time the investment is to be included within the VCT's qualifying holdings.

"Substantial", though not defined in statute, is interpreted by HM Revenue & Customs to mean more than 20 per cent. By contrast the ignoring of any incidental purposes is taken by HM Revenue & Customs to allow only the disregard of "any trivial or incidental activity". It will be appreciated that this distinction can mean that the trading requirement may in certain situations be more readily complied with by a group than by a standalone company carrying on precisely the same activities. For this reason it is not unknown for an otherwise standalone company to form a subsidiary (possibly left dormant) so as to ensure that it is dealt with under the rules pertaining to groups.

In the particular case where a standalone company intends to acquire one or more other companies with a view to their becoming qualifying subsidiaries carrying on qualifying trades, the trading requirement will be applied as if the company was the parent company of a group including those companies. This deeming provision ceases to have effect if the intention is abandoned.

It should be noted that, contrary to popular belief, neither here nor in the definition of "qualifying trade" (considered below), is there any requirement as to the location of the trade. Territorial restrictions exist only in relation to the companies actually utilising the funds (in which regard see Section 11.2.6.4 below) and are in any event to be replaced by the "UK permanent establishment requirement" summarised at Section 11.2.6.5 below. The trading requirement itself does not restrict multinational groups from raising funds under the venture capital schemes.

A "qualifying trade" is one which:

1. is conducted on a commercial basis and with a view to the realisation of profits; and
2. does not consist wholly or as to a substantial extent in the carrying on of "excluded activities".

The meaning of "substantial" is discussed above, but the concept of "excluded activities" requires further clarification. The venture capital schemes exist to encourage investment in small trading companies which would otherwise struggle to raise funding. In view of this the legislation seeks to exclude businesses operating in certain sectors and industries, using a "black list" of "excluded activities".

This list of excluded activities is periodically updated and currently includes:

1. dealing in land, in commodities or futures or in shares, securities or other financial instruments;
2. dealing in goods otherwise than in the course of an ordinary trade of wholesale or retail distribution;
3. banking, insurance, money-lending, debt-factoring, hire-purchase financing or other financial activities;
4. leasing (including letting ships on charter or other assets on hire);
5. receiving royalties or licence fees;
6. providing legal or accountancy services;
7. property development;
8. farming or market gardening;
9. holding, managing or occupying woodlands, any other forestry activities or timber production;
10. shipbuilding;
11. producing coal;
12. producing steel;
13. operating or managing hotels or comparable establishments or managing property used as a hotel or comparable establishment;
14. operating or managing nursing homes or residential care homes or managing property used as a nursing home or residential care home; and

15. providing services or facilities for a business which itself includes substantial excluded activities in cases where, broadly, there is a person with a "controlling interest" in both businesses.
16. subsidised generation or export of electricity including:
     (a) where a person is in receipt of feed in tariff;
     (b) a renewable obligation certificate is issued; and
     (c) schemes which fall within s.32 Electricity Act and similar schemes established in non UK territories.
17. subsidised generation of heat and subsidised production of gas or fuel, includes renewable heat incentives.
     The generation of heat, or production of gas or fuel, is "subsidised" if a payment is made, or another incentive is given, under—
     (a) a scheme established by regulations under s.100 of the Energy Act 2008 or s.113 of the Energy Act 2011 (renewable heat incentives); or
     (b) a similar scheme established in non UK territories.

However there are certain carve outs for example community schemes or where electricity, gas or fuel is generated by anaerobic digestion the activity will not be treated as excluded.

The legislation provides further detail as to the scope of the items on the list of excluded activities and HM Revenue & Customs have also provided extensive guidance on their interpretation of the various terms used. Space constraints prevent a full discussion here, but some brief comments are appropriate in relation to the perennial problem area of receiving royalties and licence fees.

The receipt of royalties and licence fees is not an excluded activity where they are attributable to the exploitation of "relevant intangible assets". These are intangible assets the whole or greater part of which by value has been created by either the issuing company or its subsidiaries at a time when they were its subsidiaries. The intention behind the inclusion of royalties and licence fees on the list is understood essentially to exclude companies with an acquired stream of passive income, but the limited exception means that many other situations are caught.

The problem particularly affects software and technology companies and can mean that where a number of such companies are brought together to form a group the resultant group does not in fact qualify, as the greater part by value of the underlying intellectual property ("IP") was not developed whilst the companies were within the group. The issue is particularly acute in cases where as a result of a group reorganisation a new holding company is formed. Unless certain stringent conditions are met the same analysis is deemed to apply – the result is a new group and IP developed previously will not be a relevant intangible asset.

A strict reading of the legislation can therefore result in companies being denied relief in situations which it seems unlikely were ever intended to be excluded by Parliament. HM Revenue & Customs in their guidance have in some cases been willing to take a more pragmatic approach, accepting that in some circumstances a company's activities should be more properly regarded as the supply of goods or services notwith-standing the fact that the legal form of some element of the company's income is that of a royalty or a licence fee.

The Special Commissioners upheld this type of purposive approach to the legislation in the case of *Optos Plc v Revenue and Customs Commissioners* [2006] S.T.C. (S.C.D.) 687 a case dealing with a company receiving leasing income. The company provided an extensive range of services to customers leasing its units, without which the units could not be used effectively. The Special Commissioner found that the different elements of the (single) fee received by the company were inextricably linked and that it was impossible to bifurcate them so as to identify a substantial excluded activity of leasing.

HM Revenue & Customs have been known to accept similar arguments in respect of technology companies where extensive services are provided, but the approach taken is not always consistent and this remains something of a contentious area. Potential investee companies would be more than usually recommended to seek advance assurance (see Section 11.2.8 below) at an early stage so as to allow time for discussion with HM Revenue & Customs if required.

11.2.7.3   The qualifying activity requirements

Both venture capital schemes contain requirements in relation to "qualifying activities". For the EIS these include a requirement that the purpose of the issue of shares under the scheme is to raise money for a qualifying business activity and a requirement that the activity in question is carried on for at least four months following the issue. For investment by VCTs there is a requirement that, if the investment is to form part of a VCT's qualifying holdings at a particular point of time, the investee company or one of its 90 per cent subsidiaries must have been carrying on a qualifying business activity at all times from the issue of the relevant shares and securities until the time in question.

There is a further requirement applying to investment under both schemes, that the "qualifying business activity" is carried on by the issuing company or one of its qualifying 90 per cent subsidiaries and by no other person. In a technical note released in conjunction with the Pre-Budget Report 2009 HM Revenue & Customs announced that they now interpreted this requirement so as to exclude activities carried on in partnership from being qualifying activities, on the basis that there would be a person (i.e. one of the partners) other than the company and its qualifying 90 per cent subsidiaries carrying on the activities. One of the drivers behind the new interpretation was the number of structures being adopted, particularly in the film industry, which relied on a creating a series of EIS qualifying companies operating in partnership to allow investors to benefit from the EIS reliefs in situations far removed from those the venture capital schemes were designed to support.

A "qualifying business activity" is, broadly, an activity of carrying on of a qualifying trade, preparing to carry on a qualifying trade, or carrying on research and development from which it is expected that either a qualifying trade will be derived or a qualifying trade will benefit.

There is a requirement for the Company (ie the issuing company) to have a UK permanent establishment ("the UK permanent establishment requirement") – see Section 11.2.6.5 below. Prior to April 2011 the requirement was that the trade was carried on wholly or mainly within the UK.

11.2.7.4 *The use of the money raised requirements*

The concept of the "qualifying business activity" is particularly important when it comes to the requirements governing the use of the monies raised under the venture capital schemes. The basic requirement, common to both schemes, is that the monies raised under the schemes must have been employed for the purposes of a qualifying business activity within two years of the investment being made. The time limit is extended in cases where the qualifying business activity is one of "preparing to carry on a qualifying trade" to two years from the commencement of that trade.

As observed in the previous section, it is a requirement of the EIS that monies be raised "for the purpose of a qualifying business activity"; it should be noted that the requirement for the use of money is correspondingly strengthened to a requirement that the money be employed for the purposes of the qualifying business activity for which it was raised. The lack of equivalent restrictions in the VCT legislation mean that in theory there is potentially more flexibility in using funds invested by a VCT should a company's plans change, although this is a point that is rarely seen in practice. Unlike the EIS rules, the VCT legislation also deems the requirement to be met if the only amount not used for the purposes of a qualifying business activity is "not a significant amount".

The effect of the interaction between the requirements governing the employment of funds and the qualifying activity requirements discussed in Section 11.2.6.3 above is that funds may only be employed in either the issuing company itself or a "qualifying 90 per cent subsidiary". Originally a "qualifying 90 per cent subsidiary" meant only a subsidiary of the issuing company, not under the control of any other company, in which the issuing company held at least 90 per cent of the issued share capital and voting rights and was entitled to at least 90 per cent of any profits available for distribution or assets on a winding up. This definition was extended by Finance Act 2007, however, so that a company C will also be a qualifying 90 per cent of company A if either:

1. company C is a qualifying 90 per cent subsidiary of company B which is a qualifying 100 per cent subsidiary of company A; or
2. company C is a qualifying 100 per cent subsidiary of company B which is a qualifying 90 per cent subsidiary of company A.

There is no similar extension to the definition of "qualifying 100 per cent subsidiary" (which otherwise largely mirrors that of "qualifying 90 per cent subsidiary") and so in effect it is never possible to use funds raised under the venture capital schemes other than in the top three tiers of an investee group. This can necessitate some flattening of the group structure, which will of course carry its own commercial, legal and tax considerations.

Although not usually a problem, companies seeking investment should be comfortable that they will be able to spend the money within the required time frame. In order to keep track of the money and to make it easier to demonstrate how it has been employed should the point be enquired into, it is often advisable to hold the funds in a separate bank account. HM Revenue & Customs do not insist on this, however. The holding of funds on deposit account prior to employment in a qualifying trade is generally acceptable, but companies should be extremely wary of using any funds not immediately required to, for example, acquire short term investments, as this will generally cause the requirement to be failed.

Difficulties can arise in situations where a company needs to meet significant expenditure other than for the purposes of a qualifying business activity. Historically, HM Revenue & Customs have accepted that in this type of scenario a business might raise funds under the venture capital schemes to meet the costs of its qualifying business activities, freeing the income of those activities for use in funding non-qualifying expenditure. The effectiveness of this type of planning is no longer as certain, given comments made in the course of the decision in *Skye Inns Ltd v Revenue and Customs Commissioners* [2009] UKFTT 366 (TC). There is yet to be any clear indication of a change in approach by HM Revenue & Customs, but companies relying on being able to structure funding in this way would be advised to seek advance assurance (see Section 11.2.8) on the point.

In order to obtain State Aid approval from the European Commission for the venture schemes, the UK Government was obliged in 2009 to agree to make certain modifications to the schemes, including the removal of this territorial restriction on the employment of funds. The agreed changes were finally legislated for in Finance (No.3) Act 2010, and effective from 6 April 2011.

11.2.7.5 The UK permanent establishment requirement

In parallel with the change to the definition of "qualifying business activity" to remove the requirement that the activity be carried on "wholly or mainly in the UK" a new requirement, "the UK permanent establishment requirement" has been introduced. The basic requirement is that the issuing company has a permanent establishment in the UK. This requirement will need to be met continuously from the time the shares are issued until the third anniversary of issue (or, if later, of the company starting to trade) for EIS purposes. For the purposes of determining whether an investment is included within a VCT's qualifying holdings the requirement must have been met continuously from the time the investment was made until the time the test is being applied.

There are already multiple definitions of "permanent establishment" in use for the purposes of UK tax law. The draughtsman unfortunately, failed to resist the temptation to create another, which is now set out at ss.191A and 302A of the Income Tax Act 2007 ("ITA 2007"). In broad terms, the issuing company will need to have either a fixed place of business in the UK, or an agent acting on behalf of the company which habitually exercises authority in the UK to enter into contracts on behalf of the company. It should be noted that the requirement applies to the issuing company (i.e. the parent company in a group scenario) not the company ultimately employing the funds.

Most UK AIM companies will have no difficulty in meeting this requirement and will therefore welcome the flexibility given by the rules for them to then employ the funds raised in overseas subsidiaries.

Companies which do not currently have a permanent establishment in the UK should remember that this will generally constitute a taxable presence in the UK if created, meaning that a variety of tax issues would need to be taken into account before undertaking any restructuring designed purely to comply with this requirement. It should be noted that the presence of a UK subsidiary will not in itself constitute a permanent establishment.

11.2.7.6 *The financial health requirement*

A requirement introduced by Finance (No.3) Act 2010, is the "financial health requirement". The requirement is that, at the time the investment is made, the issuing company is not "in difficulty".

The phrase "in difficulty" takes its meaning from the Community Guidelines on State Aid for Rescuing and Restructuring Firms in Difficulty (2004/C 244/02). Whilst it will be important to have regard to this new requirement, for an AIM company the fact that it is able to raise funds from investors sufficient to continue the business as a going concern will normally be prima facie evidence that the company is not in fact in difficulty. HMRC have also indicated in published guidance that companies which are within the first three years of operations in the relevant field of activity at the time of the EIS or VCT investment will not usually be regarded as "in difficulty" within the meaning of the Community Guidelines referred to above.

11.2.7.7 *The unquoted status requirement*

The basic requirement is that the investee company be "unquoted". AIM companies are not regarded as quoted for these purposes as AIM is not a recognised stock exchange.

For investment under the EIS the test applies only at the time the shares are issued, although anti-avoidance provisions apply to cases where at the time of issue there exist arrangements for the investee company to cease to be unquoted. In the absence of such arrangements there is no claw back of relief on, for example, the investee company becoming fully listed.

By way of contrast, for investment by VCTs the requirement is ongoing. Provided that the investee company met all the qualifying conditions at issue, however, the legislation allows a five-year period of grace in which the requirement will be deemed to still be met following the company ceasing to be unquoted.

11.2.7.8 *The control and independence requirements*

The "control requirement" is that the investee company (whether alone or with a person connected to it) must not control any company which is not a qualifying subsidiary.

The "independence requirement" is that the investee company must not be under the control of another company (or of another company and any person connected with it).

The requirements must be met at issue and continue to be met until the third anniversary of the issue (or if later the third anniversary of the company starting to trade) for EIS purposes or indefinitely for VCT purposes. Anti-avoidance rules catch situations where there are arrangements for control of or by the investee company in breach of the above requirements.

Although superficially straightforward there are certain subtleties in the rules that can cause problems for the unwary. For example, the meaning of "qualifying subsidiary" is considered further at Section 11.2.6.12 below, but it may be noted here that a key element of the definition requires the investee company to hold, directly or indirectly, more than 50 per cent of any subsidiary company's ordinary share capital. Such a requirement is incapable of being met by a group company without ordinary share capital, such as a company limited by guarantee. Although companies without ordinary share capital are rare in a purely UK context, international groups may encounter difficulties. Notoriously Delaware Limited Liability Corporations ("DLLCs") may or may not have ordinary share capital for UK tax purposes. Groups containing entities such as this will need to consider what steps are available to them to support an argument that the entities in question do in fact have ordinary share capital and are thus capable of being qualifying subsidiaries.

A second potential pitfall exists in relation to joint venture companies. The problem here is the fact that both the control and the independence requirement catch situations where control is by a company and a person connected to that company. A company will be connected to another person if, in particular, it acts together with that person to secure or exercise control of some other company. In relation to joint venture companies there is some risk that the joint venture partners will be acting together to secure or exercise control of the joint venture company in this way. Thus in cases where the company receiving the EIS and VCT investment is party to joint venture or is itself a joint venture vehicle some care is required to ensure the control and independence requirements are not breached. The decision of the Court of Appeal in *Steele*

(Inspector of Taxes) v EVC International NV (formerly European Vinyls Corp (Holdings) BV) [1996] S.T.C. 785 contains useful guidance on how the courts approach the question of connection in relation to joint ventures and Revenue Interpretation 160 sets out the analysis adopted by HM Revenue & Customs in respect of that decision.

11.2.7.9   The gross assets requirement

The gross assets requirement is that the gross assets of the investee company must not exceed:

1. £15 million immediately before the issue of the relevant holding; and
2. £16 million immediately after the issue of the relevant holding.

Where the investee company is the parent of a group the gross assets of all the group companies are aggregated for the purposes of this test, ignoring any rights against, or shares in or securities of another group company. It is important to appreciate that this aggregation exercise is not the same as an accounting consolidation. The main point of difference is that assets recognised only on consolidation, for example goodwill arising on share acquisitions, will not count towards the gross assets limit.

HM Revenue & Customs have published guidance on their approach in applying the gross assets requirement. This states that they will usually take the value of a company's gross assets to be the aggregate value of any assets that would be shown on the company's balance sheet if it were drawn up at the relevant time, without any deduction for any liabilities. Such a balance sheet should be drawn up on a basis consistent with the company's accounts for earlier periods and in accordance with generally accepted accounting practice.

It is also worth noting that in certain situations it may be possible to structure the fundraising in such a way that a company with gross assets in excess of the prescribed limits may nonetheless access EIS and VCT funding. The key considerations in connection with this are discussed in Section 11.2.8 below which includes the possible use of a new holding company.

11.2.7.10   The number of employees requirement

There is a requirement that the total number of full-time equivalent employees in the investee company and any subsidiaries be less than 250 at the time the shares are issued.

Again as with the gross assets limits, there may occasionally be situations in which it is possible to structure the investment in such a way that the employee limit does not bite – see Section 11.2.8 below.

11.2.7.11   The annual maximum requirement

From 6 April 2012 there is a cap of £5 million on the amount that a company can raise under venture capital schemes in any 12 month period. If an issue of shares would cause this limit to be breached then no shares in the issue will qualify.

The EIS and VCT schemes fall within the European State Aid regime and recent amendments to the legislation have arisen following negotiations with the European Commission. From 6 April 2012 a suitably qualifying company can raise up to £5 million in a 12 month period from the above schemes in aggregate but this must also take into account any other investment made which is State Aid received by it pursuant to a measure approved by the European Union in accordance with the principles laid down in the Community Guidelines on Risk Capital Investments in Small and Medium sized Enterprises – typically Equity based state aid. Unfortunately there is no definitive list of such aid but the documentation in respect of any such investment should make it clear whether or not it applies. It is very important to identify whether any such aid has been received in the 12 months including any current proposed financing as the whole of the issue which takes the company over the annual limit would be disqualified. For example – if a company raised £3 million 9 months ago from VCTs and under the EIS and now raises a further £2 million from VCTs but after the issue it is discovered that it had also 3 months ago raised £50,000 from EU state aided funding falling within the above definition then the whole of the current fund raising of £2 million would be disqualified from VCT status and not just the amount of £50,000 which is the excess over the annual limit of £5 million. Accordingly, VCTs are extremely concerned about this danger and are often seeking additional assurances.

In determining the funds raised for the purposes of this restriction it is necessary to take account of any investment in respect of which the company has issued an EIS certificate, regardless of whether the recipient has in fact claimed relief. In consequence it is advisable where possible to only issue EIS certificates to those investors intending (and capable – see Section 11.2.3 above) of claiming relief.

11.2.7.12   The qualifying subsidiaries requirement

Any subsidiary of the investee company must be a "qualifying subsidiary". This requirement applies for EIS purposes from the date the shares are issued through to the third anniversary of the issue (or, if later, to the third anniversary of the company commencing to trade). For VCT purposes the requirement must be met at any time the investment is to be included within the VCT's qualifying holdings.

A "qualifying subsidiary" is a subsidiary of the investee company meeting the following conditions:

1. the subsidiary is a "51 per cent subsidiary" of the investee company;
2. no person other than the investee company (or another of its subsidiaries) has control of the subsidiary; and
3. no arrangements exist by virtue of which either of the above conditions would cease to be met.

The term "51 per cent subsidiary" means that the investee company must own, directly or indirectly, more than 50 per cent of the subsidiary's ordinary share capital. Difficulties potentially arise in situations where the ownership is indirect as the legislation only takes account of the investee company's effective interest in the subsidiary. Thus if, for example, the investee company holds 60 per cent of the ordinary share capital of company A which itself holds 60 per cent of the ordinary share capital of company B, the qualifying subsidiaries requirement will be failed. This is because company B is indeed a subsidiary of the investee company, but the investee company is regarded as owning only 36 per cent (i.e. 60 per cent of 60 per cent) of its ordinary share capital, below the 50 per cent threshold.

11.2.7.13 *The property managing subsidiaries requirement*

Any "property managing subsidiary" of the investee company must be a "qualifying 90 per cent subsidiary". This requirement applies for EIS purposes from the date the shares are issued through to the third anniversary of the issue (or, if later, to the third anniversary of the company commencing to trade). For VCT purposes the requirement must be met at any time the investment is to be included within the VCT's qualifying holdings.

A "property managing subsidiary" is a subsidiary of the investee company whose business consists wholly or mainly in the holding or managing of land or any property deriving its value from land.

The meaning of "qualifying 90 per cent subsidiary" is discussed at Section 11.2.7.4 above.

11.2.7.14 *The "no disqualifying arrangements" test*

The "no disqualifying arrangements" were introduced in respect of shares issued on or after 6 April 2012 under s.178A of ITA 2007.

The legislation bites when there are "disqualifying arrange-ments" and either Condition A or Condition B are met, the two conditions are defined as follows the legislation;

"Condition A is that as a (direct or indirect) result of the money raised by the issue of the relevant shares being employed as required, an amount representing the whole or majority of the amount raised is, in the course of the arrangements, paid to or for the benefit of a relevant person(s)."

"Condition B is that, in the absence of the arrangements, it would have been reasonable to expect that the whole or greater part of the component activities of the relevant qualifying business activity would have been carried on as part of another business by a relevant person(s)."

"Relevant person" is defined as a person who is a party to the arrangements or a person connected with such a party

The disqualifying arrangements will not apply to existing trading companies seeking new finance. If disqualifying arrangements are likely to be an issue then advice should be sought from an appropriate specialist.

11.2.8 EIS and VCTs: structuring the investment

11.2.8.1 Overview

With some thought it may be possible to structure investment under the venture capital schemes in such a way as to enable relief to be obtained in cases where it would otherwise not be available; conversely a lack of care can easily cause relief to be forfeited. To take a very straightforward example, a company with gross assets of £14.5 million intends to raise £3.5 million. If it were to do so by way of a single issue of shares, its gross assets would stand at £18 million – higher than the £16 million limit set by the gross assets requirement (see Section 11.2.6.9 above). On the face of it venture capital funding is not available therefore. If, however, the fundraising were split into two issues (of £1.5 million and £2 million respectively), it will readily be seen that the gross assets limit will be complied with in relation to the first issue. If the other criteria are met, funding under the venture capital schemes may therefore be obtainable in respect of the first issue, and funding from other sources can then be used for the second issue without disturbing the qualification of the first issue.

11.2.8.2 Meaning of "issue"

Although the basic principle of breaking the fundraising up into a number of issues to facilitate compliance with the venture capital schemes requirements is one which is simple to understand, the actual implementation can involve some complicated issues. This is because it is necessary to take account of what the word "issue" itself actually means.

The meaning of "issue" was considered at length in *National Westminster Bank Plc v Inland Revenue Commissioners* [1995] 1 A.C. 119 (a case dealing with shares issued under the Business Expansion Scheme – a precursor of the EIS). In the House of Lords the majority held that, in the words of Lord Templeman, the word "issue" is "appropriate to indicate the whole process whereby unissued shares are applied for allotted and finally registered". This means that shares are not issued until completed, this usually means,in particular, the company's register of members is written up. If a fundraising is structured in such a way that reliance is placed on there being a number of distinct issues, therefore, it will be vital that after each issue the register is written up.

Although registration is a necessary condition for the issue to be completed, it is certainly not a sufficient condition. Where the subscription is made subject to a condition, this condition must be satisfied before the shares concerned can be said to be issued. In the context of AIM companies it is common practice for shares to be subscribed for subject to a condition that the shares concerned are subsequently admitted to trading on AIM. If such a condition is in place and all the shares subscribed for are admitted together at the end of the process, the "issue" will not be completed until at least this point. This would usually cause any planning based around the fragmentation of the fundraising into separate issues to fail.

The easy solution is to arrange for a separate admission following each issue, although this will usually cause the process to extend over several days as the London Stock Exchange are only able to effect one admission for a particular class of shares in a company in one day. Furthermore on IPO this is unlikely to be appropriate should the entire proceeds of the issues be required to enable the company to make its working capital statement. A more elegant alternative is to arrange for shares comprised in issues other than the last one usually to EIS investors and VCTs to be made unconditionally, although this can itself have a number of consequences that should be discussed with potential investors as early as possible.

If any part of the investment is to be obtained under the EIS a further complication is introduced by the fact that the meaning of "issue of shares" for EIS purposes (only) is modified, such that "references (however expressed) to an issue of shares in any company are to such of the shares in the company as are of the same class and are issued on the same day". The broad effect of this is that any planning that relies on the fact that a number of issues will be regarded as distinct for EIS purposes will normally necessitate the issues taking place on separate days.

11.2.8.3 *Use of a new holding company*

It is not uncommon for a group considering flotation on AIM to form a new holding company as part of the process. It is worth noting that where this is to be done an opportunity may be thereby created to access funding through the venture capital schemes. This is because where such a new company is formed with a view to acquiring an existing trading group many of the requirements of the schemes (for example the trading requirements) will take account of this intention, but others (for example, the employee limit and gross assets limits) are tested purely on the basis of the position of the new company at the time the shares are issued. It is thus perfectly possible for such a new company to raise £5 million (the annual maximum) under the venture capital schemes prior to the acquisition of an existing trading group (with over 250 employees and aggregate gross assets in excess of £16 million) without giving rise to any breach of the limits.

There are other commercial and tax considerations that should be borne in mind before implementing this type of planning.

11.2.9 EIS and VCTs: advance assurance

11.2.9.1 Overview

Clearly for many prospective investors the question of whether a company fulfils the requirements for their investment to qualify under the EIS, or for investment by a VCT to form part of its qualifying holdings, will be key to their decision making process.

No statutory clearance process exists through which a prospective investor or company seeking investment may obtain confirmation of a prospective investments status. HM Revenue & Customs do, however, operate a non-statutory process to provide issuing companies assurance on certain aspects of proposed investments. It should be noted that whilst recognising that there will often be a number of interested parties, HM Revenue & Customs are only able to liaise directly with the investee company itself, or its authorised advisers, in relation to any request for advance assurance. It should also be noted that where the fundraising is to be carried out by a new company (for example, where a new holding company is formed as part of the admission process), HM Revenue & Customs will not consider an application made on behalf of a company that is "to be formed" and that sufficient time must therefore be factored in for the application to be dealt with after incorporation of the new entity.

Investors, in particular VCTs who are subject to established internal compliance procedures will typically insist on such advance assurance being obtained and it is therefore important that companies seeking to raise new funds ensure that their schedule allows sufficient time for this to be done.

11.2.9.2   Scope of the advance assurance

There continues to be some confusion as to the precise scope of the advance assurance available from HM Revenue & Customs. Whilst an advance assurance can provide considerable comfort it falls a long way short of guaranteeing that relief will in fact be available to a particular investor, a point that any prospective investor would do well to bear in mind.

The aspects of a proposed investment on which HM Revenue & Customs are able to give advance assurance are:

1.   whether HM Revenue & Customs would expect to be able to authorise the company to issue EIS certificates to investors (i.e. whether it appears that the conditions relating to the company and the shares to be issued will be met);
2.   whether HM Revenue & Customs would expect shares and securities issued by the company to be capable of forming part of a VCT's qualifying holdings; and
3.   whether HM Revenue & Customs would expect shares issued by the company to a VCT to be eligible shares.

The advance assurance relates only to the outcome expected by HM Revenue & Customs for the very good reason that many of the conditions to be met by companies seeking investment under the EIS and from VCTs must continue to be met for some time after the investment is made. In the event that circumstances change such that these conditions cease to be met, the existence of an advance assurance will not prevent any withdrawal of relief.

HM Revenue & Customs note in their guidance that they are "normally bound by any assurance given, *provided the information supplied was correct and complete at the time it was given and has not been superseded by subsequent events*" (emphasis added).

It is extremely important if comfort is to be derived from the advance assurance process that appropriate care is taken to ensure that the information provided is comprehensive and accurate and that any potentially contentious matters are adequately disclosed. Indeed, the internal compliance requirements of VCTs usually stipulate that they will invest only where advance assurance has been received and in such cases the VCT will often require sight of the application for advance assurance submitted to HMRC in order to confirm that comprehensive disclosure has been made.

Should details of the proposed investment change following the submission of an application for advance assurance serious consideration should be given making a further submission outlining the changes.

11.2.9.3 *Applying for advance assurance*

The venture capital schemes are administered from the specialist Small Company Enterprise Centres ("SCECs") located in Cardiff and Maidstone. If a company has previously dealt with one of the SCECs it should send any application for advance assurance to that SCEC. In all other cases applications should be sent to: Small Company Enterprise Centre, Medvale House, Mote Road, Maidstone, ME15 6AF. The application will usually be allocated to an inspector in Maidstone or Cardiff in accordance with the location of the registered office of the applicant company. Broadly those in the North and M4 corridor will be dealt with at Maidstone whilst the Midlands and London will be dealt with by Cardiff.

The information that HM Revenue & Customs expect to be provided with in support of any application comprises:

1. a copy of the latest available accounts of the company and of any subsidiaries;
2. details of all trading or other activities carried on, or to be carried on, by the company and its subsidiaries, and details of which companies will use the money raised;

3. the approximate sum the company hopes to raise and how it will be used;
4. an up-to-date copy of the memorandum and articles of association of the company and each of its subsidiaries and details of any proposed changes;
5. a copy of the latest draft of any prospectus or similar document (ie AIM Admission Document) to be issued to potential investors;
6. details of any subscription agreement or other side agreement to be entered into by the shareholders; and
7. (for EIS purposes only) confirmation that the company expects to be able to complete the declaration on form EIS 1 in due course.

For EIS purposes HM Revenue & Customs have created a form, EIS(AA), to assist companies in making advance assurance applications. Use of this form is not compulsory, and in the author's view, inadvisable in all but the most straightforward of cases given the importance referred to above of ensuring full disclosure. There is currently no equivalent for the purposes of VCT investment. In most cases AIM companies will be seeking VCT investment in addition to (or indeed in preference to) investment under the EIS and so will be unable to make use of this form.

11.2.9.4 Timing of advance assurance

The allotted SCEC may call for the tax files from the local inspector. This may take time and it is worth checking that the relevant information has been received. Applications are dealt with in the order of post received and historically had been dealt with and a reply given within 15 working days. Due to the volume of applications received by the SCEC this time-frame is now between 5-8 weeks and it is advisable to call the SCEC in order to find out current status and plan a transaction timetable accordingly. There is, however, no statutory obligation on HM Revenue & Customs to provide a response to applications within a set timeframe (or indeed at all).

11.2.10   EIS and VCTs: administration

11.2.10.1   EIS investment

An individual's entitlement to claim EIS income tax relief is dependent upon the investor having been issued with a "compliance certificate" (often referred to as an "EIS certificate" or "EIS 3") by the investee company. This also applies for the purposes of the EIS deferral relief.

The company itself is prohibited from issuing such certificates without the authority of an officer of HM Revenue & Customs; the unauthorised issue of certificates is punishable by a fine of up to £3,000.

To obtain authority to issue compliance certificates to its investors, a company must first submit a "compliance statement" to HM Revenue & Customs. The "compliance statement" is a statement in relation to a given share issue to the effect that, except so far as they fall to be met by the individuals to whom shares have been issued, the requirements for EIS relief are currently met and have been met at all times since the shares were issued.

This statement is made using a form EIS 1, with a separate form required for each share issue. The form cannot be submitted until the qualifying activity for which the funds were raised has been carried on for at least 4 months, but must be submitted within two years of this point (or, if later, two years from the end of the tax year in which the issue took place). It is sadly not unknown for the completion of form EIS 1 to be completely overlooked and it is important therefore that investee companies clearly understand their responsibilities in this regard.

A change in the law made as a result of the recent tax law re-write project means that once a form EIS 1 has been filed, the officer of HM Revenue & Customs responsible for processing the form must notify the company whether or not the issue of compliance certificates is to be authorised (although there is no statutory time limit for the decision to issue certificates to be made). A decision not to authorise the issue of certificates may be appealed.

If the officer of HM Revenue & Customs concerned is satisfied that the relevant requirements of the legislation have been met, formal authorisation to issue compliance certificates will be given by the issue of form EIS 2. This will be accompanied by an appropriate number of blank forms EIS 3 for the company to complete and pass to its investors.

11.2.10.2 *VCT formal approval*

There is no formal approval procedure for investments made by VCTs. VCTs are subject to ongoing monitoring, however, and have to provide HM Revenue & Customs with annual returns detailing investments made in the VCT and qualifying investments by the VCT.

Although strictly obliged to do so only if the investor requests, VCTs will usually routinely issue individual investors with certificates which confirm that, so far as the VCT is aware, eligible shares have been issued to the investor for genuine commercial reasons and are not loan linked.

11.2.10.3 *Ongoing HMRC review*

EIS/VCT qualifying companies and VCTs are subject to ongoing review by HM Revenue & Customs (in the case of EIS, for the relevant period). Companies which have received funding under the EIS should be aware that they are obliged to inform HM Revenue & Customs within 60 days of any event triggering a loss or reduction of EIS relief given in respect of shares included on a form EIS 1 submitted by the company.

11.3 Loss Relief For Share Disposals

11.3.1 Background

The disposal of shares at a loss by an individual or a company will (with certain limited exceptions) give rise to a capital loss. For both individuals and companies the use of such losses is highly restricted, broadly to offset against capital gains arising in the year of disposal or a subsequent year.

In the case of a disposal of subscriber shares in a qualifying trading company or in the case of an individual, shares to which EIS relief is attributable, however, it is possible to elect for the loss to be offset against the taxpayer's general income. The requirements to be a "qualifying trading company" are discussed further below, but may particularly be noted as including a requirement that the company be unquoted at the time the shares concerned were originally issued. AIM companies are unquoted for these purposes.

An individual may claim the loss against their income of the current or previous year (or both); a company may offset the loss in the current accounting period and then, to the extent it is not fully relieved, carry it back up to twelve months.

The existence of this relief increases the probability that the taxpayer will be able to obtain relief for the loss and, in the case of an individual, ensures relief is available at the individual's top rate of tax (potentially 45 per cent) rather than only the CGT rate (currently 18 per cent /28 per cent).

11.3.2 Disposals qualifying for relief

Relief is only available for a disposal which is:

1. by way of a bargain made at arm's length;
2. by way of a distribution in course of dissolving or winding up the qualifying trading company;
3. a deemed disposal on the entire loss, destruction, dissipation or extinction of the shares; or

4. a deemed disposal arising from a claim under s.24(2) of the Taxation of Chargeable Gains Act 1992 that the shares have become of negligible value.

11.3.3 Investors qualifying for relief

11.3.3.1 Individuals qualifying relief

There are no restrictions on individuals who may claim relief beyond a requirement that they subscribed for the shares now disposed of so as to crystallise a loss for UK CGT purposes. The relief available on EIS shares is not subject to the income tax loss relief cap introduced by Schedule 3 to the Finance Act 2013.

11.3.3.2 Companies qualifying for relief

A company seeking to claim relief must also have subscribed for the shares in question, but in addition must meet a number of other requirements.

First, the investing company must be an "investment company" at the time of the disposal. An "investment company" is a company whose business consists wholly or mainly in the making of investments and which derives the principal part of its income from the making of investments, but excludes the holding company of a trading group.

Secondly, the investing company must either have been an investment company throughout the six-year period preceding the disposal, or, if only an investment company for some shorter period, have not previously been either a trading company or an "excluded company". An "excluded company" is a company which:

1. has a trade which consists wholly or mainly of dealing in land, in commodities or futures or in shares, securities or other financial instruments;

2.   has a trade which is not carried on, on a commercial basis, and in such a way that profits in the trade can reasonably be expected to be realised;
3.   is a holding company of a group other than a trading group; or
4.   is a building society or a registered industrial and provident society.

Thirdly, the investing company must not have been associated with, or a member of the same group as, the qualifying trading company at any point between the original investment and the disposal. Companies are "associated" for the purposes of this test if one controls the other or they are under common control.

11.3.4   Investments qualifying for relief

11.3.4.1   Overview

The relief applies to shares in a "qualifying trading company" subscribed for by the investor. The conditions to be met by a "qualifying trading company" are numerous and complex. They do, however, broadly replicate the requirements to be met by an investee company under the venture capital schemes (EIS and VCT). These requirements are discussed above and so to avoid duplication are simply summarised here.

11.3.4.2   Requirements to be met at and prior to disposal

On the date of disposal the investee company must meet each of the following conditions:

1.   the trading requirement (see Section 11.2.7.2 above);
2.   the control and independence requirement (see Section 11.2.7.8 above);
3.   the qualifying subsidiaries requirement (see Section 11.2.7.12 above); and
4.   the property managing subsidiaries requirement (see Section 11.2.7.13 above).

If the requirements are not met at disposal a company may nonetheless continue to qualify provided that the requirements were met at a time no more than three years prior to the disposal and since that time the investee company has not been an excluded company, an investment company or a trading company.

In each of the above scenarios the requirements must have been met either for a continuous period of six years, or have been met for a shorter period before which the company was not an excluded company, an investment company or a trading company.

11.3.4.3   Requirements to be met at the time of issue

At the time the shares were issued, the investee company must have met:

1.   the gross assets requirement (see Section 11.2.7.9 above); and
2.   the unquoted status requirement (see Section 11.2.7.7 above).

There is no automatic exclusion of relief should the investee company cease to be unquoted in the time between the original subscription and the disposal in respect of which relief is claimed.

11.3.4.4   UK permanent establishment requirement

The Company is required to have a UK permanent establishment throughout the period:

1.   beginning with the incorporation of the company or, if later, 12 months before the shares in question were issued; and
2.   ending with the date of the disposal.

11.4 Capital Gains Tax Gift Relief

11.4.1 Background

There is no general relief from CGT for gifts of assets such as shares, although transfers between spouses or civil partners will usually be deemed to take place for an amount of consideration such that no gain or loss would arise. For gifts in general, however, the legislation in fact deems the donor to have disposed of the asset in question at its market value. This may expose the donor to a CGT liability – a liability that can be particularly onerous given that the donor has not in fact received any consideration for the disposal.

A corollary of the above is that the recipient of a gift will, on a subsequent disposal of the asset by them, usually be regarded for CGT purposes as having acquired the asset at its then market value.

For gifts of shares or securities of certain unquoted companies (which includes AIM companies) it is possible, however, to make an election such that the consideration deemed to have been received by the donor and given by the donee is reduced by the amount of the gain that would have otherwise accrued to the donor. This in effect means that the donor is not liable to CGT as a result of making the gift but because the donor is not taxed on the gain that would have arisen, when the donee subsequently disposes of the shares or securities in question the acquisition cost deductible on disposal is effectively restricted to the donor's cost plus expenses subsequently incurred by the donee.

As a claim for relief affects the tax position of both parties, the statute requires the claim to be made by both the transferor and the transferee rather than just by the transferor acting unilaterally except where the transfer is to trust.

11.4.2 Gifts qualifying for relief

11.4.2.1 Requirements for the transferor

The principal relief is only available for disposals made by individuals. It should be noted in this context, however, that for these purposes transactions entered into by a partnership are regarded as transactions entered into by the individual partners and accordingly certain disposals by a partnership may qualify (Note that for this, and most tax purposes, a limited liability partnership (LLP) is treated in the same way as a general partnership so long as it carries on a business).

Provisions also exist which can extend the relief to certain disposals made by the trustees of a settlement.

11.4.2.2 Requirements for the transferee

Relief will not be available if the transferee is either a company or a person neither resident nor ordinarily resident in the UK. Special rules apply in situations where the transferee, though resident or ordinarily resident in the UK at the time the gift was made subsequently ceases to be either. These rules are outlined briefly at Section 11.4.3 below. Care is also needed in relation to gifts to non-resident trusts: there are specific residence rules for trusts and specialist advice is needed in the case of any transfer to a trust.

11.4.2.3 Requirements for the shares or securities transferred

Relief is potentially available for gifts and other disposals otherwise than under a bargain at arm's length of shares and securities in AIM companies which are either trading companies or the holding companies of trading groups.

A "trading company" is a company carrying on trading activities whose activities do not include to a substantial extent activities other than trading activities. Similarly a "trading group" is a group, one or more of whose members carry on trading activities, and the activities of whose members, taken together, do not include to a substantial extent activities other than trading activities.

The term "substantial" lacks statutory definition, but HM Revenue and Customs guidance indicates that, as in relation to the venture capital schemes (see Section 11.2.6.2 above), they interpret this as meaning 20 per cent or more of the company's activity measured in terms of assets, turnover or use of resources. This is not an area in which the rules can be regarded as hard and fast and some negotiation with HM Revenue & Customs may be necessary to establish trading status in marginal cases.

Whilst the definitions clearly also have some similarity with those used for the venture capital schemes, there are some differences which should not be overlooked. The legislation governing Business Asset Gift Relief has no equivalent of the "black list" of excluded activities which applies to the venture capital schemes. The treatment of a standalone company is also more favourable for the purposes of Business Asset Gift Relief, with the threshold simply being that the company should not have substantial non-trading activities.

If the company or its subsidiaries hold non-business assets, i.e. assets not used for the purposes of the trade of the company or its subsidiaries, the gift relief available on a transfer of shares or securities in the company may be restricted. This rule only bites, however, if at some point within the 12 months prior to the disposal the transferor held at least 5 per cent of the voting rights (if an individual) or 25 per cent of the voting rights in all other cases.

11.4.3 *Emigration of transferee*

If the transferee ceases to be either resident or ordinarily resident in the UK within six years of the end of the tax year in which the disposal was made, and the transferred assets are still held by them at that time, the deferred gain will crystallise. A limited exception to this rule is available in cases where the reason for an individual's emigration is employment abroad and within three years they again become resident or ordinarily resident in the UK, without having disposed of the transferred assets.

Clearly there may be practical difficulties facing HM Revenue & Customs in the collection of tax falling due under these rules from an individual who has severed all ties with the UK. To protect against this the legislation allows HM Revenue & Customs, in cases where the tax due remains outstanding for 12 months or more, to collect the tax from the transferor instead.

11.5 Inheritance Tax ("IHT") Business Property Relief

11.5.1 Background

A charge to inheritance tax ("IHT") will potentially arise on the reduction in value of the estate of a transferor of property (most commonly but not exclusively by way of a gift) or on the assets comprised in his or her estate on death. A number of exemptions and reliefs exist to mitigate this charge, however, among the most important of which is business property relief ("BPR").

The effect of BPR, where available, is to reduce the value of "relevant business property" which is chargeable to IHT by up to 100 per cent. Investments in unquoted companies, which for these purposes include investments in AIM companies, are, subject to meeting certain qualifying conditions (see below), eligible for relief at the full rate of 100 per cent.

11.5.2 *Investments qualifying for relief*

11.5.2.1 *Size of holding*

Shares in an unquoted company will qualify for relief, if the remaining requirements outlined below are met, regardless of the size of the holding.

For unquoted securities others than shares, however, the availability of relief is considerably more limited. Such securities qualify for relief only if they, either by themselves or together with other unquoted securities and shares held by the individual, give that individual control of the company concerned. HM Revenue & Customs take the view that only securities which themselves actually contribute to this control can qualify for relief. Thus unquoted non-voting securities (in contrast to unquoted non-voting shares) will not qualify for relief.

11.5.2.2 *Business of the company invested in*

Relief will not be available if the business carried on by the company consists wholly or mainly of one or more of:

1. dealing in securities, stocks or shares;
2. dealing in land or buildings; or
3. making and holding investments.

These exclusions do not prevent shares in the holding company of a group from qualifying, provided that company is the holding company of one or more companies not caught by the above exclusions.

The exclusions similarly do not apply to disqualify the shares in a company whose business is wholly that of a market maker or discount house and is carried on in the UK. It should be noted that it is only in cases where this exemption is relied upon that there is a requirement as to the location of the company's business.

Particular problems can arise as a result of the restriction on companies dealing in land or buildings. A business which consists principally of letting property will be excluded whereas a land-based business which consists predominantly of active management and service provision may still qualify for the relief

11.5.2.3 Companies being wound up

BPR is not available in relation to transfers which take place at time when a winding-up order has been made in respect of the company, the company has passed a resolution for voluntary winding-up, or the company is otherwise in the process of liquidation.

An important exception to this general rule exists for cases where the business of the company is to continue to be carried on after a reconstruction or amalgamation and the reconstruction or amalgamation is either the purpose of the winding-up or liquidation or takes place not later than one year after the transfer of value.

11.5.2.4 Minimum period of ownership by the transferor

Shares or securities will not qualify for BPR unless they have been owned by the transferor throughout the two years preceding the transfer on which IHT is chargeable. In the case of shares or securities acquired from a spouse or civil partner there is an automatic aggregation of the periods of ownership but only where the acquisition was a result of the death of that spouse or civil partner, i.e. not for lifetime transfers.

The period of ownership of shares which replaced a previous holding in a reorganisation to which the CGT share reorganisation provisions applied will include the period of ownership of the previous holding. However, this only applies to shares – there is no equivalent provision for other securities.

11.5.2.5 *Contracts for sale*

BPR will not be available in relation to a transfer of shares or securities if, at the time of the transfer, a binding contract has been entered into for their sale, unless the sale is made for the purpose of reconstruction or amalgamation.

11.5.2.6 *Ownership by the transferee*

Gifts from one individual to another during their lifetime (so-called potentially exempt transfers) will usually only be subject to IHT if the transferor dies within seven years of the transfer. In relation to such transfers, and any other chargeable transfers within the seven years preceding the death of the transferor, BPR will be available only if the transferee continues to own the shares or securities throughout the period ending with the death of the transferor and either the investment continues to be unquoted throughout that period or (unusually) the transferee has a controlling interest in the company concerned at the time of the transferor's death. Once again, there are provisions for including previous holdings of shares replaced in a reorganisation to which the CGT reorganisation provisions applied.

11.5.3 *Excepted assets*

If an investment qualifies for BPR, the BPR will only apply to shelter that part of the value transferred which is not attributable to "excepted assets" held by the investee company. Calculation of the reduction in relief arising from the existence of "excepted assets" can be complicated and where this is an issue specialist advice will be needed.

An asset held by the company will be an "excepted asset" unless either:

1. it has been used wholly or mainly for the purposes of the business concerned throughout the two years preceding the transfer; or

2. it is required at the time of the transfer for future use for those purposes.

It should be noted that the requirement is simply in relation to the company's business. A company may well have part of its business that falls within the exclusions described in Section 11.5.2.2 above, but nonetheless qualifies for BPR because its business as a whole does not consist "wholly or mainly" of such activities. In such situations there is no requirement that an asset be used for the "qualifying" part of the company's trade if it is avoid classification as an excepted asset.

11.6   Conclusion

It will be seen from the commentary above that significant tax benefits are potentially available to investors in AIM companies. The venture capital schemes in particular can provide a material incentive to encourage investment, even (as we have seen in recent years) when market conditions are difficult and traditional institutional investors are less willing to invest in AIM companies. Ability to access funds through the venture capital schemes can therefore be critical to the success of (particularly smaller) growing companies. An awareness of the available reliefs is thus important to any practitioner working with AIM companies and it is hoped that the summary provided in this chapter will go some way to fulfilling this need.

Nonetheless, the warning made at the start of this chapter that the legislation is complex and liable to change, must be repeated, together with the strong recommendation that, in light of this, specialist advice always be sought in matters of tax law.

Chapter 12

The Broker and the Trading Rules

John Wakefield

Director, Corporate Finance, WH Ireland Limited

12.1   Introduction

Where a company has been successfully admitted to trading on AIM, an investor – whether a private individual or institutional fund manager – intending to buy or sell shares in the company is likely to be concerned with three main issues: price, payment and delivery. How do investors find out about the company, in particular how shares are bought and sold, and what are the practicalities of dealing on AIM?

This Chapter examines the trading and regulatory environment in which shares in an AIM company are traded and which regulate the trading activities of the market practitioners – the Nominated Adviser ("Nomad"), the broker and the market maker.

12.2   The trading system

Information on AIM quoted shares is disseminated by the trading services operated by the London Stock Exchange ("LSE") via its Millennium Exchange™ technology and published via a public display system including the LSE's own system, Proquote and other third-party service providers, such as Fidessa, Reuters, Thomson and ICV Datastream. Millennium Exchange™ operates several different trading platforms, including SEAQ, SETS and SETSqx, each of which is used to trade AIM securities by enabling LSE member firms to publish and access the prices of AIM securities in real time. The most liquid securities are traded on SETS, the LSE's flagship electronic order book on which shares comprised in the FTSE 100 and FTSE 250 indices, FT Small Cap, Exchange Traded Funds and the most liquid AIM shares are traded. As at November 2013, 177 AIM securities were traded on SETS. All Main Market and the next most liquid AIM securities (that are not traded on SETS) are traded on SETqx (Stock Exchange Electronic Trading Service-quotes and crosses). SETSqx, is a hybrid trading mechanism and provides additional functionality by supplementing the electronic order book and the stand-alone quote-driven market maker facility available on SEAQ with electronic auctions which take place four times each day. SETSqx is also compliant with the obligation imposed by the Market in Financial Instruments Directive (MiFID) which requires EU regulated exchanges to enable trading on a best execution basis. Although AIM securities are outside the scope of MiFID, SETSqx trading enables limit orders to be input into the system so that the trade does not execute if the price identified by the limit order is not available. Currently, 354 AIM securities are traded on SETSqx.

SEAQ ("Stock Exchange Automated Quotations") is the LSE's non-electronic, quote-driven trading service in which a minimum of two market makers display continuous two-way prices for AIM securities that are not traded on SETS or SETSqx and for which there is a "European market size" or EMS, (i.e. the minimum quantity of securities in which the market makers are obliged to quote a firm two-way price). At the time of writing, most AIM securities are traded on SEAQ though the trend is towards more trading on the electronic order book in order to narrow bid/offer spreads, reduce costs and improve liquidity. Currently, 586 AIM securities (approximately 54 per cent of all AIM companies as at December 2013) are traded on SEAQ.

12.3 Information requirements

A public display system will usually give the following information on an AIM security to enable investors to make appropriate judgments on whether to buy or sell:

1. the date the information was last updated;
2. the SEDOL ("Stock Exchange Daily Official List") or ISIN ("International Securities Identification Number") code;
3. the industry sector;
4. the number of shares in issue;
5. the approximate free market capital ("FMC") as a percentage of shares in issue; FMC excludes shares owned by directors, their spouses and minor children, and shareholders owning five per cent or more;
6. the expected dates of announcement of preliminary and interim results;
7. the company's final or interim turnover, whichever is later;
8. the net interim and (if available) final net dividend figure;
9. the volume of shares traded in the last 12 months; and
10. the volume of shares traded during the current month.

This information is usually inputted by the company's corporate broker.

Despite the trend towards electronic trading, most AIM listed shares are still currently traded on SEAQ. A typical SEAQ page on an AIM traded security, would appear as shown in fig.1.

The example shows that Pittards Plc (AIM:PTD) has six market makers. The best "bid" price at which they will buy is 185p and the best "offer" price at which they will sell is 190p, giving a 5p "spread", from which the market makers will derive their "turn" or profit on the trade. The "touch", indicated by the strip in the centre of the screen shows the most competitive quotes and these are provided by LIBC and PEELwhich will each buy at 185p, LIBC in 500 shares and PEEL in 1000 shares; and PEEL will sell 1000 shares at 190p.

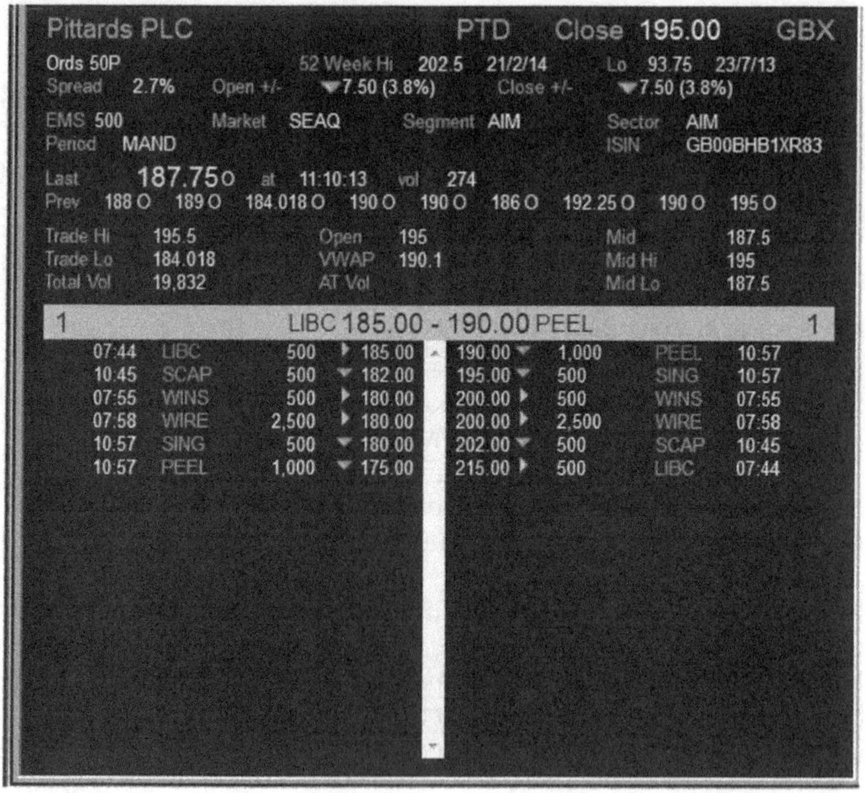

Figure 1. Source: Alpha Terminal.

A more liquid share, dealt in on SETSqx, would appear as shown in fig.2.

There are eight market makers in Wessex Exploration and the best "bid" price at which up to 75,000 shares may be sold is 0.65p and 0.75p is the best "offer" price at which up to 75,000 may bebought. In addition, the screen has a facility to show the order book prices at which various market participants are prepared to buy and sell in various sizes. An example of an AIM share traded on SETS is ASOS Plc, currently the largest company (by market value) on AIM is shown in fig.3.

As SETS is purely an electronic order book, there are no market makers making continuous two-way prices and the blue strip

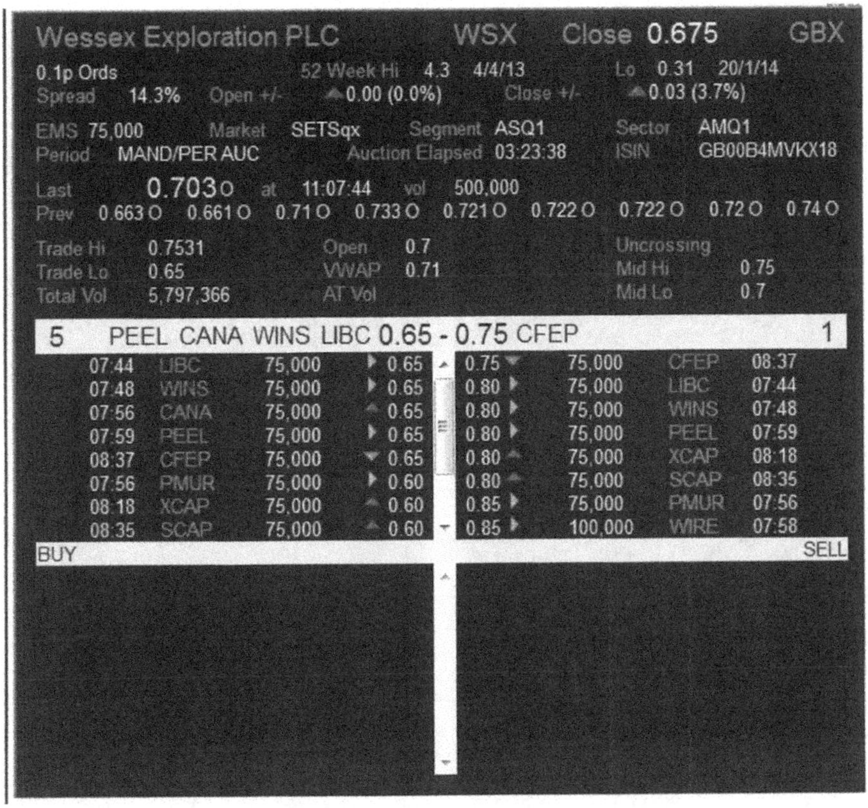

Figure 2. Source: Alpha Terminal.

reflects the best bid and offer prices from the displayed orders. The left hand column shows the prices at which shares are being bid for, the right hand shows the price at which they are offered. The example shows that 523 shares are being bid for at 5,101p and 270 are offered for sale at 5,107p.

12.4 The market practitioners

One of the distinguishing features of AIM is the relative simplicity of the formal procedures governing eligibility and admission to the market, in contrast to the more onerous requirements of the Official List. This is also generally true of

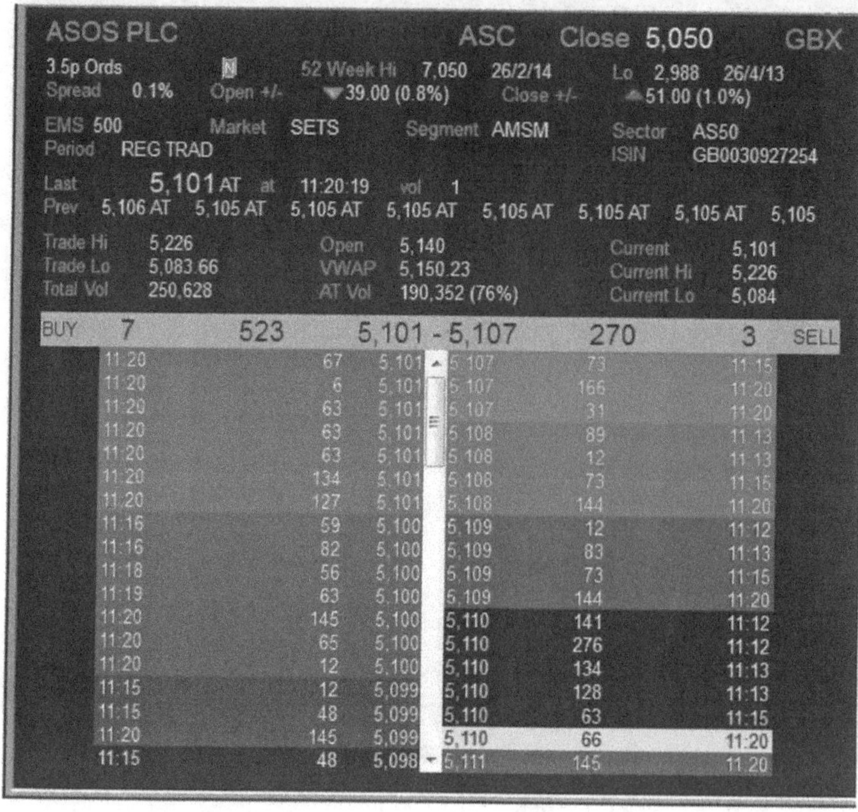

ASOS PLC				ASC	Close 5,050		GBX

Figure 3. Source: Alpha Terminal.

the environment in which AIM quoted securities are traded following admission. By and large, it is up to the market practitioners to ensure a satisfactory trading environment in which the securities can be freely traded within the regulatory framework established by the LSE. The AIM Rules for Companies include the obligation to ensure that any new developments which, if made public, would be likely to lead to a significant movement in the price of a company's shares, are announced without delay (AIM Rules for Companies r.11). The AIM Rules for Nominated Advisers, first introduced in

February 2007, confirm that the Nomad is responsible for advising the company on its continuing obligations under the AIM Rules for Companies.

Although the Nomad is responsible to the LSE for confirming that the company is "appropriate" to be admitted to AIM and ensuring compliance by the company and its directors with the AIM Rules for Companies, the Nomad is not required to be a member firm of the LSE. The trading rules are contained in the London Stock Exchange Rules (not the AIM Rules for Companies or AIM Rules for Nominated Advisers) which apply to member firms, and compliance with them is the principal responsibility of the broker who is such a member firm. In addition, the (buying or selling) broker (who need not be the corporate broker) is responsible for trade reporting and settlement, generally within the CREST system (see Chapter 12, Section 12.8). Currently, 132 member firms are authorised to act as brokers in AIM securities.

The role of the Nomad is the subject of Chapter 3.

12.4.1 *The role of the broker*

It is a requirement of the AIM Rules for Companies that a company whose shares are quoted on AIM "must retain a broker at all times" (AIM Rules for Companies r.35). Although there are no specific duties imposed on the broker under the AIM Rules for Companies, the mandatory language of r.35 effectively makes the appointment of a broker a requirement of achieving admission and the retention of a broker a continuing requirement of maintaining the dealing facility.

The Guidance Notes contained in Pt 2 of the AIM Rules for Companies explain that, by agreeing to act as broker to the company, the firm (an LSE member firm) is required to use its best endeavours to match bargains in AIM securities in which there is no registered market maker during the mandatory quote period (08:00–16:30 during business days). This means finding a willing buyer to "match" a willing seller (or vice versa), which is an order-driven process using the Bulletin

Board facility, rather than responding to opportunities generated by the competing quotes published by market makers.

It should be noted that, where AIM securities are traded on such a matched bargain basis, the price may not be a true reflection of market value in the absence of firm continuous two-way prices.

In addition, the LSE may declare prices to be "indicative only" in certain specified circumstances and to maintain an orderly market. A firm order will also be treated as indicative for a limited period of 30 minutes following an announcement by the company on the Regulatory News Service ("RNS") operated by the LSE.

In practical terms, the broker supplies liquidity by identifying and matching buyers and sellers without taking a principal position, unlike the market maker.

12.4.2 The role of the market maker

Market makers are central to the process of price formation and the supply of liquidity and therefore, although the way in which they undertake business is changing to a more order driven basis, at least for more liquid shares, a word of explanation is needed.

The defining characteristic of a security that is publicly quoted and traded on the LSE is the presence of a market maker. A market maker is a member firm of the LSE that wholesales lines of stock and takes a principal position by owning securities for re-sale on its own account. This enables shares to be freely traded and, as a result, the price fluctuates or "floats" according to the market makers' perception of supply and demand.

Unlike the broker, who is remunerated by charging clients (buying or selling) a commission based on the value of the transaction, the market maker earns its revenue by exploiting the difference between the price at which it is prepared to buy (the "bid" price) and the price at which it is prepared to sell (the "offer" price) the shares. The difference between the two prices is called the "market maker's turn".

Most AIM securities are currently traded on SEAQ, requiring the presence of at least two market makers. Only a member firm that is registered as a market maker in a security can quote firm continuous two-way prices on SEAQ or SETSqx.

A registered market maker in an AIM security is required to display firm continuous two-way prices in not less than the minimum quote size of 500 shares. If at least one market maker is displaying firm continuous two-way prices in a security, all market makers' prices in that security must also be "firm continuous two-way prices".

Where a market maker quotes a price on the telephone that is higher than the one on display, it is obliged to deal at that price and size; where a market maker quotes a price over the telephone to another market maker in a security for which it is registered, but is displaying an indicative price, that quotation will be treated as firm and the market maker is obliged to deal at the quoted price.

There are three control mechanisms which the market maker can use to regulate its risk in holding securities in an AIM company and to encourage trading:

1. to mark the price up or down in response to demand; and/or
2. to widen the bid/offer spread; and/or
3. to increase or reduce the size at which it is prepared to buy or sell (but not below the minimum quote size of 500 shares).

As the market maker's income derives from its level of trading activity, its role in judging market supply and demand is crucial both as regards its own profitability and generally in providing liquidity. In doing so, the market maker's price formation effectively determines the current market value of the company.

The choice and selection of a market maker is generally dealt with by the broker. The broker will take care to ensure that the market maker is kept informed of developments in the company's trading activities and also that the market maker has an opportunity to participate in issues of new shares and significant transactions in existing shares conducted "on exchange".

Currently, there are 52 member firms registered with the LSE as market makers authorised to make markets in AIM securities. The latest available LSE statistics show that nearly all AIM companies have at least two market makers. As at 31 December 2013, 1,087 companies were quoted on AIM, comprising 861 UK companies and 226 international companies with market capitalisations ranging from under £1 million to over £5 billion, with the majority of companies falling within the £10–100 million band. In practice, there is a correlation between the size of the company and the number of market makers registered to deal in its stock, with the most liquid shares attracting most competition for business.

Detailed rules govern how firm and indicative orders may be executed in a particular security, depending on whether the order is "all or nothing" or a "limit order", and when the order was first given in relation to competing orders in the same security. For example, before completing a transaction, a market maker must check to see whether there are any firm exposure orders at the same price or at a more competitive price. If there are, it must satisfy the displayed order unless it is an "all or nothing" order and the proposed transaction is for a lesser number of shares with the result that the price available for completing the balance of the order would be prejudiced.

12.5 Liquidity

The price of quoted securities is driven by supply and demand which, actual or perceived, is influenced by many factors, but none more so than the trading performance of the company in relation to market expectations.

A great many influences affect liquidity, ranging from macro economic factors such as interest and exchange rates (which are for the most part outside the company's control) to sector and stock-specific factors. Certainly, the size of company is an important factor, if only for the reason that larger companies tend to be more dependent on outside capital and therefore have a wider "free market capital" ("FMC") – the number of shares in the marketplace which are available for trading in response to market demand – so increasing opportunities for active trading to take place.

The ease with which AIM shares can be freely bought and sold is determined by the availability of shares at prices and in sizes which will attract investors wishing to deal. In practice, liquidity is supplied by the market makers' preparedness to quote continuous bid/offer prices, and their willingness to do so will reflect their perception of demand for a share relative to supply in the marketplace. While investors wish to trade shares in order to earn an investment return, the availability of shares is a function of FMC. Consideration must be given to ensuring that the supply of, and demand for, a share do not come out of kilter, resulting in prices getting distorted in relation to the underlying financial characteristics such as, price/earnings and dividend yield, by which a share is ultimately valued.

The ideal scenario is a trading environment where company performance is in accordance with, or better than, market expectations, and the FMC is such that shares are readily available for trading in response to judicious pricing by competing market makers.

This creates a virtuous cycle in which there is sufficient trading activity for several market makers to provide competing quotes at the keenest prices.

Generally speaking, it is usually the case that the smaller the company, the lower the FMC and the greater the reluctance of the market makers to make "keen" prices, which is reflected in a wide bid/offer spread. However, this should not be seen as a function of AIM, but of the size of the company in terms of market capitalisation and the limited number of shares held in public hands as opposed to tightly held by the directors and their families. As a company expands, so generally does its need to access outside capital, which in turn results in the issue of further shares, so increasing the FMC and trading opportunities.

For the year to 31 December 2013, the average number of AIM shares traded on a daily basis was 1,152.8m, the highest since AIM was established in June 1995.

12.6 The after-market

Liquidity is, of course, also influenced by the activity and effectiveness of the broker in publicising information amongst its client base and creating and managing a demand environment.

Brokers take on companies where they are convinced of the prospects for above average growth, either because of the quality of the management or the products/services on offer, or market sentiment towards the sector. If brokers are unable to assess such factors, it is unlikely that they will wish to be associated with the stock and actively encourage their clients to make an investment.

As far as new issues are concerned, brokers look to price companies at a level which is designed to give investors a modest premium, of around 10 per cent in initial dealings, as an inducement for the risk of holding a newly floated share.

Ideally, the opening price should go to, and remain at, this level until there is an announcement justifying a price adjustment, usually the first set of figures after flotation. To maintain an active and orderly after-market, brokers will be in frequent contact with companies; estimates for the current year and future performance are updated in the light of trading conditions. Certainly, brokers would look to publish research notes following the interim results or preliminary announcement of full-year results, as well as general and more comprehensive updates on companies following significant transactions or further capital-raising exercises (unless the company is in a "quiet period" as, for example, when it is in an "offer period" (as defined by the City Code) when publication of any forecasts could risk divulging price-sensitive information, or which would lead to further unhelpful rumour and speculation. It has become market practice for the house broker not to publish research material at these times).

The relationship between the broker and the company will usually be defined by an agreement which would be expected to cover such routine matters as publication of research notes, organising institutional presentations and shareholder analysis, as well as one-off, specific projects.

12.7 Relations with investors

The broker is responsible for maintaining an active dialogue between the company and its investors, who might otherwise only hear from the company on a twice-yearly basis (on publication of its interim results and preliminary announcement), as well as at the annual general meeting. The broker will also arrange institutional presentations at which the executive directors, usually the chief executive/managing director and finance director would have one-to-one meetings with the institutional shareholders.

This process is crucial if the company has ambitions to raise further equity capital, such as an acquisition to be financed by an entitlement issue (rights issue or open offer), or a vendor consideration placing. In such circumstances, the broker will normally seek the agreement of the institutional shareholder that it be made an insider prior to the commencement of discussions designed to establish the level of support for a particular transaction. In addition, the broker will seek to involve the market maker in "agency crosses" (riskless transactions in the existing shares between member firms) to allow the market maker to fulfil any order limit or to level a long or short position.

12.8   Reporting and settlement

Most transactions conducted on the LSE are settled in CREST. CREST is the system used for settling stock exchange bargains in uncertificated (or dematerialised) form and has been operational since 15 July 1996.

CREST effectively matches all buying and selling transactions (by crediting and debiting stock and consideration electronically) to or from the buyer's or seller's account, which is operated by the 20 or so CREST member accounts.

The London Stock Exchange Rules require CREST trades to be reported by 21:00 on the day of the trade if the transaction was carried out during the trade reporting period (07:15–17:15 on days when the LSE is open for business), or by 20:00 on the following day if it was conducted outside the trade reporting period.

Where a trade report is required, the trade must be submitted to the LSE within three minutes of the execution of the transaction, except where it is effected outside the trade reporting period, in which case it must be reported to the LSE between 07:15 and 08:00 during the next trade reporting period. The London Stock Exchange Rules prescribe the detailed information to be included in a trade report. All AIM transactions must be trade reported except "riskless principal transactions" (matched bargains, sometimes referred to as "agency crosses") or where the transaction is "put through" the LSE, at the same price and size.

All risk trades are published three business days after the day of trading; riskless transactions are published as soon as the LSE receives details.

Settlement, unless otherwise agreed, is three days after the transaction date (the date on which the transaction is effected). The minimum period for settlement on CREST is delivery on the same day and the maximum period is delivery within one year.

An alternative method of settlement is "residual settlement" (for very illiquid stocks). This involves the physical delivery of share certificates to the buyer generally within three days of the transaction.

12.9 Market regulation

12.9.1 *Insider dealing*

12.9.1.1 *Criminal liability*

An individual must ensure that he does not deal in an AIM (or any publicly quoted) security on the basis of "inside information". This prohibition is, therefore, not confined to AIM and is part of the general criminal law contained in Pt V of the Criminal Justice Act 1993 ("CJA 1993").

In summary, the legislation creates an offence of "insider dealing" and prohibits the use of inside information, which may be defined generally as confidential price-sensitive information, for the purposes of dealing in the securities of a quoted company and thereby deriving an advantage. The legislation, which only applies to individuals, extends beyond any individuals in possession of inside information who themselves deal in the securities in question; it also applies to encouraging or procuring another person to deal, whether or not that person knows he is dealing on the basis of inside information.

The difficulty is to identify confidential price-sensitive information. Section 56 of the CJA 1993 defines "inside information" as information which:

1. relates to a particular security or issuer, and not to securities or issuers generally;
2. is specific or precise;
3. has not been made public; and
4. if it were made public would be likely to have a significant effect on the price.

According to s.57 of the CJA 1993, a person has information as an insider if and only if:

1. it is, and he knows it is, inside information; and
2. he has the information and knows that he has it from an inside source, that is from:
    1. a director, employee or shareholder; or
    2. a person who has access to such information by virtue of his employment, office or profession; or
    3. directly or indirectly from any such person referred to in (a) and (b).

The general principle is that any information which is not already in the public domain and can reasonably be construed as having a bearing on the value of quoted securities (thereby requiring an announcement to be made in accordance with r.11 of the AIM Rules for Companies), constitutes confidential price-sensitive information. In borderline cases, caution must be exercised and an announcement must be made before dealings take place to prevent a false market from arising.

Under s.53 of the CJA 1993, it is a defence if the individual:

1. does not expect the dealing to result in a profit because the information is price-sensitive;

2. believes on reasonable grounds that the information has been disclosed sufficiently widely, so that no-one taking part in the transaction could be prejudiced by not having the information; or
3. still would have dealt even if he did not have the information.

12.9.1.2 Special defences

Paragraph 1 of Sch.1 to the CJA 1993 provides a defence if an individual acted in good faith in the course of his business as, or his employment in the business of, a market maker.

For these purposes, a market maker is defined as a person who "holds himself out at all normal times in compliance with the rules of a regulated market or an approved organisation as willing to acquire or dispose of securities". An "approved organisation" is defined as "an international securities self-regulating organisation approved by the Treasury under any order made under s.22 of the Financial Services and Markets Act 2000". It therefore appears that a market maker registered as such under the London Stock Exchange Rules is clearly covered by this definition and so is within the scope of the defence.

12.9.1.3 Civil liability

In addition, it is possible to institute civil proceedings for insider trading (effectively for breach of statutory duty) with a view to obtaining restitution or compensation, as appropriate, from the defendant.

There have been remarkably few successful prosecutions and even fewer civil actions. Successful action under either criminal or civil law would not necessarily render the offending transaction void, voidable or otherwise unenforceable.

12.9.1.4   Further developments

The Financial Services and Markets Act 2000 (the "FSMA 2000") created a new offence of "market abuse". The intention appears to be to catch behaviour which is damaging to markets but which does not constitute any of the existing offences. This is partly in response to technological developments such as the wider use of the internet and increased levels of execution-only trading, which have seen instances of unscrupulous behaviour by some stock tipsters buying securities for their own account shortly before publishing "buy" recommendations.

The legislation applies to all persons (individuals and corporations) and has an extra-territorial dimension in that it applies to prevent market abuse on a "prescribed market" (including the LSE), regardless of where the abuse takes place.

In addition, s.89 of the Financial Services Act 2012 (previously s.397 of the FSMA 2000) creates an offence of making or engaging in misleading statements and practices in relation to the market in or price or value of listed or quoted shares.

The Market Abuse Directive ("MAD"), which came into force with effect from 1 July 2005, imposes additional requirements on fully listed companies to maintain lists of persons (including employees and advisers) who are privy to confidential price-sensitive information. The FCA's Guidance Manual confirms that the MAD does not apply to AIM listed companies.

12.9.1.5   LSE requirements

For directors and "applicable employees", r.21 of the AIM Rules for Companies imposes additional constraints on dealing. Directors and certain employees are considered to be generally in possession of more information regarding a company's affairs than is publicly available. An "applicable employee" is defined in the Rules as someone who, together with his family, has an interest directly or indirectly in 0.5 per cent of a class of AIM securities; or is likely to be in possession of unpublished price-sensitive information in relation to the company because of his employment with the company or a member of the group.

An AIM company must ensure that its directors and applicable employees do not deal in its securities during a "close period". A close period is defined in the AIM Rules for Companies as any one of the following:

1. the two-month period preceding the publication of the company's annual results or, if shorter, the period from its financial year end to the time of publication;
2. the two-month period immediately preceding the notification of the company's half-year results (or, if shorter, the period from the relevant financial period end up to and including the time of notification):
    (a) where the company reports on a half-yearly basis; or
    (b) where it reports on a quarterly basis the period of one month immediately preceding the notification of its quarterly results or, if shorter, the period from the relevant financial period end to the time of notification;
3. any other period when the company is in possession of unpublished price-sensitive information; and
4. any time when it has become reasonably probable that such unpublished price-sensitive information will be required by the AIM Rules for Companies to be notified to the Company Announcements Office.

These particular obligations mirror the principal restrictions contained in the Model Code of Directors' Dealings in the Listing Rules of the UK Listing Authority. It is good practice to require the chairman's approval to be obtained in all cases before dealings by a director or applicable employee take place.

It is important to emphasise that these restrictions are in addition to the criminal law which applies at all times and in all cases.

In certain instances, discussions will need to take place between a company looking to raise further capital (e.g. to finance an acquisition or improve its balance sheet) and its major shareholders. In these circumstances, the position is regulated by general company law. Where an underwriting or capital raising is in prospect by way, for example, of a selective marketing (or placing), discussions will need to be held with a company's major shareholders for the purposes of determining the level of support for the proposals and as part of the pricing mechanism. In practice, most firms of brokers seek to make their major institutional clients insiders, thereby depriving those shareholders of the opportunity of dealing until a full public announcement is made. When the outcome is known and the acquisition, for example, can proceed, an announcement will be required under r.11 (and, if the acquisition is a "substantial transaction", r.12) of the AIM Rules for Companies.

12.9.2 Dealing announcements

Announcement of certain transactions is required in accordance with general company law, as supplemented by the AIM Rules for Companies.

12.9.2.1 Dealings by directors

Any deal by a director or his spouse or minor children must be disclosed in accordance with r.17 of the AIM Rules for Companies, by the company "without delay".

12.9.2.2 Substantial interests

A person (or persons acting in concert) who acquires an interest in shares amounting to three per cent or more of a company is required under the Disclosure and Transparency Rules ("DTR") (made in accordance with powers granted to the secretary of state under the FSMA 2000) to inform the company within two business days of the transaction. Thereafter, any subsequent dealing which takes the shareholder(s) through one whole percentage point, upwards or downwards, or as a result of which the shareholder(s) ceases to have a substantial interest (i.e. less than three per cent), must be reported to the company, which must then make an appropriate announcement by the next business day.

Under para.5.1.5 of the DTR, an interest in shares held by a market maker for the purposes of his business (only in so far as it is not used for the purpose of intervening in the management of the company) is disregarded. For these purposes a market maker is a person authorised under the law of a Member State to deal in securities and to deal on a relevant stock exchanges. He holds himself out at all normal times as willing to acquire and dispose of securities at prices specified by him, and in so doing is subject to the rules of that exchange.

Market makers are therefore exempt from the requirement to notify companies of their substantial interests, but they must nevertheless inform the LSE which publishes announcements via the RNS at its discretion.

12.9.3 *Integrated Monitoring and Surveillance System*

The LSE operates an integrated surveillance system to monitor trading on the London markets. Integrated Monitoring and Surveillance System (IMAS) is a sophisticated computer system which highlights irregularities such as large fluctuations in share prices or volumes of trades.

The system works in real time during market hours. It monitors trades and quotes continuously and pinpoints deviations from the norm.

Generally speaking, an unexplained price movement of 10 per cent or more on one day will lead to an informal enquiry of the company's broker by the LSE surveillance team.

12.10   Information about AIM companies

Where does an actual or prospective investor in an AIM company look for information about the company?

There are seven main sources of information:

1.   SEAQ, SETS and SETSqx, which can be accessed by a member firm, usually a broker acting on behalf of the investor;
2.   The LSE produces indices of the leading AIM companies, by market capitalisation. Details of the companies which constitute the top 50 and 100 AIM companies, as well as the FTSE AIM All-Share can be found on the LSE's website;
3.   Brokers' research notes – information prepared by corporate brokers for their private and institutional clients, include a résumé of the company and the nature of its business, an estimate of projected trading performance for the next two to three years, and a commentary on the latest published figures;
4.   Financial press – the FT publishes the latest share prices of AIM quoted companies on a daily basis. It should be noted that the price/earnings ratios ("PERs") quoted by the FT are historic (based on published results) as opposed to the PERs in brokers' notes which derive from the brokers' own estimates of future earnings. Other publications, such as *Investors Chronicle* and *Shares* magazine, follow the more actively traded and fashionable AIM stocks;
5.   Published annual and interim report and accounts; the FT provides a free distribution service for many AIM companies.
6.   The websites of companies whose securities are quoted on AIM. Rule 26 of the AIM Rules for Companies requires an AIM company to make the following information available on its website (words in italics refer to definitions in the AIM Rules for Companies):
     (a)   a description of its business and, where it is an *investing company*, its *investing policy* and details of any *investment manager* and/or key personnel;

(b) the names of its *directors* and brief biographical details of each, as would normally be included in an *admission document*;

(c) a description of the responsibilities of the members of the board of *directors* and details of any committees of the board of *directors* and their responsibilities;

(d) its country of incorporation and main country of operation;

(e) where the *AIM company* is not incorporated in the *UK*, a statement that the rights of *shareholders* may be different from the rights of *shareholders* in a *UK* incorporated company;

(f) its current constitutional documents (e.g. its articles of association);

(g) details of any other exchanges or trading platforms on which the *AIM company* has applied or agreed to have any of its securities (including its *AIM securities*) admitted or traded;

(h) the number of *AIM securities* in issue (noting any held as *treasury shares*) and, insofar as it is aware, the percentage of *AIM securities* that is *not in public hands* together with the identity and percentage holdings of its *significant shareholders*.

This information should be updated at least every six months and the website should include the date on which this information was last updated;

(i) details of any restrictions on the transfer of its *AIM securities*;

(j) The annual accounts published pursuant to r.19 for the last three years or since admission, whichever is the lesser and all half-yearly, quarterly or similar reports published since the last annual accounts pursuant to r.18;

(k) all *notifications* the *AIM company* has made in the past 12 months;

(l) its most recent *admission document*together with any circulars or similar publications sent to *shareholders* within the past 12 months;

(m) details of the corporate governance code that the AIM company has decided to apply, how the AIM company complies with that code, or if no code has been adopted this should be stated together with its current corporate governance arrangements;

(n) whether the AIM company is subject to the UK City Code on Takeovers and Mergers, or any other such legislation or code in its country of incorporation or operations, or any other similar provisions it has voluntarily adopted; and

(o) details of its *Nomad* and other key advisers (as might normally be found in an *admission document*).

7. In addition, the website of the LSE provides information on all AIM quoted securities: *www.londonstockexchange.com*.

12.11   Conclusion

The role of the broker is key to promoting the investment profile of the AIM company to the market, as represented by existing investors and market makers, and also to prospective investors.

The broker's functions broadly cover the following:

- maintaining a two-way dialogue between the company and the market, including regular updates on actual and expected performance of the company and its peer group;
- equity distribution to finance acquisitions or rights issues; and
- advising the company on the presentation of corporate information to the market and generally acting as a "sounding board" on the appropriateness and proposed financing of acquisitions.

The broker is, therefore, a key member of the company's team and supplements the work of the company's other advisers in ensuring that actual and prospective investors, including the market makers, are kept regularly informed of all material developments as well as the broker's views on expectations and trends.

In addition, the AIM Rules for Companies require the broker, in cases where there is only one registered market maker, to supplement the role of the market maker in using its best endeavours to match buyers and sellers of the company's shares.

Chapter 13

Overseas Companies on AIM

Nick Williams
Partner, Edwin Coe LLP

13.1 Introduction

As the economies of the world have become increasingly globalised, so too have its capital markets. Competition between the markets for overseas members continues to be strong. This Chapter considers AIM's success in attracting overseas companies and outlines some of the regulatory considerations particularly relevant to an overseas company considering a listing on AIM.

13.2 Why might an overseas company choose AIM?

13.2.1 AIM's objectives

The London Stock Exchange Plc ("LSE") promotes AIM as "the international market for smaller growing companies" and is keen to attract overseas companies. It has been successful in doing so, because of AIM's balanced approach to regulation, its accessibility for new and early-stage companies, the availability of funding through an international investor base and the public profile obtained by international companies on AIM. Since May 2003, admission to trading on AIM has been potentially easier for certain companies quoted on one of a number of overseas exchanges. These are exchanges which have been designated by AIM as "AIM Designated Markets". Companies which have been quoted on an AIM Designated

Market for at least 18 months may take advantage of the "fast-track route", which is an expedited procedure for admission to trading on AIM. The fast-track route is considered at Section 13.5 below.

13.2.2 Flexible regulation

One of AIM's key attractions is that it is more flexible than many other international markets. For instance, AIM has limited requirements for shareholder approval in relation to transactions (see Chapter 8), no requirement for a trading track record and no minimum market capitalisation requirement. Under the AIM Rules for Companies there is no prescribed requirement for a minimum number of shares to be in public hands, but an applicant company's Nominated Adviser ("Nomad"), when assessing whether it is appropriate to be admitted to AIM, will consider whether a sufficient proportion of its AIM securities are in public hands. Under the AIM Rules for Companies there is also no maximum market capitalisation for AIM companies, although an applicant company would not normally be expected to have a market capitalisation in excess of £500 million on admission.

13.3 How successful has AIM been in attracting overseas companies?

In December 2013, of the 1,087 companies admitted to AIM, 226 (approximately 21 per cent) were companies incorporated outside the UK, Channel Islands and Isle of Man.

The overseas countries with companies admitted to AIM were (as at December 2013): Cayman Islands (42 companies); British Virgin Islands (36 companies); Australia (28 companies); Republic of Ireland (26 companies); Bermuda (20 companies); Canada (18 companies); United States (17 companies); Cyprus (7 companies); Singapore (5 companies); and Israel (4 companies). There were 15 other countries with three companies or fewer admitted to AIM.

It should be borne in mind that these figures do not take account of overseas businesses which have, for whatever reason, decided to establish a domestic (UK, Channel Islands or the Isle of Man) holding company prior to admission to AIM. It should also be noted that the jurisdiction in which the holding company is established is not necessarily that in which the principal business of the group is carried on. For instance, Chinese businesses which have come to AIM typically have a group holding company incorporated in a jurisdiction such as Jersey, the Cayman Islands or the British Virgin Islands.

It is accordingly interesting to contrast the above statistics with the categorisation of AIM companies according to their main country or region of operation. The clear leader in December 2013 was the UK with 624 companies, with the remaining companies principally operating in: Africa (82 companies); Western Europe (64 companies); United States (50 companies); China (48 companies); Asia Pacific (42 companies); Russia and the former CIS countries (41 companies); Australia (26 companies); Latin America (25 companies); India and Bangladesh (24 companies); Central and Eastern Europe (19 companies); Canada (15 companies); Israel (10 companies); Middle East (9 companies); Isle of Man (3 companies); Channel Islands (2 companies); and Other Offshore jurisdictions (3 companies).

It should be noted that in assessing an overseas company's suitability to be admitted to trading on AIM, the prospective Nomad will normally wish to see that the company's business is or is becoming international and not limited to its local market.

13.4 Legal and regulatory considerations for overseas companies

13.4.1 Eligibility requirements under the AIM Rules for Companies

Overseas companies, as is the case for all applicant companies, are subject to the eligibility requirements described in Chapter 2. The first paragraph of the Guidance Notes to the AIM Rules for Companies also states that an AIM company or applicant for admission to AIM must be appropriate for AIM's regulatory framework, and if not a UK public limited company, should usually be a similar structure. Further, an AIM company should not be complex in terms of its structure and securities, and should issue primarily ordinary shares (or equivalent). *The following requirements have particular relevance to overseas companies.*

The shares in an AIM company must be freely transferable (r.32). There are two exceptions. The first is where, in any jurisdiction, statute or regulation places restrictions upon transferability. The second is where the AIM company is seeking to limit the number of shareholders domiciled in a particular country to ensure that it does not become subject to statute or regulation. The Guidance Notes to r.32 state that where an AIM company wishes to rely on the exceptions stated in r.32, its Nomad should apply to the AIM Regulation team for confirmation that this is acceptable. The AIM Regulation team is contactable using the email address aimregulation@lseg.com and on +44 (0)20 7797 4154.

A new holding company may be set up in a suitable jurisdiction, if the method of transferring shares in an overseas company is not compatible with AIM.

Rule 36 states that an AIM company must ensure that appropriate settlement arrangements are in place. In particular, all AIM securities (including where the relevant AIM company is incorporated outside the UK) must be eligible for electronic settlement save where the LSE otherwise agrees. Although

CREST is the usual form of electronic settlement used by AIM companies, r.36 does not expressly limit "electronic settlement" to CREST, or even to an electronic settlement system administered in the UK. The Guidance Notes to the AIM Rules for Companies state that the LSE will only grant a derogation from the requirement to be eligible for electronic settlement in the most exceptional circumstances, such as where none of the current electronic systems can cope with settling the AIM company's securities, or where the local law of an AIM company prohibits such settlement.

Advisers should therefore liaise as appropriate with AIM, Euroclear UK & Ireland Ltd (the operator of the CREST system) and/or the company's registrars at an early stage in the admission process about the above issues. Where companies are incorporated outside the UK, Guernsey, Jersey, the Isle of Man or Ireland, "depository interests" ("DIs") representing their shares have to be constituted to participate in the CREST settlement system. DIs are usually issued by the company's UK registrars on its behalf, and constitute an interest in the underlying shares of the company. Shares are transferred or issued to the company's UK registrars who then issue DIs to individual investors' CREST accounts. "CREST Depository Interests" or "CDIs" may also be issued, and this service is restricted to stock issued by companies in certain jurisdictions. CDIs and DIs are dematerialised securities which trade on CREST. Chapter 15 considers particular aspects of electronic settlement for overseas companies in more detail.

DIs should be distinguished from depository receipts, which are another form of instrument representing underlying shares, and commonly used by overseas companies to obtain a listing on an exchange outside of their jurisdiction of incorporation, if they are restricted from listing the shares directly. Issue 1 of "Inside AIM", published by the LSE in December 2009 and available on its website at www.londonstockexchange.com/aim, states that depository receipts will only be considered appropriate for admission to AIM when the AIM company is incorporated in a jurisdiction which prohibits, or unduly restricts, the offering or admission of its securities outside of that country.

The AIM Regulation team expressed the view in Issue 5 of "Inside AIM", published by the LSE in October 2012, that an AIM company or applicant must take care to ensure that it can comply with its AIM obligations, including r.41 (cancellation of admission). Any less stringent local laws do not override r.41 and where local laws do impact Nomads should seek to ensure that where possible a company's AIM obligations are enshrined in its constitutional documents.

13.4.2 The Admission Document and Prospectus Rules

If an overseas applicant company is not taking advantage of the fast-track route (see Section 13.5 below), it will have to produce an admission document including the information required by Sch.2 to the AIM Rules for Companies. Schedule 2 requires, among other things, that certain of the content requirements set out in Annexes I and III of the Prospectus Rules are included in the admission document. If the admission document is issued in respect of an offer to the public which is not exempt from the obligation to publish a prospectus, the content requirements of the Prospectus Rules will apply in full (see Chapters 6 and 7 for more details). These requirements of the AIM Rules for Companies and, where applicable, the Prospectus Rules, are applicable to overseas companies. In certain circumstances, the content requirements of the Prospectus Rules address local law and practice, for instance compliance with the corporate governance regime of the country of incorporation. The other legal requirements for marketing securities in the UK and other relevant jurisdictions will also need to be complied with.

13.4.3 Using a new holding company

Rather than an overseas company itself seeking admission to AIM, it can carry out a reorganisation prior to admission so that a UK plc, or a company established in another jurisdiction, such as the Channel Islands, the Cayman Islands or the British Virgin Islands, becomes the parent company, owning 100 per cent of the shares in the overseas company.

The decision to do this may be driven by tax considerations or because a UK plc, or a holding company established in another jurisdiction, is seen by institutional investors as a preferable form of entity in which to invest, or because the method of transferring shares in the overseas company is not compatible with r.32 (see Section 13.4.1 above). As the views of investors on the suitability of a particular jurisdiction for incorporating a holding company to be admitted to AIM may change, it would be advisable to obtain the advice of the appointed or prospective Nomad on which jurisdiction to choose.

Apart from the legal issues involved in such a reorganisation, there may be UK or overseas securities regulations and tax and stamp duty implications to consider.

13.4.4   Continuing obligations

The Introduction to the AIM Rules for Companies states that AIM companies need to comply with any relevant national law and regulation as well as certain European Commission standards where applicable, such as the Disclosure and Transparency Rules published by the UK Financial Conduct Authority and the Prospectus Rules. An overseas AIM company is also subject to the continuing obligations under the AIM Rules for Companies described in Chapter 8. *It will need to address the following requirements in particular*:

13.4.4.1   Rule 10 (Principles of disclosure)

Where an AIM company is required to make an announcement through a regulatory information service, the information must be announced no later than it is published elsewhere. This means that, for instance, if an AIM company is also quoted on another exchange, the announcements must be coordinated.

13.4.4.2 *Rule 17 (Disclosure of miscellaneous information)*

The AIM Rules for Companies distinguish between a DTR company (defined as an AIM company that is required to make disclosures in accordance with the Disclosure and Transparency Rules ("DTR") published by the UK Financial Conduct Authority from time to time) and a non-DTR company (a company that is not required to make disclosures in accordance with the DTR). An AIM company is a DTR company, if it is a public company within the meaning of the UK Companies Act or any other body corporate incorporated in and having a principal place of business in the UK. All AIM companies are required under r.17 to announce without delay any relevant changes (changes above 3 per cent, excluding treasury shares, which increase or decrease a holding through any single percentage) in any legal or beneficial interest, whether direct or indirect, in the AIM securities of a significant shareholder. A significant shareholder is defined as any person with a holding of 3 per cent or more in any class of AIM security, excluding treasury shares, including family (as defined) holdings, and the acquisition or disposal of such a holding must be announced. The definition of "holding" in the Glossary of the AIM Rules for Companies provides that when determining whether a person is a significant shareholder, a holding also includes a position in a financial instrument, which is defined as any financial instrument requiring disclosure in accordance with DTR 5.3.1. The definition of "financial instrument" also provides that for the purposes of the definition, all AIM companies shall be treated as if they are DTR Companies regardless of their country of incorporation. AIM Notice 32, published on 28 May 2009, states that shareholders in a non-DTR company should be encouraged to disclose a shareholding represented by a holding of a long position in a contract for differences, or similar financial product, on a delta-adjusted basis, although disclosure on this basis will not be mandatory. Further details, including the information to be disclosed, are set out in Chapter 8.

The Guidance Notes to r.17 state that non-DTR companies are required to use all reasonable endeavours to comply with r.17, notwithstanding that the local law applicable to some AIM companies does not contain provisions that are similar to the DTR. In that instance, such an AIM company is advised to include and maintain provisions in its constitution (articles of association, or equivalent) requiring significant shareholders to notify the AIM company of any relevant changes to their shareholdings in similar terms to the DTR, noting certain differences described in the Guidance Notes. These differences are that notwithstanding the time limits for disclosure set out in the DTR, DTR companies are required under r.17 to announce such information "without delay"; and the information required to be released pursuant to r.17 must be announced to the market through a regulatory information service rather than "made public" in accordance with the DTR. Non-DTR companies are also advised to make appropriate disclosure of the fact that statutory disclosure of significant shareholdings is different and may not always ensure compliance with the requirements of r.17.

Also, r.17 requires that the admission to trading (or cancellation from trading) of AIM securities (or any other securities issued by an AIM company) on any other exchange or trading platform, where such admission or cancellation is at the application or with the agreement of the AIM company, must be announced without delay. This information must also be submitted separately to the LSE. An announcement in relation to the trading of an AIM company's securities on any other exchange or trading platform should include details of which exchange or platform (including details of any segment, tier or similar) and which securities this relates to.

13.4.4.3 Rule 19 (Annual accounts)

AIM companies which are incorporated in a European Economic Area (EEA) country (which is deemed to include for the purposes of the AIM Rules for Companies only, the Channel Islands and the Isle of Man) must prepare and present annual audited accounts in accordance with International Accounting Standards (standards adopted for use in the European Union in accordance with Article 3 of the IAS

Regulation (EC) No.1606/2002, as adopted from time to time by the European Commission). There is a carve-out for this requirement in relation to AIM companies incorporated in the EEA which, at the end of the relevant financial period, are not parent companies (as interpreted in accordance with applicable law). Such companies may either prepare and present their accounts in accordance with International Accounting Standards, or in accordance with the accounting and company legislation and regulations that are applicable to them due to their country of incorporation.

AIM companies which are not incorporated in the EEA have a choice of International Accounting Standards; Canadian, US or Japanese Generally Accepted Accounting Principles (GAAP); or Australian International Financial Reporting Standards (as issued by the Australian Accounting Standards Board). The LSE encourages all AIM companies to use International Accounting Standards, both on admission and in the preparation of all post-admission financial information. The choice of accounting standards should be consistently implemented and any change between those standards available to a particular AIM company should only be made with the prior approval of the AIM Regulation team. Any queries over the interpretation of these provisions should be addressed by the AIM company's Nomad to the AIM Regulation team at the earliest opportunity.

In addition, since February 2010, non-UK companies have been able to satisfy the requirement in r.19 to send accounts to shareholders by sending such accounts by electronic communication (any communication sent by e-mail or made available on an AIM company's website pursuant to r.26) to shareholders. This is subject to the constitution (articles of association, or equivalent) of the company and any legal requirements in its jurisdiction of incorporation. Where a company is not subject to the UK Companies Act 2006, the following requirements have to have been satisfied:

1. a decision to use electronic communication to shareholders has been approved by shareholders in a general meeting of the AIM company;

2. appropriate identification arrangements have been put in place so that the shareholders are effectively informed; and

3. shareholders individually:
    (a) have been contacted in writing to request their consent to receive accounts by means of electronic communication and if they do not object within 28 days, their consent can be considered to have been given;
    (b) are able to request at any time in the future that accounts be communicated to them in writing; and
    (c) are contacted alerting them to the publication of the accounts on the AIM company's website.

13.4.4.4   Rule 26 (Website)

There are a number of ongoing requirements in relation to the contents of an AIM company's website, but of particular note for an overseas company are that the website must include the following: the company's country of incorporation and main country of operation, a statement that the rights of shareholders may be different from the rights of shareholders in a UK incorporated company, details of any other exchanges or trading platforms on which the company has applied or agreed to have any of its securities (including its AIM securities) admitted or traded, details of any restrictions on the transfer of its AIM securities and details of the takeovers regime to which it is subject (see Section 13.4.5 below). Additional guidance on certain of these requirements is given in the Guidance Notes to r.26.

AIM companies and Nomads are reminded in the AIM Note for Mining and Oil & Gas Companies (see Section 13.4.9 below) that where an AIM company is also admitted to trading on another exchange, the AIM Rules for Companies need to be complied with irrespective of the regulatory requirements of the other exchange. Any specific issues in relation to an AIM company's ability to comply with the AIM Rules for Companies or the Note as a result of the rules of the other exchange should be referred to the AIM Regulation team.

13.4.4.5   Rule 30 (Language)

All admission documents, any documents sent to holders of AIM securities and any information required by the AIM Rules for Companies must be in English. Where the original document or information is not in English, an English translation may be provided.

13.4.5   UK Takeover Code

An AIM company whose registered office is in the UK, the Channel Islands, or the Isle of Man is subject to the UK City Code on Takeovers and Mergers ("Takeover Code"), and this should be disclosed as a matter of good practice in its admission document. If an AIM company is incorporated elsewhere, it will not be subject to the Takeover Code, and this similarly should be disclosed in its admission document, together with the relevant matters provided by r.26 (see below). Such a company should consider whether certain provisions of the Takeover Code, in particular Rule 9 of the Takeover Code (providing for a compulsory takeover offer in certain circumstances), should be reflected in the company's constitutional documents (articles of association, or equivalent) to give shareholders protection similar to that afforded under the Takeover Code. Whether such provisions are capable of being satisfactorily enforced is subject to debate.

Rule 26 requires AIM companies to include information on their website as to whether the AIM company is subject to the Takeover Code, or any other such legislation or code in its country of incorporation or operation, or any other similar provisions it has voluntarily adopted.

13.4.6   Legal opinions

The principal legal adviser to an applicant company is invariably a UK law firm, which will work with local legal advisers in any jurisdiction where the company or any of its other group members has a significant presence. In addition to carrying out a legal due diligence review, it is best practice for a legal opinion to be given by the relevant overseas legal counsel in relation, among other things, to the good standing of an overseas applicant company and/or any companies in a group which are incorporated outside the UK. Such an opinion would typically cover matters such as due incorporation, solvency, ownership of assets and enforceability of material contracts. The opinion would normally be addressed to both the applicant company and Nomad/broker. The AIM Note for Mining and Oil & Gas companies (see Section 13.4.9 below) states that where an AIM applicant company's assets (as defined in the Note) exist outside the UK, as well as performing usual due diligence, a formal opinion letter should be obtained from an appropriate legal adviser authorised to practice in the jurisdiction in which the assets are located and in the law under which they are governed. Such opinion should deal with matters including: (a) issues of jurisdiction (such as the proper incorporation and good standing of any incorporated subsidiary or interest); and (b) the title to or validity and enforceability of any assets (including for the avoidance of doubt licences and agreements), as is appropriate to the applicant company. The LSE would usually expect that details of the adviser providing such opinion should be included in the advisers' section of the applicant company's admission document.

13.4.7 Restrictions on directors' authority to allot shares

The directors of companies incorporated in jurisdictions outside the UK often have wide powers to allot shares. In these circumstances, the Nomad may require that the constitutional documents of an applicant company (articles of association, or equivalent) be amended to contain provisions restricting the ability of the directors to allot shares or to grant subscription or conversion rights over shares, in line with the UK Companies Act and UK institutional guidelines.

13.4.8   Differences from UK law and market practice

In addition to the issues described above, it is considered good practice for an admission document prepared in relation to an applicant company incorporated outside the UK, to identify any material differences between the law and practice of the country of incorporation of the applicant company and of the UK. Such differences are sometimes addressed in the "Risk Factors" section, if appropriate.

13.4.9   AIM Note for Mining and Oil & Gas Companies

The LSE publishes a Note for resource companies, such as exploration, development and production companies, operating in the mining and oil & gas sectors. The Note forms part of the AIM Rules for Companies and AIM Rules for Nominated Advisers. The Note does not, however, apply to companies which purely invest in or provide consultancy, advice or other such services to resource companies. This Note is relevant here as the assets of resource companies will usually be situated outside the UK. If a Nomad believes that provisions set out in the Note are not applicable or appropriate to a particular AIM company, for instance, if the requirements of the AIM company's home exchange conflict with the Note, they should contact the AIM Regulation team at aimregulation@lseg.com.

13.4.10   US-Specific Issues

In view of the broad reach of United States securities laws and regulations, these may be relevant to companies applying for admission to and admitted to trading on AIM. US-specific issues are considered in Chapter 14.

13.4.11   UK Bribery Act

Nomads and overseas companies admitted to trading on AIM and applying for admission should consider the UK Bribery Act 2010, which came into force on 1 July 2011. As well as applying to UK persons and companies, the Act applies to companies incorporated outside the UK which carry on a business, or part of a business, in any part of the UK. The overseas company will itself be guilty of an offence, if a person associated with it bribes another person on its behalf anywhere in the world, but it is a defence for the company to prove that it had in place adequate procedures designed to prevent persons associated with it from undertaking such conduct. Overseas companies applying for admission to AIM and already admitted should refer to their UK legal advisers for advice on the Bribery Act and its application, in particular, whether they would be treated as carrying on business, or part of a business, in the UK. Non-binding guidance issued by the UK Ministry of Justice at the time the Act came into force suggests that for this purpose the mere fact a company's securities have been admitted to the UKLA Official List (by way of example) would not, in itself, qualify that company as carrying on a business or part of a business in the UK. However, comments made on behalf of the UK Serious Fraud Office have suggested that it may be sufficient.

The AIM Regulation team considers the Bribery Act in Issue 4 of "Inside AIM" and states that each overseas company needs to consider whether it could fall within the scope of the Act, and that Nomads may wish to make sure that overseas client companies are aware of the legislation and have undertaken this review. In this context, while AIM Regulation goes on to state that it would expect Nomads to consider any significant and relevant legislation, its impact on their clients and the extent to which it may impact appropriateness for AIM, it acknowledges the significance of the Bribery Act to a company will inevitably vary depending on business type and jurisdiction.

It is suggested that it would be good practice to make reference to the Bribery Act in the admission document published by an overseas company, and in particular describe the extent to which the overseas company has put in place procedures to comply with it.

13.4.12   The role of the Nomad in relation to overseas companies

Rule 18 of the AIM Rules for Nominated Advisers states that in deciding whether a Nomad has complied with those Rules and the undertakings it has provided to the LSE in its Nomad's declaration, the LSE will have regard to the matters set out in Sch.3 to the AIM Rules for Nominated Advisers, which should be exercised with due skill and care and after due and careful enquiry. The Nomad responsibilities in Sch.3, which are described in more detail in Chapter 3, consist of numbered principles in bold followed by a list of actions. The provisions of Sch.3 apply to all AIM companies, wherever incorporated.

While Sch.3 is applicable to Nomads acting for all types of AIM companies, certain provisions in the "Admission Responsibilities" section highlight issues in relation to overseas companies, in particular that:

1.   in assessing the appropriateness of an applicant company and its securities for AIM and achieving a sound understanding of the applicant and its business (AR1), Nomads should take into account and consider any issues relating to its country of incorporation and operation; and

2.   in assessing the suitability of directors and proposed directors and the efficacy of the board (AR2), Nomads should, in the case of directors who are not UK-based, undertake appropriate investigations. The AIM Regulation team expressed the view in Issue 5 of "Inside AIM" that for overseas directors particularly, they would expect it to be normal practice rather than the exception for a Nomad to undertake third party due diligence, typically the appointment at the expense of the company of a firm of specialist investigators who will carry out background checks on the directors. This is in addition to the internet based searches and searches of local public records, which are carried out to supplement directors' questionnaires, interviews and references. The objective of third party due diligence is to provide substantive and reliable independent information which will be beyond what Nomads are

able to ascertain from desktop searches. The Nomad should also consider the board of directors as a whole, including in relation to the fact that the applicant will be admitted to a UK-based, English-language public market. Typically, it will be considered appropriate for an AIM company with its principal business situated outside the UK to have at least two suitably experienced and independent UK-based non-executive directors.

If one or more directors are not English speaking, consideration will need to be given during the admission process to having dual language documents and using translators, and thereafter the Nomad will need to be satisfied that the board will be able to meet the English language requirements of AIM and its investor base.

Apart from the above specific matters addressed in Sch.3, the Nomad will need to consider any particular issues arising from the country of incorporation of an applicant company and the place or places where it carries on its business. For instance, in certain jurisdictions, principles of corporate governance may be less developed and information may be less readily available. Site visits may also be more difficult because of the distances involved.

Issue 4 of "Inside AIM", published by the LSE in September 2011, has a section on "Chinese companies on AIM", which includes a commentary on "Points to consider relating to due diligence and ongoing governance".

13.5 The fast-track route for certain companies quoted on AIM Designated Markets

13.5.1 *Key features of the fast-track route*

In May 2003, the AIM Rules for Companies were amended to provide for an expedited admission procedure (often referred to as the "fast-track route" or "AIM Designated Markets route") to be available to certain companies quoted on certain overseas exchanges, as well as companies transferring to AIM from the Official List.

Rule 3 provides that a company which has had its securities traded upon an AIM Designated Market (see below) for at least 18 months prior to applying to have those securities admitted to AIM, and which seeks to take advantage of that status in applying for the admission of its securities ("a quoted applicant"), is not required to produce an admission document, unless it is required to publish a prospectus in accordance with the Prospectus Rules in relation to the issue of AIM securities which are the subject of admission, in which case the Guidance Notes confirm that the requirements of Schedule 2 to the AIM Rules for Companies apply in addition to the requirements of the Prospectus Rules. The Guidance Notes to r.2 make it clear that a company, which could qualify as a quoted applicant and take advantage of the expedited route, is still able to use the usual form of admission process for AIM involving a pre-admission announcement and an AIM admission document at any time. The 18 months requirement is in place to ensure that there has been a sufficient period of disclosure in the home market about the business in the form in which it is seeking admission to AIM. A company exploring this route is highly recommended to discuss the details with its Nomad at an early stage, and Nomads should, in turn, discuss with the AIM Regulation team at the earliest opportunity, before any significant work is undertaken, whether it is appropriate for an applicant company to take advantage of the fast-track route. This is particularly the case where the applicant company has been subject to a significant change or event during the 18-month period prior to its application to be admitted to AIM, and further guidance on this is provided in Issue 2 of "Inside AIM" published by the LSE in July 2010.

The LSE publishes a list of AIM Designated Markets, which may be downloaded from its website at *www.londonstockex-change.com*. The AIM Designated Markets are the main markets of:

1. NYSE Euronext;
2. Deutsche Börse Group;
3. NASDAQ OMX Stockholm;
4. Swiss Exchange;
5. NASDAQ;
6. Australian Securities Exchange;
7. Johannesburg Stock Exchange;
8. New York Stock Exchange (NYSE);
9. TMX Group; and
10. UKLA Official List.

A company seeking admission via the AIM Designated Markets route must have been listed on the top tier/main board of the above exchanges. The LSE may at any time remove a market from its list of AIM Designated Markets.

It will be noted that the Official List is an AIM Designated Market. The reference to an applicant being listed on the top tier or main board of an AIM Designated Market would tend to suggest that in respect of the Official List, this may only apply to applicants which have a Premium Listing. However, the AIM Regulation team has confirmed that they would consider whether a company with a Standard Listing could avail itself of the fast track route, in which case the proposed Nomad should discuss this with the AIM Regulation team at the earliest opportunity. Where a company listed on the UK Official List is considering admission to AIM via the AIM Designated Markets route, this is available in principle to companies incorporated in the UK or overseas.

13.5.2 *Disclosure and other requirements*

If an applicant company is seeking to rely on the fast-track route, the requirements for it to make a pre-admission announcement (in accordance with r.2 of the AIM Rules for Companies – see Chapter 7 for further details) are modified in two ways. First, the information specified in Sch.1 to the AIM Rules for Companies must be provided to the LSE at least 20 (as opposed to 10) clear business days (being any day upon which the LSE is open for business) before the expected date of admission. In addition, a quoted applicant must provide at the same time the information specified in the supplement to Sch.1 to the AIM Rules for Companies.

The supplement to Sch.1 to the AIM Rules for Companies requires a quoted applicant to provide the LSE with the following additional information:

(a) The name of the AIM Designated Market upon which its securities have been traded;

(b) The date from which its securities have been so traded;

(c) Confirmation that, following due and careful enquiry, it has adhered to any legal and regulatory requirements involved in having its securities traded upon such market, or details of where there has been any breach. The Guidance Notes provide that disclosure as to any breach should only be made after prior consultation with the AIM Regulation team;

(d) A website address where any documents or announcements which it has made public over the last two years (in consequence of having its securities so traded) are available. The Guidance Notes provide that such documents or announcements must be made available following admission at the website required pursuant to r.26 of the AIM Rules for Companies;

(e) Details of its intended strategy following admission including, in the case of an investing company (any company which has as its primary business or objective, the investing of its funds in securities, businesses or assets of any description), details of its investing policy;

(f) A description of any significant change in the financial or trading position of the quoted applicant which has occurred since the end of the last financial period for which audited statements have been published. The Guidance Notes provide that this should include any significant change to indebtedness;

(g) A statement that its directors have no reason to believe that the working capital available to it or its group will be insufficient for at least 12 months from the date of its admission;

(h) Details of any lock-in arrangements pursuant to r.7 of the AIM Rules for Companies;

(i) A brief description of the arrangements for settling transactions in its securities;

(j) A website address detailing the rights attaching to its securities. The Guidance Notes to r.2 state that the website may also, to the extent permitted by law, contain other information which the quoted applicant considers may be useful to investors;

(k) Information equivalent to that required for an admission document which is not currently public, including any information that would be required as part of an admission document by the Notes published by the LSE from time to time. The Guidance Notes state that in ascertaining whether disclosures are required, the requirements of Sch.2 to the AIM Rules for Companies should be fully considered. The Guidance Notes also state that information made public is that which is made available at an address in the UK or at a website address accessible to users in the UK;

(l) A website address of a page containing its latest published annual accounts which must have a financial year end not more than nine months prior to admission. The annual accounts must be prepared in accordance with r.19 of the AIM Rules for Companies, although the Guidance Notes concede that a reconciliation to an applicable accounting standard under r.19 (see Section 13.4.4.3 above) may be presented where the accounts are not prepared under r.19 standards, although the requirements of r.19 will apply on an ongoing basis. Where more than nine months have elapsed since the financial year end to which the latest published annual accounts relate, a website address must also be provided of a page containing a set of interim results covering the period from the financial year end to which the latest published annual accounts relate and ending no less than six months from that date; and

(m) The number of each class of securities held as treasury shares.

Other consequences of using the fast-track route are:

1. Rule 2 of the AIM Rules for Companies provides that if there are any changes to the information contained in a pre-admission announcement prior to admission, the applicant must advise the LSE immediately by supplying details of such changes. The LSE may delay the expected date of admission for a quoted applicant by 20 clear business days (as opposed to 10 clear business days for other applicant companies), if in the LSE's opinion the information contained in the pre-admission announcement has significantly changed prior to admission. The LSE will make an announcement via RNS of information it receives;

2. Under r.5 of the AIM Rules for Companies, a quoted applicant is required to submit to the LSE at least three clear business days before the expected date of admission an electronic version of its latest annual accounts (instead of an electronic version of an admission document, which is the requirement where the fast-track route is not being used). All applicants are required in addition to submit a completed application form and a Nomad's declaration and to pay the invoiced AIM fee when due;

3. The AIM Regulation team has made it clear in Issue 4 of "Inside AIM" that a company which is being admitted to AIM by the fast-track route is subject to r.7 (lock-ins) even where that company's shareholders are free from restrictions on another exchange, on the basis that if a company is seeking investors through AIM, which the LSE would expect usually to be the case, the same rules should apply as for all other applicants.

4. A Nomad to a quoted applicant is required to make a declaration in the form set out in Sch.2 to the AIM Rules for Nominated Advisers that, among other things, to the best of its knowledge and belief, having made due and careful enquiry and considered all relevant matters under the AIM Rules for Companies and the AIM Rules for Nominated Advisers, the requirements of Sch.1 to the AIM Rules for Companies and its supplement (contents of the pre-admission announcement) have been complied with and otherwise all applicable requirements of the AIM

Rules for Companies and the AIM Rules for Nominated
Advisers have been complied with; and
5. The AIM Note for Mining and Oil & Gas Companies
    contains a statement under "Dual-listed resource com-
    panies" confirming that for the avoidance of doubt quoted
    applicants taking advantage of the AIM Designated
    Markets (fast-track) route will be required to comply with
    the contents of the Note. Similarly, the definition of
    "applicant" in the Note specifically includes a quoted
    applicant, reflecting the definition in the AIM Rules for
    Companies.

13.5.3   *The Prospectus Rules and the fast-track route*

Companies intending to use the fast-track route and simultaneously raise funds by offering shares in the UK will have to
consider whether the fund-raising amounts to an "offer to the
public" in the UK that is exempt from the requirement to
publish a prospectus for the purposes of the Prospectus Rules.
If it is not exempt, the fast-track route will be of marginal
assistance, since a prospectus complying with the content
requirements of the Prospectus Rules will have to be produced.
The Guidance Notes to r.3 provide that where a quoted
applicant is making an offer to the public, whether in the UK
and/or other jurisdictions, it should satisfy itself that there are
no legal or regulatory requirements outside the AIM Rules for
Companies which compel it to produce any form of prospectus. Where there is a requirement for such a prospectus, it
should be made available to the public under para.(o) of Sch.1
to the AIM Rules for Companies as if it were an admission
document.

Certain types of offers of shares in the UK are treated as
exempt offers to the public. Common examples in the context
of an AIM fund-raising are offers to fewer than 150 persons in
the UK and offers to persons who are "qualified investors" (for
more on these exemptions see Chapter 6). In these cases, a
prospectus complying with the content requirements of the
Prospectus Rules is not required to be published, although any

offer made by a quoted applicant falling within the exemptions is still likely to involve the production of an information memorandum.

Accordingly, the fast-track route will provide the most significant advantage over a standard AIM admission where a quoted applicant seeks admission to AIM by way of an introduction, that is, without undertaking a fund-raising, since no information memorandum will be necessary.

13.5.4 Nomads and the fast-track route

In view of the specific and general responsibilities of a Nomad, it is not likely that any lesser standard of due diligence would be applied to a quoted applicant as opposed to other applicant companies. Indeed, the LSE has expressed the view that in the case of a quoted applicant, a similar level of due diligence and preparation for admission needs to be taken as for a standard admission. Schedule 3 to the AIM Rules for Nominated Advisers is applicable to Nomads acting for all types of AIM companies (the preamble to the "Admission Responsibilities" ("AR") section makes it clear that they apply also to quoted applicants), and only distinguishes quoted applicants in noting at AR4 that quoted applicants are not required to produce an admission document and therefore some of the provisions of AR4 will not be applicable. However, it is further noted that para.(k) of the supplement to Sch.1 to the AIM Rules for Companies will necessitate a full consideration of the requirements of Sch.2 to the AIM Rules for Companies. In addition, the statements required to be given pursuant to the supplement to Sch.1 to the AIM Rules for Companies should be given after due and careful enquiry.

To comply with AR4, the Nomad should be satisfied (in the terms of the Nomad's declaration) that any appendix prepared by a quoted applicant in relation to para.(k) in the supplement to Sch.1 to the AIM Rules for Companies complies with those Rules, liaising with the AIM Regulation team to the extent that rule derogations or interpretations may be required.

It is also worth noting that the working capital statement which is given by the directors of a quoted applicant (as required by para.(g) of the supplement to Sch.1 to the AIM Rules for Companies) is that the "directors have no reason to believe that the working capital available to it or its group will be insufficient for at least 12 months from the date of its admission". This appears less robust than the statement required in an admission document, to the effect that in the opinion of the directors, "having made due and careful enquiry, the working capital available to the [applicant company] and its group will be sufficient for its present requirements, that is for at least twelve months from the date of admission of its securities". However, an equivalent degree of care is likely to be required in validating such statements.

13.6 Conclusion

As will be gathered from this Chapter, AIM is continuing to attract a significant number of overseas companies. While an overseas company, or an overseas business which may have a domestic holding company, may present challenges, these will generally be overcome with the assistance of the applicant company's Nomad and other professional advisers. The popularity of AIM as an international market appears set to continue.

Chapter 14

US Company Considerations

Bryce D. Linsenmayer

Partner, Baker & Hostetler LLP

14.1 Introduction

Over the past few years, a number of US companies have accessed the public markets through non-traditional routes. As the capital markets continue to globalise, US companies increasingly have the opportunity to locate capital abroad. The London Stock Exchange ("LSE"), in particular, the AIM Market provides international companies with an alternative means to going public in the United States.

AIM affords smaller cap companies access to capital markets through a more streamlined process than an IPO in the United States. The inability of smaller companies to interest investment bankers and analysts as well as the limited liquidity of small cap companies has hurt or destroyed the US public markets for small companies. Despite the passage of laws such as the Jumpstart Our Business Startups Act, which were enacted to ease the restrictive nature of the Sarbanes-Oxley Act of 2002 and other corporate governance requirements, some of the requirements still make it prohibitively expensive for smaller public companies in the US to comply. Accordingly, smaller companies are looking abroad for capital. Some ten to fifteen years ago, smaller companies would have gone public, raised $10 to $30 million and listed on NASDAQ. The average AIM offering for companies outside the UK is between $20 and $80 million, although this number is increasing and offerings in excess of $100 million are not uncommon. Now, many small cap companies are taking a more serious look at deals in

London. AIM, in particular, and the international markets in general, represent a significant funding source, especially for smaller US entities.

14.2 Why US Companies Pursue AIM Offerings

14.2.1 Sarbanes-Oxley and the Regulatory Environment

Issuers who go public on AIM are sponsored by a Nominated Adviser (a "Nomad"), who is responsible not only for maintaining the profile of the listed security, but also vouching for the company's good name. The diligence process in an AIM offering is extensive since the reputation of the Nomad is on the line. The Nomad confirms that the company is suitable to list on AIM and advises on the content of the offering materials. There is no regulatory body similar to the US Securities Exchange Commission ("SEC") once the company is admitted for listing on the AIM market. As AIM-listed companies report financial information semi-annually (as opposed to quarterly in the US), the rules and regulations of the market are generally considerably less burdensome, and the overall cost of compliance is correspondingly less.

14.2.2 Expenses

Nomad and broker fees tend to be less in the UK, compared to traditional investment banking fees in the US. There are also lower fees associated with audits and financial statement preparation (primarily due to the regulatory environment). Other professional fees such as attorneys' fees tend to be commensurate with US offerings. However, corporate govern-ance and reporting requirements are considerably lower.

14.2.3 Institutional and Sophisticated Market

The institutional investors active on AIM form a relatively small group. Those investors get to know the company and its management and business model. Typically, they also invest for the long term. With relatively few "retail" shareholders, a company's securities typically are held by 15–40 institutional investors who comprise a sophisticated shareholder base. Many AIM-listed companies raise additional capital from their existing shareholder base over time through secondary placings. Generally, these investors tend to be significantly less demanding than US private equity, hedge or venture capital ("VC") funds.

14.2.4   Similar Process

The IPO process in the US is similar to the IPO process on the AIM Market. Just like any offering in the US, issuers on the AIM Market are required to prepare an offer document containing background and financial information. Contrastingly, the diligence process in an AIM offering tends to be a bit more exhaustive than a US offering, but the Nomad and broker are taking a calculated risk in bringing any issuer to market. As such, they are very careful in preparing the offer document and conducting appropriate diligence.

14.2.5   Exit Strategy

As opposed to US private equity and fund deals, AIM recognises and approves of VCs using an offering to sell some or all of their venture stock. This is a better exit strategy for the VCs and fund participants than exists in other early stage companies.

14.3   US Law Considerations

14.3.1   The Rule of Numbers

One of the advantages of AIM is the relatively small number of placees in an offering. Because AIM is a largely institutional market, the stock in an AIM IPO is typically sold to fewer than 50 institutional holders. For US companies, in particular, this is a distinct advantage. Under US securities laws, an issuer is only required to register with the SEC once it has either (i) more than 2,000 shareholders or (ii) 500 or more shareholders who are not accredited investors. Accordingly, an issuer can come into an AIM IPO with 400 existing shareholders (in the US or elsewhere) and remain under the US law threshold (assuming an IPO with fewer than 1,600 new shareholders or 100 new unaccredited investors). In this manner, US companies can complete an AIM offering to raise additional capital, remain a "private" company for purposes of US Securities laws, and avoid tedious compliance and reporting obligations to the SEC. US companies listing on AIM have found this approach to be a more efficient means of accessing the capital markets. It is important to note that once a US company has either (i) 2,000 shareholders or (ii) 500 or more shareholders who are not accredited investors anywhere, not just in the US, it will be required to register with the SEC and begin reporting as a public company.

14.3.2 Regulation S Offerings

Regulation S under the US Securities Act was enacted in 1990 with the aim to allow private placements of shares outside the US without the burden and expense of registering such offerings with the SEC. Specifically, Regulation S provides that for the purposes of the US Securities Act, the terms "offer," "offer to sell," "sell," "sale," and "offer to buy" are deemed not to include offers or sales of securities that occur outside of the US. Rule 903 of Regulation S provides a safe haven for issuances of securities made outside the US, and therefore most US companies use this exemption for their AIM IPOs.

Rule 903 provides three (3) categories under which issuances of equity securities may fall:

- *Category 1* includes (a) equity securities issued by a foreign issuer that reasonably believes at the commencement of the offering that there is no substantial US market interest in the securities being offered or sold; (b) overseas directed offerings, which includes offerings of equity securities by a foreign issuer that is directed into a single country other than the US to the residents thereof and made in accordance with the local laws and customary practices of such country; (c) offerings where the securities are backed by the full faith and credit of a foreign government; or (d) securities offered and sold to employees of the issuer pursuant to an employee benefit plan established and administered in accordance with the law of a country other than the US.

- *Category 2* includes the equity securities of a reporting foreign issuer.
- *Category 3* includes all issuances of securities made outside the US that do not fall under category 1 or 2 above. These generally include (a) all offerings of equity securities by US domestic issuers and (b) offerings of equity securities by non-reporting foreign issuers where there is substantial US market interest for the securities being offered.

Most US companies listed on AIM are category 3 issuers. This is typically the case because they are established companies with existing operations in the US. As such, there can be negative tax consequences of modifying their jurisdiction of incorporation. In order to receive the protections of r.903, category 3 issuers must meet several requirements. The most significant implication of being a category 3 issuer for purposes of Regulation S is the requirement for certificating shares of the company's stock. This is a disadvantage to US companies since the CREST system is not available for one year following an IPO. See Section 14.4.1 for a further discussion of the CREST system as it applies to US companies.

14.3.3 Resales under Regulation S

Rule 904 of Regulation S provides that any offer or sale of securities by any person other than the issuer, a distributor, any of their respective affiliates, or any person acting on behalf of any of the foregoing shall be deemed to occur outside the US if the transaction is made offshore and no directed selling efforts are made in the US. Resales by distributors and affiliates of the issuer have additional restrictions placed on them. Distributors, generally the purchasers of US company securities in an AIM IPO using Regulation S, can sell their shares to other purchasers in the IPO, provided that the shares maintain the restrictive legend for one year following the IPO. Affiliates of the US company (as defined by US securities laws, but specifically excluding directors and officers of the issuer who are affiliates solely by virtue of holding such positions) must follow these resale restrictions for so long as they own the shares. As such, it is more difficult for affiliates of the issuer to sell their shares post-IPO.

14.3.4 *Regulation D*

The rules comprising Regulation D have evolved over the years to permit US companies to complete "private" offerings of their securities. Specifically, Regulation D provides certain aggregate offering amounts and number of investors thresholds in rr.504, 505 and 506, under which rules a private offering of securities in the US will not be considered a "public offering" under the US Securities Act. This means that a company may offer shares without registration in the US so long as the Regulation D restrictions are observed. Thus, an AIM IPO for an English company may have a Regulation D "component" in that the IPO is completed on AIM, but a simultaneous US placing is made privately to accredited investors in the US. Similarly, a US issuer might conduct a simultaneous Regulation S and Regulation D offering to complete an AIM IPO. In either case, the AIM Admission Document contains a US "wrapper" that contains the relevant US securities law requirements, disclaimers and legends. Because of Regulation D, more AIM IPOs have a US component and a number of placees in the US.

14.3.5 *US Blue Sky Laws*

It is important to note that each of the 50 states has its own securities laws. As such, any US placements must comply with these state securities regulations commonly referred to as "Blue Sky Laws". Fortunately, Regulation D offerings fall into a category of offers that are typically exempt from registration in any particular state. Still, it is important for US and other AIM issuers to know where their offerees reside, as the state of residence for each offeree determines the applicable Blue Sky Laws.

14.4　Hurdles for US Companies

14.4.1　CREST and Electronic Settlement

As discussed in Section 14.3.2 above, category 3 issuers under Regulation S must use certificated shares bearing a restrictive legend for one year following issuance of such shares of stock. This means that such an issuer's shares cannot be traded via the CREST system. This certification requirement not only presents a logistical problem for an issuer's Nomad and broker, but it makes it more difficult to market a US listing. The LSE has initiated a formal process with the SEC, whereby the SEC would waive this one-year requirement. However, the SEC has not granted the requested relief. Accordingly, most US issuers on AIM convert their trades to CREST on the one-year anniversary of their admission to trading.

14.4.2　UK Holdco v US Issuer

The UK's CREST system, which is the paperless, electronic means by which stocks trade on AIM, cannot easily accommodate legend stock. As discussed above, most US issuers rely upon Regulation S as the exemption to issue the securities outside the US, as all US company stock contain a restrictive legend preventing its sale to a US person. As such, many Nomads advise US issuers to form a UK Plc as a holding company above the US subsidiaries or assets. However, for reasons ranging from tax implications to simple matters of national pride, most US issuers choose to remain domiciled in Delaware, New York, California, Texas or their original states of incorporation.

14.4.3   Liquidity

The AIM financial community may be viewed as relatively small, sophisticated and "clubby". Investors know the good Nomads and brokers; their reputation is everything; and they tend to take a longer-term view than most US investment houses. The trading volume in AIM listed stocks is correspondingly low. The investment market is comprised of typically larger, institutional investors, who take the time to understand the company's business and tend to be more forgiving of a difficult fiscal quarter. However, given the thinner trading volumes (especially in the smaller market caps), liquidity is somewhat low.

14.4.4   UK Style Verification

Just as US entities may find the diligence process painful in a US offering, the same holds true in London; perhaps more so. Because the Nomad's name and reputation are on the line, they require independent verification of all assertions made in the offering document, and UK securities laws support this exacting process. In the end, however, the issuer is left with an offer document that has been fully vetted, thereby limiting the risks to the company, its management and directors.

14.4.5   Accounting

US issuers may prepare their admission documents using UK or US GAAP and continue reporting in either UK or US GAAP. The long-form and short-form financial reports required by an AIM listing may require an issuer to report financial information a bit differently. However, such reporting is easily adapted from US GAAP.

14.4.6   International/Global Focus

Foreign issuers, particularly US companies, face the initial question, "why London?" In the early years of the AIM Market (1995–2004), relatively few foreign issuers came to AIM, and many bankers and brokers encountered a bias against foreign companies listing on AIM. Since the beginning of 2005, the market opened to issuers from across the globe, and now sees its future expansion primarily among non-UK issuers. For all the reasons listed above, AIM is attractive to US issuers. However, it is often important that a US issuer demonstrates an international or global market (or market potential) for its products and services, although this is not an absolute requirement. By establishing more than a local reach, an AIM issuer not only presents a large potential market, it shows that it is an international player worthy of being traded in one of the world's financial capitals. A US company with a sole US-base of clients/customers/markets will raise questions in the AIM investing community.

Chapter 15

Settlement Arrangements – The CREST system

Christopher Twemlow

Head of Legal Affairs, UK for Euroclear SA/NV

15.1   Introduction

The AIM Rules for Companies require that every AIM company must have appropriate settlement arrangements in place. Unless the London Stock Exchange ("LSE") otherwise agrees, this means that the securities traded on AIM must be admitted to one of the electronic settlement systems. While the CREST system is not the only such system, it is the one most commonly used by the AIM market. The LSE will grant a derogation from this rule in only the most exceptional of circumstances. As a consequence of the popularity of AIM with overseas companies, a mechanism had to be found for overseas securities (not normally eligible for admission to CREST) to become transferable by means of the CREST system.

This Chapter is an update of a version originally drafted by Jane Tuckley, a partner at Travers Smith LLP.

15.2   What is the CREST system?

The CREST system is an electronic system for the holding and transfer of securities in electronic form. Its arrangements also facilitate:

1.   the making of payment simultaneous with transfer; and

2.   the effecting of various corporate action-related operations in relation to securities held within its system (proxies can be appointed by means of the CREST system; takeovers accepted; rights taken up and so on).

The CREST system is operated by Euroclear UK & Ireland Limited (referred to in this Chapter as "EUI"), a member of the Euroclear group. The CREST securities settlement system settles exchange-traded and over-the-counter securities trans-actions for a range of securities including UK, Irish, Jersey, Guernsey and Isle of Man equities, warrants and covered warrants, UK government bonds and money market instru-ments and investment funds, including exchange-traded funds.

Unless an AIM company were to decide that all its shares were to be capable of being held *solely* in the CREST system (a very unusual step), the system enables holders to decide whether they want to become members and hold their securities within the system, or whether they would prefer to continue to hold them in paper form. Securities held in the system are termed "uncertificated"; securities in paper form are "certificated". The system facilitates the transfer of securities from certificated to uncertificated form and vice versa. These facilities are known as the paper interface.

15.3   The CREST legal framework

15.3.1   *General*

Until the CREST system became operational in 1996, English company law provided that shares were to be evidenced by means of a share certificate and transferred by means of a stock transfer form. Legal changes were therefore required to enable title to be transferred by means of an electronic system: these came in the form of the Uncertificated Securities Regulations 1995. While the regulations, often referred to as the "USRs", make no mention of EUI, they provide a framework which generally fits the manner in which the CREST system operates.

EUI has been approved as an operator for the purposes of the USRs. The USRs have been re-enacted and amended a number of times since the original 1995 version.

The USRs apply to both shares and other securities or interests in securities, for example debenture and loan stocks, bonds, warrants, nil-paid and fully-paid rights and depository interests (depository receipts). The USRs in some senses are little more than a piece of framework legislation. They amended the key legal obstructions to the operation of an electronic settlement system in the UK and address certain regulatory and other issues. It was always intended, however, that any system operating under the USRs would be complemented by a detailed contractual structure. In relation to AIM companies, the key relevant elements of the contractual structure are:

1. the CREST Security Application Form (see Section 15.4.2 below);
2. the CREST Manual; and
3. the CREST Rules.

15.3.2 *Non-UK securities*

The USRs only govern the holding and transfer in the CREST system of securities constituted under the laws of England and Wales, Scotland or Northern Ireland. Securities constituted under the laws of the Republic of Ireland, Jersey, Guernsey or the Isle of Man can also be held and transferred in the CREST system under similar regulations passed in each of those jurisdictions. These securities are together referred to as "domestic securities".

The securities of no other jurisdiction can be admitted *directly* to the CREST system. These securities ("international securities") are settled by the CREST system using an indirect mechanism (see Section 15.6 below).

15.4 Admitting domestic securities to the CREST system

15.4.1 *Are the securities eligible for CREST settlement?*

In relation to any transaction involving the issue of securities by an AIM company, early consideration should be given to whether the securities are eligible for CREST. Eligibility is determined by a combination of jurisdictional issues (see above), the USRs, the terms of issue of the securities and the CREST Rules. In particular, in the case of shares:

1. the company's articles of association must be consistent with the USRs and the holding and transfer of the shares in uncertificated form or an overriding directors' resolution must have been passed in accordance with reg.16 of the USRs and remain in effect; and
2. the conditions set out in the CREST Rules must be met (most notably CREST r.7). The rules contain provisions which, for example, relate to the fungibility of the shares within the class (so, for example, partly paid shares cannot be admitted to CREST because they are required by law to be individually numbered and are therefore not fungible), the free transferability of the shares and their unconditional issuance.

Additional rules apply in respect of depositary interests (CREST r.9) and to other securities which are not shares.

It is not necessary for securities to be listed or subject to any trading facility in order for them to be eligible for CREST. Theoretically, therefore, the shares of any private company might be eligible for CREST, although there is little demand for such a facility in relation to these shares. Where, however, the allotment or issue of a security is *conditional* upon, say, admission to trading on AIM, the security must not be admitted to the CREST system until that condition has been satisfied (see Section 15.4.2 below).

15.4.2 *The admission mechanics*

Admission is made by means of a CREST Security Application Form ("SAF"). This is available from the Euroclear website, but the company's registrar is also likely to have a ready supply. The company's registrar will assist the company with the completion of the form – EUI has published guidance notes for the completion of the form, which form part of its application procedures. The registrar will submit the form to EUI on the company's behalf. However, the form must be signed by the company itself. EUI guidelines require the submission of the form no later than two business days before the security is to be enabled in the CREST system. When the timetable permits (as might be usual in the case of an initial public offering ("IPO")), the registrar will usually try to submit the form to EUI approximately 10 business days in advance of the date on which the shares are to become enabled within the CREST system. Arrangements can often be made to expedite the processing of the form by EUI, including when necessary the emailing of the completed form to EUI and its processing on the same day, but such arrangements are at EUI's discretion and allow no leeway for identification and correction of errors. If the form is emailed to EUI, the hard copy must follow promptly.

It is not necessary for all of the criteria for the security to be eligible for CREST to be satisfied at the time the form is submitted. It is possible to indicate on the form that some conditions for admission to the CREST system remain to be satisfied – a special box is included for this purpose. If the form indicates that the conditions are not satisfied, EUI may take some preparatory steps in relation to setting the security up in its system, but will not enable the security in the system until it receives confirmation that all conditions for admission of the security have been satisfied. This confirmation, commonly referred to as an enablement letter, must be given in writing by either the issuer or its agent. It is common that the last condition to be satisfied will be the admission of the securities to trading on AIM, since the allotment and issue of at least some of the securities to be admitted to CREST will normally be expressed to be conditional upon this event.

The preparatory steps taken by EUI to set a security up in its system prior to receipt of an enablement letter will permit steps to be taken to ensure prompt settlement of securities once enablement occurs. These may include the entering into the system of settlement instructions (e.g. for the delivery of securities to the placees) or the provisional crediting of CREST accounts by the registrar in preparation for the enablement of the security. If provisional credits are made, the credits will be of no legal effect until the security is enabled in the system.

The SAF requires the company to state the date on which the company would like the security to be enabled in the CREST system. If no outstanding conditions exist at the time the form is submitted, EUI will adhere to this date (unless it receives notification to the contrary before the security has been enabled). If there are outstanding conditions EUI will only adhere to this date if it has received an enablement letter.

An approximate CREST application timetable in relation to a typical AIM IPO will therefore run as follows:

D minus 14 days:	Security Application Form completed and sent to EUI. (Form indicates that some conditions remain outstanding. Form sets the security start date at D.)
D minus 3 days:	Settlement instructions entered into the system and/or provisional crediting of the relevant CREST accounts by the registrar.
D:	Securities admitted to trading on AIM. Enablement letter emailed to EUI. EUI enables the security and settlement commences.

15.4.3   *Admitting further securities to the CREST system*

The permission for securities to be admitted to CREST does not apply to a fixed number of securities; it applies to the whole class and to any further securities of that class which may be issued from time to time provided that they are absolutely identical. Therefore, no further application needs to be made in relation to a new issue where this is the case. However, it is common to see further issues of shares of an existing class made on terms that the new shares will not qualify for a dividend in relation to a period just ended or about to end. In this case, the new shares would not be absolutely identical and a new application would need to be made for the further shares. Arrangements would be made with EUI for the two lines to be merged once the old shares are marked ex dividend.

15.5   The relationship between the AIM company and EUI

The relationship between EUI and the company operates on a number of different levels.

15.5.1   *The technical interface*

Almost all companies appoint agents (registrars and receiving agents) to send and receive messages through the CREST system on their behalf. Therefore, there is normally no need for the company itself to have the technical capabilities required for a link to the CREST technical system.

15.5.2   *The legal relationship*

Notwithstanding that a company does not communicate electronically with the CREST system, each company whose securities are admitted to CREST has a contractual relationship with EUI. This contract is entered into on the terms of the SAF, which incorporates the CREST Rules and the CREST Manual as from time to time in force. Changes to the rules and manual are not notified directly to issuers – they are sent to their registrars.

EUI's liability to a company is subject to the limitations and exclusions set out in the CREST Manual.

15.5.3 Registers of securities – England and Wales, Scotland and Northern Ireland

The USRs governing UK securities make provision for a system known as electronic transfer of title, or "ETT". In essence, this means that certain records maintained within the CREST system are the prima facie evidence (or, in relation to Scottish securities, sufficient evidence) that the persons named are the holders of the number of securities stated in the record. Therefore, in relation to securities held in uncertificated form, the CREST computer records themselves constitute the relevant register of holders. The principal effect of this is that transfer of title occurs in relation to UK securities simultaneously with settlement of a transaction within the CREST system.

Where the securities are shares, the company is still required to keep a composite register of members, containing the details of the holders of shares in certificated form (which it, not the CREST system, holds) and copy details (obtained from the CREST system) of the holders of shares in uncertificated form. To the extent that the details of uncertificated holders shown on the company's (composite) register of members and those shown on the CREST register differ, the CREST register prevails.

EUI has made detailed rules identifying which of the CREST system records form part of the register of securities (see CREST r.14).

As each transaction settles in the CREST system, the relevant issuer (through its registrar) receives details of the transfer which has been effected. This enables the registrar to maintain a running record of the holders (in effect, a duplicate of the register maintained in CREST). It is this record which the issuer uses for day-to-day purposes, for example in processing corporate actions. The USRs provide that, as long as a company has regularly reconciled its record with the register in the CREST system, a company will not be liable if it relies on its record for processing purposes and that record subsequently proves to be incorrect.

15.5.4 *Registers of securities – Ireland, Jersey, Guernsey and the Isle of Man*

An equivalent of the ETT regime has not yet been adopted for the other (i.e. non-UK) domestic securities and therefore the CREST system does not maintain the register of holders of legal title to these securities. Accordingly, in these jurisdictions, legal title does not pass at the point of settlement in CREST: at the point of settlement an equitable interest (or its equivalent in the relevant jurisdiction) is acquired by the transferee. Simultaneously, the relevant registrar is notified electronically (through the CREST system) of the transaction and legal title transfers when the registrar updates the register of holders (normally within two hours of CREST settlement). The limited grounds on which a registrar can decline to update the register are set out in the relevant regulations.

15.6   International securities – depository interests

15.6.1 *General*

The CREST legal framework permits only those securities constituted under the laws of one of the domestic jurisdictions to be admitted to the CREST system. The mechanism for permitting CREST settlement of international securities therefore involves creating a domestic security which represents the underlying international security, but is separate and distinct from it. A number of slightly different structures can be used, although all tend to involve the creation of a type of depository interest, similar to the American depository receipts and global depository receipts with which the markets are familiar, under which a depository holds the relevant underlying international securities on trust for the holders from time to time and issues to the holders (i.e. the beneficiaries under the trust) depository interests which represent the entitlement to the international security. Typically, one unit of a depository interest represents one share of the international security held. The depository may either hold the international securities in its own name or appoint a nominee to hold them on its behalf. The structure is created by a deed poll or similar instrument.

The depository interests are typically constituted under the laws of England. They are therefore governed by the USRs (and any relevant EUI requirements) and will behave in the CREST system much as any other UK security, with a register maintained by the CREST system.

In addition to complying with the rules generally applicable to securities admitted to CREST, depository interests are required to comply with the additional rules contained in CREST r.9.

While there is no prescribed depository interest mechanism, a number of structures are commonly seen. These are described below and a comparative table of their key features is included at Section 15.6.6.

15.6.2   CREST Depository Interests

EUI operates an international service which relies on a series of automated links which it has established with counterparts in other jurisdictions. The service is based on a depository interest mechanism – an EUI subsidiary holds (directly or indirectly) the international securities on trust for the relevant CREST members who are issued with CREST Depository Interests ("CDIs") representing their international securities.

The CDIs are not themselves admitted to trading on AIM. The international securities will be admitted to trading in the normal way and will be allocated an international securities identification number (known as an "ISIN" – the unique identification number by which securities are identified in trading, settlement and other systems). The CDIs are regarded as a mere settlement mechanism – a trade in the underlying international security will be settled by means of a transfer of

CDIs which represent the securities traded. For this reason, the CDIs are identified within the CREST system by the same ISIN as the underlying international security.

The CDIs are generally only capable of existing in uncertificated form – there is therefore no effective paper interface in relation to these securities, but otherwise they behave in the CREST system in broadly the same way as other domestic securities admitted to the system.

The CREST International Service, as an established structure, is convenient and does not involve the overseas issuer in additional cost in the establishment or ongoing operation of its own depository interest structure (the costs are borne by the CREST members holding the CDIs and not the issuers). It does not, however, have universal coverage and not all links operate on a with-payment basis (some of the links facilitate the transfer of the securities but not payment for them, with the result that separate bilateral payment arrangements need to be made between the parties to the transaction). The CREST International Service is described in detail in the CREST International Manual (see the Euroclear website) and includes facilities for the processing of corporate actions.

Companies wishing to establish a CREST settlement facility for their international securities should contact EUI at an early stage in order to identify whether the security is already settled by means of the international service (this is quite often the case where the security has an overseas listing). If it is not, the company should check whether it would be eligible for the service and, if so, the service to which it would be admitted. The arrangements for introducing new securities to the service can also, of necessity, vary considerably depending on the local requirements in the relevant overseas jurisdiction. Therefore, this should also be raised with EUI at an early stage.

It is important to identify whether a security has already been admitted to the CREST International Service, even if a company proposes to establish its own bespoke depository arrangements. The CREST system has no means of distinguishing between two different securities (a CDI and a bespoke depository interest) which bear the same ISIN within its system and, for this reason, will only admit one security per ISIN.

15.6.3 Bespoke Depository Interests

The bespoke depository interest ("DI") structure emerged initially to permit a form of CREST settlement for those securities which are not eligible for the CREST International Service, although some companies whose securities would be eligible have since established a DI service.

These DI structures tend to be offered by some of the larger registrar groups. They involve a member of the registrar's group acting as depository and (either itself or through a nominee or custodian on its behalf) holding the underlying international securities on behalf of the holders; and, as with the EUI structure, issuing DIs (typically constituted under English law) representing the underlying securities in uncertificated form in the CREST system to those holders. Since the number of international securities held within the DI structure tends not to be static (it is a requirement that there is a ready facility for the crediting and withdrawal of the underlying securities to and from this structure), the registrar may also either itself hold the register of international securities or have arrangements with an entity which does.

At the time these DI structures were developed confirmation was obtained from the LSE and the UK listing authority respectively that the same ISIN as the underlying security could be used for the DI and that no separate listing would be required for the DIs, provided that the DIs meet the following criteria:

1. they are created as legal instruments in their own right;
2. they are created under and subject to UK law;
3. they are subject to the USRs;

4. they use the same ISIN code as the underlying security to which they relate and, accordingly, they are not separately traded or priced from those underlying securities;
5. they will be available for use by the underlying security's holder at its sole discretion;
6. they are freely convertible into the underlying listed security (subject only to fair and reasonable costs);
7. they benefit from all the rights attaching to the underlying security, including voting rights, dividends and participation in corporate actions;
8. they are settled electronically through a "relevant system" for the purposes of the USRs (the CREST system is currently the only such system);
9. they are created and used in respect of a UK listed security issued by a non-UK incorporated issuer;
10. they are structured and established such that the promotion of the DIs is not subject to the restrictions on financial promotions under s.21 Financial Services and Markets Act 2000; and
11. that the use of the DIs to effect electronic settlement will not contravene the law of the jurisdiction governing the underlying security.

The same criteria are applied in relation to DIs representing AIM traded securities.

Accordingly, like CDIs, DIs have no separate trading facility on AIM and no separate ISIN and issuers of prospectuses have limited the securities the subject of the offer to the underlying securities, not the DIs. The DIs are merely regarded as a settlement mechanic – a trade in the underlying international security can be settled by the delivery of DIs through the CREST system. As if to emphasise this, requirement (6) necessitates an interchange between the uncertificated DIs and the certificated underlying security (the DIs themselves not being permitted to exist in certificated form outside the CREST system). The normal CREST paper interface messaging and forms are used to achieve the conversion, although additional support is required either from the constitutional documents of the underlying issuer or appropriate board or other resolutions (depending on the requirements of local law). The provisions must achieve the following key objectives:

1. That on receipt of a dematerialisation request form (which ordinarily simply requests the conversion of a security from certificated form to uncertificated form in the name of the same holder):
    (a) the company may treat this as a request to transfer the securities to the depository's nominee to be held for the account of the holder; and
    (b) the depository may treat it as a request to issue DIs to the CREST account of the holder.
2. That on receipt of a CREST transfer form (which ordinarily simply requests the conversion of a security from certificated form to uncertificated form in the name of a new holder):
    (a) the company may treat this as a request to transfer the securities to the depository's nominee to be held for the account of the new holder; and
    (b). the depository may treat it as a request to issue DIs to the CREST account of the new holder.
3. That on receipt of a stock withdrawal message in the CREST system (which ordinarily simply requests the conversion of a security from uncertificated to certificated form either in the name of the same holder or a new holder, as specified in the message):
    (a) the depository may treat this as a request to collapse the affected DIs; and
    (b) the company may treat it as a request to transfer the underlying securities from the depository's nominee to the person specified in the message.

To establish a DI structure the following documents and resolution must be put in place:

1. A depository agreement – entered into by the depository and the issuer. This is a framework agreement which sets out the terms on which the depository agrees to establish the DIs for the company;

2. A deed poll – executed solely by the depository. This key document constitutes the DIs and contains the declaration of trust which sets out the terms on which the depository holds the issuer's securities on trust as DIs for CREST member holders; and

3. A board resolution of the issuer – the deed poll contains the necessary provisions to establish the mechanics of the paper interface (as described above) and the overseas company's constitution must permit these arrangements. Accordingly, the issuer normally passes a board resolution (or, depending on the requirements of local law, other arrangements for the amendment of its constitution) confirming that the paper interface arrangements are valid under its constitution.

Once the DI structure is in final form, the depository must apply to EUI for admission of the DI. It is the depository, and not the underlying issuer, which has the legal relationship with EUI in relation to the DIs. Application to EUI involves the submission of the following documents:

1. A legal opinion provided by a firm of English solicitors (assuming that the deed poll is governed by English law) acting for the depository in the standard CREST form which confirms key legal criteria, under English law, in relation to the DI structure and the depository, and, under the relevant foreign law, in relation to the issuer. Accordingly, in order to be able to give the opinion, the solicitors acting for the depository will need to procure a foreign legal opinion. If the issuer maintains a share register in a jurisdiction other than (a) that in which it is incorporated, or (b) the UK, an additional opinion in relation to the jurisdiction in which the register is located will also be required. The legal opinion must also confirm whether or not transfers of the DIs will be subject to SDRT. The pro forma opinion is available from EUI.;

2. An International Security Application Form – this is a similar form as for the admission of domestic securities and the same process as described in Section 15.4.2 above applies save that, for a DI, the issuer of the security to be

admitted to the CREST system is the depository and not the overseas company and, therefore, the depository arranges for the submission of the form; and

3. An operational bulletin – this is provided by the depository and published by EUI. It sets out, for informational purposes for CREST members and the market, the date of admission of the DI and the arrangements in relation to the paper interface. The pro forma bulletin is available from EUI or registrar depositories.

EUI can ask for additional support for an application. It is likely in particular to ask for additional confirmations and/or legal opinions if the underlying securities are subject to restrictions, such as those under the US Securities Act 1933. In these circumstances additional time should be allowed to ensure the requirements can be understood and then met.

All of the above documents must be received by EUI either 5 or 10 clear business days prior to the date of admission of the DI to the CREST system. The deadline depends on whether trades in the international company's securities (of the same ISIN as the proposed DI) are already being settled through the CREST residual settlements mechanism or are used for transaction reporting purposes. (The residual settlements mechanism makes use of parts of the CREST paper interface functionality to facilitate traditional certificated settlement on a T+10 timeframe.) If not, the deadline will be 5 business days and, if so, 10 business days (to allow such trades to settle) prior to the admission date. On a new primary listing or issue of a new class of share the deadline will typically only be five days before the admission date. This should be checked with EUI early on in the process.

15.6.4 Global Depository Interests

While based on the same basic depository interest concept, global depository interests ("GDIs") differ from CDIs and DIs in a number of key respects:

1. they are admitted to trading on AIM as a security in their own right, with their own ISIN (distinct from any ISIN allocated to the underlying security);
2. as such, for the purposes of the prospectus requirements and the AIM Rules for Companies, the provisions specifically applicable to depositary receipts must be complied with – albeit the greater emphasis is on the issuer of the underlying securities; and
3. if a certificated option is available, it is the GDI itself which will be available in certificated form – the GDI is not simply a settlement mechanic and can (if its terms provide) have an existence outside the CREST system.

15.6.5 Comparison of key aspects of the different depository interest mechanisms

	CREST International Service	Bespoke Depository Interests	Global Depository Interests
Are the costs of the service borne by the company?	No. EUI makes no charge to the company.	Yes. Charges typically include a one-off establishment fee plus ongoing costs.	Yes. Charges typically include a one-off establishment fee plus ongoing costs.
Are the depository interests separately traded on AIM?	No. It is the underlying international security and not the CDI which is admitted to trading.	No. It is the underlying international security and not the DI which is admitted to trading.	Yes. The trading facility relates to the GDI itself and not the underlying international security.

Do the depository interests share the same ISIN as the underlying security?	Yes.	Yes.	No. The GDIs have their own ISIN.
Can the holder participate in corporate actions relating to the underlying security?	Yes.	Yes.	Yes.
Is the holder able to exercise voting rights on the underlying security?	Not a standard service.	Yes.	Yes.
Can the CREST paper interface be used to obtain a certificate?	No.	Yes. The DI will be cancelled and a certificate for the underlying international security will be issued to the holder.	Yes. The GDI can normally exist in certificated or uncertificated form.

15.7 Conclusion

The requirement in the AIM Rules for Companies that appropriate electronic settlement arrangements should be in place is met simply in relation to UK and other domestic securities. It has been necessary to become more innovative in order to meet the settlement requirements for trading other overseas securities. However, over time a range of products has been developed so that it is normally possible to find a solution suitable for each issue.

Appendix 1 – AIM Documents List

Abbreviations:

[The Company]	–	**"Company"**
[Nominated Adviser]	–	**"Nomad"**
[Company Solicitors]	–	**"CoSols"**
[Solicitors to the Issue]	–	**"IssueSols"**
[Reporting Accountants]	–	**"Rep Accts"**
AIM Admission Document/Prospectus	–	**"Admission Document"**
[Registrars]	–	**"Reg"**
[Public Relations]	–	**"PR"**
[Broker (if separate Nomad and Broker)]	–	**"Broker"**
[Printers]	–	**"Printers"**

References are to AIM Rules unless otherwise stated

Document		Primary Responsibility
A.	**Administrative and preliminary documents**	
1	List of parties	Nomad
2	Timetable	Nomad
3	List of documents	CoSols/Nomad
4	Estimate of expenses	Nomad
5	Nominated Adviser [and Broker] engagement letter	Nomad/Company/CoSols
6	[Broker engagement letter]	Broker/Company/CoSols
7	Solicitor engagement letter	CoSol/IssueSols
8	Reporting Accountants engagement letter	Rep Accts/Nomad/CoSols

Document	Primary Responsibility
9 Printer engagement letter	Printers
10 PR engagement letter	PR
11 Directors' declaration forms	Company
12 Memorandum on directors' responsibilities	CoSols
13 Tax clearance	Rep Accts
14 Corporate reorganisation memorandum]	CoSols
B. Principal public documents	
15 Admission Document	All parties
16 Share certificate	Company/Reg
17 Documents on display *[not required by AIM Rules unless a prospectus]*	CoSols – see K below
C. Documents related to the placing	
18 Placing agreement	CoSols/IssueSols/Broker
19 Warranty Certificate	CoSols/IssueSols/Broker
20 Placing letters	CoSols/IssueSols/Broker

Document	Primary Responsibility
21 Presentation slides	Company/Broker/CoSols
D. Press announcements and publicity	
22 10 day announcement to AIM (Rule 2 and Schedule 1 AIM Rules for Companies)	PR/Nomad/Company
23 Announcement of commencement of dealings	PR/Nomad/Company
E. Due diligence	
24 Legal due diligence report	CoSols
25 'Long form' – financial due diligence report	Rep Accts
26 Other commercial due diligence report(s)	Company/Expert
F. Supporting documents	
27 Nominated Adviser [and Broker] Agreement	Nomad/Company/CoSols/IssueSols
28 Directors' powers of attorney and responsibility letters	CoSols
29 Directors' service contracts/appointment letters	CoSols

Document		Primary Responsibility
30	Share option schemes	CoSols
31	Verification notes (for Admission Document and presentation slides)	CoSols
32	General meeting notice and minutes	CoSols
33	'Pathfinder' Admission Document board minutes	CoSols
34	Completion board minutes	CoSols
35	Working capital report/memorandum	Company/Rep Accts
36	Financial position and prospects procedures memorandum	Company/Rep Accts
37	Tax Clearances from HM Revenue & Customs	Rep Accts
38	Registrar's agreement	Reg
39	CREST application form and enablement letter	Company/Broker
40	Terms of reference for audit, risk, remuneration and nomination committees, list of matters specifically reserved for decision of full board	Company/CoSols

Document	Primary Responsibility
41 Share dealing code	CoSols
42 Irrevocable undertakings	CoSols
43 Lock-in agreements (Rule 7 AIM Rules for Companies)	CoSols/IssueSols
44 Nomad's declaration (Rule 20 & Schedule 2 AIM Rules for Nominated Advisers)	Nomad
45 AIM compliance memorandum	CoSols
46 Publicity Guidelines	CoSols
47 AIM checklist	IssueSols
G. **Supporting correspondence/comfort letters**	
48 Comfort letter from the directors to Nomad on compliance with AIM Rules for Companies and understanding responsibilities (Rule 31 AIM Rules for Companies, Rule 20 & Schedule 2 AIM Rules for Nominated Advisers)	IssueSols

	Document	Primary Responsibility
49	Comfort letter from the directors to Nomad/Broker confirming working capital statement (Schedule 2 paragraph (c) AIM Rules for Companies)	Issue Sols
50	Comfort letters from CoSols and Reporting Accountants to Nomad/Broker on compliance with AIM Rules for Companies (Rule 20 & Schedule 2 AIM Rules for Nominated Advisers)	CoSols/Rep Accts/Issue Sols
51	Comfort letter from Reporting Accountants on working capital report/memorandum	Rep Accts
52	Comfort letter from Reporting Accountants on financial position and prospects procedures memorandum	Rep Accts
53	Comfort letter from Reporting Accountants on extraction of financial information	Rep Accts
54	Comfort letter from Reporting Accountants on no significant change	Rep Accts
55	Comfort letter from Reporting Accountants giving comfort on status of tax computations/clearances	Rep Accts

Document	Primary Responsibility
56 Comfort letter from Reporting Accountants on taxation information	Rep Accts
57 Comfort letter from Reporting Accountants on pro forma financial information in Admission Document	Rep Accts
58 Comfort letter from Reporting Accountants on any illustrative financial projections in Admission Document	Rep Accts
H. Consent and approvals	
59 AIM to provide letter confirming the shares are admitted (Dealing Notice issued pursuant to Rule 6 AIM Rules for Companies)	AIM
60 Consent letter regarding issue of Admission Document from Nomad/ Broker	Nomad/Broker
61 Consent letter regarding issue of Admission Document from the Reporting Accountants	Rep Accts
62 Consent letters from any other Expert or originator of any source material quoted in Admission Document	CoSols

Document		Primary Responsibility
I.	**Documents to be submitted to Registrar of Companies**	
63	[Re-registration to PLC/revised constitutional documents and change of name if appropriate]	CoSols
64	[Form SH01, Forms AP01 and other Companies House forms as required]	CoSols
J.	**Documents to be submitted to AIM (Rule 5 AIM Rules for Companies and Guidance Notes to Rule 5)**	
65	Company AIM application form	Nomad
66	Nomad declaration form	Nomad
67	Copy of Company minutes unconditionally allotting any securities issued on Admission	Company
68	Fee	Company
69	Electronic version of the Admission Document	Nomad/Printers

Document		Primary Responsibility
K.	**Documents to be on display *[Not required by AIM Rules unless Admission Document constitutes a prospectus]***	
70	Memorandum and Articles of Association	CoSols
71	Historical financial information	Rep Accts/Company
72	Accountants' report and report on pro forma financial information	Rep Accts
73	Expert reports/statements	CoSols
74	Nomad/Broker and accountants consent letters	Nomad/Broker/Rep Accts
75	Service agreements/letters of appointment for directors	CoSols
76	Material contracts	CoSols
77	Rules of share option schemes/long term incentive plans	CoSols
78	Any other document prepared by an expert at the Company's request referred to in Admission Document	CoSols

Appendix 2 — Specimen AIM Flotation Timetable

Abbreviations:

[The Company]	–	**"Company"**
[Nominated Adviser]	–	**"Nomad"**
[Company Solicitors]	–	**"CoSols"**
[Solicitors to the Issue]	–	**"IssueSols"**
[Reporting Accountants]	–	**"Rep Accts"**
AIM Admission Document/Prospectus	–	**"Admission Document"**
[Registrars]	–	**"Reg"**
[Public Relations]	–	**"PR"**
[Broker (if separate Nomad and Broker)]	–	**"Broker"**
[Printers]	–	**"Printers"**

Date	Event	Responsibility
Week 1		
	Initial all parties meeting	All
	Provisional timetable circulated	Nomad
	List of parties circulated	Nomad
	List of documents circulated	CoSols
	Directors' cards circulated to board	CoSols
	Engagement letters with Rep Accts, CoSols, Broker and Nomad circulated in particular agreeing scope of long form report and legal due diligence report	Nomad
Week 2		
	Directors' cards completed and returned to Nomad	Directors
	Draft power of attorney and directors' responsibility statement circulated	CoSols

Draft memorandum on directors' responsibilities circulated	CoSols
Long form report and legal due diligence report questionnaires circulated	Rep Accts/CoSols
Decide dates for organising general meeting for [group reorganisation,] authority to allot shares and disapply pre-emption rights, share option requirements, adopt new articles (if necessary)	CoSols
Consult PR on proposed programme of presentations and announcements	Company/Broker
Determine tax clearance issues	CoSols/Rep Accts
Confirm dates for drafts of long form report, working capital memorandum, report on profit forecast, memorandum on financial position and prospects procedures	Rep Accts/ Company
Finalise timetable and sign engagement letters	Nomad/CoSols/ Company
Commence work on working capital report	Company
Commence work on long form report	Rep Accts
Commence work on legal due diligence report	CoSols
Corporate governance terms of reference and share dealing code circulated	CoSols
First draft share option schemes circulated	CoSols
New memorandum and articles of association circulated	CoSols
Directors' service agreements circulated	CoSols

Week 3		
	Tax clearances sought	Rep Accts
	Comments on memorandum on directors' responsibilities to CoSols together with comments on power of attorney and directors' responsibility statement	Company/IssueSols
	First draft Admission Document circulated	Nomad
	First draft placing agreement circulatedFirst draft placing letter circulated	IssueSolsIssueSols/Broker
	First draft Nomad/Broker agreements circulated	IssueSols
	First draft "intention to float" announcement circulated	Nomad
	Comments on first draft Admission Document to Nomad	All
	Notice of general meeting to shareholders to approve new memorandum and articles, etc.	Company/CoSols
Week 4		
	Second draft Admission Document circulated including short form report and legal 'statutory and general information'	Nomad
	Audit to date completed	Rep Accts
	First rehearsal of management presentation to institutions and press	Company/Broker
	Draft estimate of expenses available	Company

	Comments on first draft placing agreement and Nomad/Broker agreements	CoSols
	Comments on second draft Admission Document to Nomad	All
Week 5		
	Circulate directors' pack including draft pathfinder board minutes, final responsibility letters, final powers of attorney, memorandum on directors' responsibilities, publicity guidelines	CoSols
	Third draft Admission Document circulated	Nomad
	First draft working capital report available	Company/Rep Accts
	First draft long form report circulated	Rep Accts
	First draft legal due diligence report circulated	CoSols
	First draft institutional presentation circulatedFirst draft verification notes available	Company/BrokerCoSols
	Presentation to Broker salesmen	Company/Broker/PR
	Comments on first draft verification notes	IssueSols

	Progress meeting to include:
	    1) drafting;
	    2) verification;
	    3) final estimate of expenses;
	    4) working capital
		All

	First draft consent and comfort letters circulated	CoSols/IssueSols/Rep Accts

Week 6		
	Fourth draft Admission Document circulated	Nomad
	Second draft placing agreement and Nomad/ Broker agreements circulated	IssueSols
	Institutional meetings start to be arranged	Broker
	Comments on consent and comfort letters provided	CoSols/IssueSols RepAccts
	Printers appointed	Nomad
	Registrars appointed	Company
	Comments on fourth draft Admission Document (drafting meeting as requested/ necessary)	All
	Circulate First Printers Proof Admission Document	Printers
	Comments to IssueSols on second draft placing agreement and Nomad/Broker agreement	CoSols
	Verification notes in final form	CoSols
	Second draft long form report available	Rep Accts
	Meeting at Nomad to discuss any final issues on working capital and long form reports	Nomad/RepAccts/ Company
Week 7		
	Board meeting to approve pathfinder Admission Document, presentation slides and verification notes and documents in final/near final draft form	All parties

AIM application forms and supporting letters	Nomad
Consent letters	Nomad/Rep Accts
Comfort letters	CoSols/IssueSols
CREST application	Broker
Press release/intention to float announcement	PR
Nomad/Broker agreement	IssueSols
Placing agreement	IssueSols
Placing letter	Broker
Memorandum on directors' responsibilities	CoSols
Directors' service agreements	CoSols
Non executives' letter of appointment	CoSols
AIM Compliance Manual	CoSols
Registrars' agreementDraft share certificate	RegReg
Estimate of expenses	Nomad
Legal due diligence report	CoSols
Powers of attorney	CoSols
Directors' responsibility statements	CoSols
Report on financial position and prospects procedures	Rep Accts
Long and short form reports	Rep Accts
Pro forma financial information	Rep Accts

	Profit forecast (if applicable)	Rep Accts
	Report on working capital	Rep Accts
	Share option scheme(s)	CoSols
	General meeting to adopt new memorandum and articles, etc.	Company
Week 8/9		
	Institutional marketing commences	Company/Broker
Week 10		
	Institutional marketing completed	Company/Broker
	Informal pricing meeting to determine price range for discussions with institutions	Company/Broker
	Any final minor amendments to pathfinder Admission Document	Nomad/CoSols/Rep Accts
	10 day notice submitted to Stock Exchange	Nomad
	Board meeting to confirm issue price, approve Admission Document as 'P' proof, approve service contracts and letters of appointment, approve verification notes, adopt working capital statement and profit forecast (if applicable), approve placing agreement and ancilliary documents, approve estimate of expenses, approve press announcement, approve number of shares subject to placing, approve share option scheme(s) and adopt terms of reference and share dealing code	All
	Agree pricing	Company/Broker

	Meeting with Press/Press release	Company/PR
	Bulk print of 'P' proof Admission Document	Printers
	Placing letters despatched to placees with 'P' proof Admission Document	Broker
	Placing letters received back by Broker	Broker
	10 a.m. completion meeting to approve all documents, sign the placing agreement, provisionally and conditionally allot new shares, appoint a board committee to deal with all matters connected with the admission, including despatch of share certificates to placees as necessary after Admission; all documentation held in escrow overnight	Company/CoSols
	Directors responsibility statement and powers of attorney signed	Company
	Approve announcement of flotation	Company
	Approve and sign off Admission Document	Company
	Bulk print admission document overnight	Printers
	Rep Accts report signed	Rep Accts
	Approve and sign all necessary documentation	All
Week 11		
	IMPACT DAY Flotation announcement released	PR

	Placing agreement and other documents released from escrow	Broker
	Documents on display (if applicable)	CoSols
	Three day information submitted to AIM: company application form, Nomad's declaration, cheque for exchange fee, electronic copy of Admission Document, and evidence of allotment of new shares	Nomad
Week 12		
	First day of dealings on AIM	Company
	Announcement from Stock Exchange	Stock Exchange
	CREST member accounts credited	Reg
	Company to receive placing monies	Nomad
	Share certificates despatched	Reg

Appendix 3 — Specimen AIM Completion Board Minutes

CONAME PLC

(the "**Company**")

Minutes of a meeting of [a Committee of] the Board of Directors of the Company [duly constituted by a meeting of the Board of Directors held on [   ] 20[   ]] held at [   ] on [   ] 20[   ] at [   ] a.m./p.m.

Present:	[ ]	(in the Chair)
	[ ]	
	[ ]	
In Attendance:	[ ]	
	[ ]	

1   Chairman Quorum, notice & previous meeting

1.1   It was noted that due notice had been given of the matters to be proposed at the meeting and that a quorum was present. Mr [   ] took the Chair.

1.2   [The minutes of the meeting of the Board held on [   ] 20[   ] were tabled and It was resolved that they be signed by the Chairman as a true and accurate record of the matters discussed at that meeting.]

2   Declaration of interest

2.1   Each Director present confirmed that such Director had no interest, direct or indirect, in the business to be discussed at the meeting which had not been previously disclosed to the Company and which such Director was required by the Articles of Association or by sections 177 and 182 of the Companies Act 2006 (the **"Act"**), or otherwise, to disclose. [If any Director has a conflict of interest to be disclosed, the above wording requires amendment and further provisions will be required with respect to the remaining Directors considering whether to authorise the conflict and any conditions which are imposed on the relevant director in respect of the conflict.]

2.2   The Chairman also referred the meeting to sections 171 to 177 inclusive of the Act and noted that each Director, in discharging his

379

duty under section 172 of the Act, must act in a way which he considers, in good faith, would be the most likely to promote the success of the Company for the benefit of its shareholders, and have regard (amongst other matters) to certain factors set out in section 172 of the Act. Each Director acknowledged that such Director understood the statutory duties set out in such section.

3 Purpose of meeting

3.1 The Chairman explained that the meeting had been convened to deal with the final formalities required in connection with the proposed placing (the **"Placing"**) of [   ] new ordinary shares of [   ]p each in the capital of the Company (**"Ordinary Shares"**) at [   ]p per share to be made by [Broker Limited] (the **"Broker"**) on behalf of the Company [and certain selling shareholders (the **"Vendors"**)], and with the admission (the **"Admission"**) of the whole of the share capital of the Company, issued and to be issued, to trading on the AIM Market of the London Stock Exchange (**"AIM"**) (all such matters being collectively referred to as the **"Proposals"**). It was noted that [Nomad Limited] (the **"Nomad"**) had agreed to act as the Company's nominated adviser as required by the AIM Rules for Companies.

3.2 The response to date of the issue of the placing letters to institutional investors (the **"Placing Letters"**) with the "P" Proof Admission Document by the Broker was reported to the meeting.

4 Documents tabled

4.1 In connection with the Proposals the following documents were tabled to the meeting:

4.1.1 a final proof (dated [   ] 20[   ]) of the admission document (the **"Admission Document"**) as required by the AIM Rules for Companies to be published by the Company in connection with the Placing and Admission;

4.1.2 verification notes to be signed by the Directors in respect of the contents of the Admission Document (the **"Verification Notes"**), together with the annexures thereto;

4.1.3 a legal due diligence report by [   ] (the **"CoSols"**);

4.1.4 responsibility statements and powers of attorney signed by each of the Directors (respectively the **"Responsibility Statements"** and **"Powers of Attorney"**);

4.1.5   a letter addressed to the Nomad [and the Broker] to be signed by the Directors giving comfort in respect of the contents of the Admission Document (the **"Responsibility Letter"**);

4.1.6   a letter addressed to the Nomad [and the Broker] to be signed by the Directors confirming the sufficiency of working capital;

4.1.7   the formal application to be signed by the Company for the purposes of Admission (the **"Application"**) and the form of declaration to be signed by the Nomad required by the London Stock Exchange (the **"Nomad Declaration"**);

4.1.8   a letter from the Directors to the Nomad confirming that they have had their responsibilities as directors of a company admitted to trading on AIM explained to them and that, having made due and careful enquiry, they have established procedures which provide a reasonable basis for them to make proper judgements as to the financial position and prospects of the Company [and its subsidiaries] (the **"Nomad Comfort Letter"**);

4.1.9   a memorandum prepared by CoSols concerning the responsibilities of the Directors in connection with the Placing and Admission (the **"CoSols Memorandum"**);

4.1.10   a memorandum prepared by CoSols concerning the obligations of the Directors and the Company following Admission and setting out certain procedures to be followed to ensure compliance with the AIM Rules for Companies (the **"AIM Compliance Manual"**);

4.1.11   a set of guidelines prepared by CoSols concerning the restrictions and obligations of the Directors and the Company during the marketing period and following Admission setting out certain procedures in relation to securities laws (the "**Publicity Guidelines**");

4.1.12   copy declarations [and supplementary declarations] relating to the Directors previously delivered to the Broker and the Nomad;

4.1.13   letters from [   ] (the **"Reporting Accountants"**) to the Company giving comfort in respect of certain statements relating to taxation and certain financial information contained in the Admission Document;

4.1.14   a long form financial report prepared by the Reporting Accountants relating to the Company [and its subsidiaries], together with a letter to the Reporting Accountants relating thereto;

4.1.15   the short form accountants' report(s) by the Reporting Accountants relating to the Company [and its subsidiaries] the text of which is to be reproduced in the Admission Document and the report on the pro forma financial information also to be reproduced in the Admission Document;

4.1.16 [a copy of the illustrative financial projections for the Company [and its subsidiaries] for the three financial periods ending [   ] 20[   ] (the **"Projections"**), together with a letter from the Reporting Accountants giving comfort in respect of the calculation of the Projections, the text of which is to be reproduced in the Admission Document;]

4.1.17 the cash flow projections dated [   ] 20[   ] of the Company [and its subsidiaries] for the period to [ ] 20[   ] (the **"Cash Flow Projections"**), together with a report thereon prepared by Reporting Accountants and reviewing the working capital statement in the Admission Document (the **"Working Capital Report"**);

4.1.18 consent letters from the Reporting Accountants, the Nomad and the Broker;

4.1.19 letters from CoSols and the Reporting Accountants to the Nomad [and the Broker] concerning the contents of the Admission Document;

4.1.20 an engrossment of a placing agreement to be entered into between the Company, the Directors, the Nomad [and] the Broker [and the Vendor(s)] (the **"Placing Agreement"**);

4.1.21 the form of the Placing Letter;

4.1.22 engrossments of service agreements to be entered into between the Company and each of [   ] and [   ] (the **"Service Agreements"**), [together with letters setting out arrangements as to the payment of bonuses to them];

4.1.23 letters of appointment relating to the appointment of each of [   ] and [   ] as non-executive directors of the Company (the **"Appointment Letters"**);

4.1.24 [certificates of title prepared by CoSols in respect of the [Company's / Group's] premises at [   ] and [   ] and by [   ], solicitors, in respect of the premises at [   ]];

4.1.25 an agreement to be entered into by the Company and [   ] concerning the provision of services by [   ] as registrars to the Company (the **"Registrars Agreement"**);

4.1.26 a specimen share certificate;

4.1.27   an application prepared by the Broker in relation to CREST together with a CREST enablement letter;

4.1.28   [draft rules of HM Revenue & Customs Approved Share Option Scheme, the Unapproved Share Option Scheme, [   ] and the Employee (Savings Related) Share Option Scheme (together the **"Share Option Schemes"**) each proposed to be adopted by the Company;]

4.1.29   draft terms of reference for each of the proposed remuneration, risk, audit and nominations committee and a list of matters specifically reserved for the decision of the full board;

4.1.30   a draft code for all directors and employees relating to the proposed rules for dealing in the Ordinary Shares (the **"Share Dealing Code"**);

4.1.31   an engrossment of an option agreement proposed to be entered into by the Company in favour of [   ] (the **"[   ] Option Agreement"**);

4.1.32   copies of letters from the HM Revenue & Customs granting clearance pursuant to Chapter 1, Part 13 of the Income Tax Act 2007 (for income tax) Part 15, Corporation Tax Act 2010 (for corporation tax) and section 137 of the Taxation of Chargeable Gains Act 1992;

4.1.33   a draft press announcement concerning the Proposals (the **"Press Announcement"**); and

4.1.34   an estimate of the expenses relating to the Proposals (the **"Estimate of Expenses"**).

5   The placing

5.1   The Chairman reminded the meeting that the Company was proposing to raise approximately £[   ] million net of expenses under the Placing. The funds raised would be used for [   ] and [   ], as described in the Admission Document.

5.2   The Placing would comprise [   ] Ordinary Shares at [ ]p per share. It was reported that the Broker had agreed to place those shares with institutional and other investors. [The Placing would include [   ] Ordinary Shares being sold by the Vendors, at the placing price of [   ]p per share.]

5.3   The Placing would be conditional upon, inter alia, Admission occurring on or before [   ] 20[   ] (or such later date as the

Nomad, the Broker and the Company agreed, but in any event not later than [   ] 20[   ]).

6   Placing Agreement

6.1   The attention of the meeting was then drawn to the terms of the Placing Agreement and in particular to the following:

6.1.1   the conditions to which the Nomad [and the Broker's] obligations under the terms of the Placing Agreement were subject, including Admission taking place on or before [   ] 20[   ], (or such later date as the Nomad, [the Broker] and the Company may agree) but in any event not later than [   ] 20[   ];

6.1.2   the fees and commissions to be paid to the Nomad [and the Broker] as set out in clause [   ] of the Placing Agreement;

6.1.3   the warranties and undertakings to be given to the Nomad [and the Broker] by the Company and the Directors pursuant to clause [   ] of the Placing Agreement;

6.1.4   the indemnities to be given by the Company [and the Directors] to the Nomad [and the Broker] and their respective officers and agents pursuant to clause [   ] of the Placing Agreement;

6.1.5   the events which would entitle the Nomad [and the Broker] to terminate the Placing Agreement prior to Admission as set out in clause [   ] of the Placing Agreement;

6.1.6   the restrictive covenants imposed on the executive Directors by clause [   ] of the Placing Agreement;

6.1.7   the tax covenant contained in schedule [   ] to the Placing Agreement to be entered into by the executive Directors; and

6.1.8   the undertaking from each of the Directors not to, and to procure that none of their connected persons will, dispose of any interest in Ordinary Shares in the Company for a period of [twelve] months after Admission and that no disposals will be made otherwise than through [the Broker] (for so long as it remains broker to the Company).

7   Share Options

7.1   The rules of the Share Option Schemes were considered, and it was noted that they would be limited to [10] per cent of the Company's issued share capital from time to time. It was noted that the rules of the approved scheme and of the SAYE scheme had previously been submitted to the HM Revenue & Customs for informal approval. It was reported that it was intended to grant options under the Approved Scheme as soon as formal approval had been obtained from the HM Revenue & Customs, and that, subject to the adoption of the Share Option Schemes in general meeting, it was proposed to grant options under the Unapproved Scheme to subscribe for [   ] Ordinary Shares at [   ]p per share and to grant options under the Approved Scheme for [   ] Ordinary Shares at [ ] per share.

7.2 **It was resolved** that the Share Option Schemes be and they are hereby approved for consideration at the General Meeting referred to in minute 8 below.

7.3 **It was resolved** that, subject to adoption by the Company in General Meeting of the Unapproved Scheme, the following options be and they hereby are granted under the Unapproved Scheme (to take effect in accordance with the Unapproved Scheme Rules), it being noted that no performance conditions were attached to those options, and the Directors and Secretary be and they hereby are instructed to execute and issue the Option Certificates for those options:

Name and address of Option Holder	Number of Ordinary Shares subject to Option	Price per share	Total Subscription Price payable
[ ]	[ ]	[ ]p	£[´]
[ ]	[ ]	[ ]p	£[ ]
[ ]	[ ]	[ ]p	£[ ]

7.4 The terms of the [   ] Option Agreement were considered and **It was resolved** that it be and it is hereby approved and executed on behalf of the Company, and that the Company hereby grants to [   ] the option to subscribe for up to [   ] Ordinary Shares in the capital of the Company at [   ]p per share, on the terms of the [   ] Option Agreement.

8 **General meeting**

8.1 As part of the arrangements necessary to implement the Proposals it was explained that it was necessary for the Company to:

8.1.1 grant authority to the Directors pursuant to section 551 of the Act to allot relevant securities up to an aggregate nominal amount of £[   ]; and

8.1.2 empower the Directors pursuant to section 570 of the Act to allot equity securities for cash otherwise than on a pro rata basis up to an aggregate nominal value of £[•].

8.2 At the same time, the Chairman reported that it was proposed that the Company adopt the Share Option Schemes, each to be governed by the draft rules tabled to the meeting.

8.3 Accordingly, there was tabled to the meeting a notice convening a General Meeting of the Company to pass resolutions necessary to carry into effect the above matters together with a form of consent to the General Meeting being held on short notice to be signed by or on behalf of the holders of all existing issued Ordinary Shares in the Company. Following consideration of the notice **It was resolved** that the same be approved and despatched to the members and that, subject to the consent to the General Meeting being held on short notice being duly given, the General Meeting be held forthwith.

8.4 The meeting adjourned at [   ] pm.

8.5 The meeting resumed at [ ] pm and it was reported that the General Meeting had been duly convened and held (the necessary consents to the General Meeting being held on short notice having been obtained) and the resolutions set out in the notice had been duly passed.

9   Appointment of Registrars

It was resolved that [   ] be and they are hereby appointed as Registrars to the Company, upon the terms of the Registrars' Agreement.

10   Working Capital

10.1 The Cash Flow Projections were carefully considered. It was noted that they had been reviewed by the Reporting Accountants and discussed with the Nomad [and the Broker], and the contents of the Working Capital Report were carefully considered. **It was resolved** that the representation letters to the Reporting Accountants in connection with the working capital statement and the letter to the Nomad [and the Broker] on working capital be and they are hereby approved and that they be signed by the Chief Executive Director and the Finance Director. It was noted that the working capital statement is being made in respect of the [   ] month period ending [   ] 20[   ].

10.2 **It was resolved** that the Cash Flow Projections be adopted and that it is the opinion of the Company, having made due and careful enquiry, that, from the time of Admission, the working capital of the [Company / Group] is sufficient for its present requirements, that is, for at least the next twelve months.

11   Illustrative financial projections

11.1   [The Projections were carefully considered, together with the assumptions relating thereto. It was noted that they had been reviewed by the Reporting Accountants and discussed with the Nomad and the Broker, and the content of the comfort letter by the Reporting Accountants upon the Projections was carefully considered. It was noted that the Directors were responsible for the Projections. The Directors confirmed that they had been prepared after due and careful enquiry and that there were no assumptions relevant or material to the Projections which ought to be considered apart from those set out in the Projections and reproduced in the Admission Document. **It was resolved** that the representation letter to the Reporting Accountants in connection with the Projections be and it is hereby approved and that it be signed by the Chief Executive Director and the Finance Director.

11.2   **It was resolved** that the Projections be and they are hereby approved and adopted.]

12   Accountants reports

12.1   The accountants' reports were carefully considered. The Directors confirmed that they had provided all relevant information to the Reporting Accountants in the preparation of them and that they were not aware of anything incorrect in, or inconsistent with, such reports. **It was resolved** that the representation letters to the Reporting Accountants in connection with the long form report and the accountants reports be and they are hereby approved and that they be signed by the Chief Executive Director and the Finance Director.

12.2   **It was resolved** that the accountants' reports be and they are hereby approved and adopted.

13   Remuneration, Risk, Nominations and Audit Committees

13.1   It was noted that in accordance with the CoSols Memorandum on aspects of corporate governance, which had been circulated to the Board by CoSols, it was appropriate that each of a remuneration, risk, nominations and an audit committee be established under defined terms of reference and that a formal list of matters specifically reserved for the decision of the full Board be adopted. Accordingly, the terms of reference for each of the remuneration, risk, nominations and audit committees and the list of matters specifically reserved for the decision of the full Board were considered and noted.

13.2   **It was resolved** that the terms of reference and the list of matters specifically reserved for the decision of the full Board be and they are hereby adopted, and that, pursuant to article [   ] of the Company's Articles of Association, each of a remuneration committee, risk committee, nominations committee and an audit committee be established, and that the non-executive Directors be and they are hereby appointed as members of such committees, [   ] to act as chairman of each committee. *[Details of the directors appointed to each committee to be inserted]*

14   Share Dealing Code

14.1   It was noted that in accordance with the CoSols Memorandum (which dealt with aspects of corporate governance) which had been circulated to the Board by CoSols, it was appropriate that a share dealing code be adopted incorporating the requirements under rules 17 and 21 of the AIM Rules for Companies.

14.2   The provisions of the Share Dealing Code were considered and noted and **it was resolved** that the Share Dealing Code be and is hereby adopted. The Company Secretary was instructed to ensure that all staff received a copy of the Share Dealing Code.

15   Service agreements and appointment letters

15.1   The Directors proceeded to consider the terms of the Service Agreements, [   ] and [   ] each declaring their interests in relation to them. It was noted that each Service Agreement was subject to [twelve] month's notice of termination (not to be given before [   ] 20[   ] in the case of [   ]). [   ] and [   ] were entitled to annual salaries of respectively £[   ] and £[   ] and were each entitled to the use of a company car, membership of a private medical scheme for the Director and his/her spouse and dependent children, permanent health insurance, life assurance and critical life cover. In addition, pension contributions are to be payable to [   ] and [   ] of, respectively, £[   ] per month and [   ] per cent. of salary. Each Service Agreement contained restrictive covenants, including post-termination non-competition covenants.

15.2   [The terms of the bonus arrangement letters were also considered, and it was noted that the bonuses were limited to a maximum of £[   ] for [   ] and £[   ] for [   ][, and that they related to the achievement of the Projections set out in the Admission Document].]

15.3   The Appointment Letters were then considered and it was noted that they were subject to termination upon [twelve] months written notice from either party. Each non-executive Director would be entitled to an initial annual fee of £[   ] payable [monthly] in arrears.

16   Approval of the admission document

16.1   The Directors were then reminded, in relation to Admission, of the following matters which had been discussed at the meeting of the full Board on [   ] 20[   ]:

16.1.1   that on the date when it is published, as required by the AIM Rules for Companies, the Admission Document will be required to contain all such information as, investors would reasonably require, and reasonably expect to find there, for the purpose of forming a full understanding of the assets and liabilities, financial position, profits and losses and prospects of the Company and its Ordinary Shares and of the rights attaching to those shares and all other matters contained in the Admission Document;

16.1.2   that each Director would be responsible for the information contained in the Admission Document and that, if such document did not contain all such information, or if any statement included therein was untrue or misleading on the date on which the Admission Document was published or a significant change affecting any matter required to be included therein occurred or if a significant new matter arose, the inclusion of information in respect of which would have been required if it had arisen when the Admission Document was prepared, each Director may incur liabilities, and may be liable in damages in connection with the information contained in, or omitted from, such document. Written confirmation of all the Directors' responsibilities in the terms of the Responsibility Statements had been obtained. The attention of the meeting was drawn to the fact that an untrue or misleading statement in the Admission Document could lead to civil and/or criminal liability as explained below and in the CoSols Memorandum which had been circulated to all the Directors and discussed with all the Directors at a meeting held on [   ] 20[   ]. Each of the Directors confirmed that he had read and understood the CoSols Memorandum;

16.1.3   it was explained that there was a regulatory requirement to publish a supplementary admission document in respect of any significant change affecting any matter contained in the Admission Document, or any significant new matter, which was capable of affecting the full understanding by an investor as mentioned in minute 16.1.2 above arising before the Ordinary Shares were admitted to trading on AIM, which was expected to be on [   ] 20[   ]. The attention of the Directors was also drawn to the terms of the Placing Agreement which obliged the Company or the Directors to notify the Nomad [and the Broker] if the Company or the Directors became aware at any time before the shares were admitted to trading on AIM that any of the representations and warranties set out in the Placing Agreement was or had become untrue, inaccurate or misleading. Each Director present confirmed that, if, prior to the commencement of dealings, such Director became aware of any fact or circumstances which would be relevant to any of the foregoing, or if he/she became aware that there was, or might be, a need to publish a supplementary admission document, then he/she would take steps immediately to inform the Nomad, [the Broker] and his fellow Directors;

16.1.4   there would, following Admission, be continuing obligations owed to the London Stock Exchange under the terms of the AIM Rules for Companies which, it was explained, would impose obligations on the Company to disclose information on a timely basis to the London Stock Exchange. It was noted that the continuing obligations imposed by the AIM Rules, including the dealing in the Company's securities, were considered in detail in the CoSols Memorandum, the Share Dealing Code and the AIM Compliance Manual.

16.2   The meeting was then reminded of the detailed consideration of the terms of the Admission Document at the meeting of the Board on [   ] 20[   ], which had particularly noted the following sections:

Key Information, including the placing statistics;
[Part I – Principal Activities;
- Principal Markets
- Products;
- Suppliers;
- Sales and Marketing Strategy;
- Intellectual Property Rights;
- Financial record;
- Current trading and prospects;
- Reasons for the Placing and use of proceeds;
- The Placing and Admission;
- Selling Shareholders;
Part 2 – Risk factors
Part 3 – Accountants' reports;
Part 4 – Pro forma financial information; and
Part 5 – Additional information.]

16.3   A report was then given on the procedures that had been conducted in order to verify the contents of the Admission Document and provide a record of the steps taken to ensure the accuracy of the Admission Document. It was noted that copies of the Verification Notes had been supplied to each of the Directors and had been considered in detail at [two] verification meetings at which all the Directors had been present. These Verification Notes had subsequently been brought up to date and circulated again to the Directors. The completed Verification Notes had been tabled to the meeting and each of the Directors confirmed that he/she was satisfied with the responses to the Verification Notes which were to the best of each Director's knowledge, information and belief, accurate in all respects.

16.4   Having considered the terms of the Admission Document each of the Directors present confirmed that:

16.4.1   the statements as to his interests in the Ordinary Shares of the Company and the other matters relating to him/her set out in paragraph [5] of Part [5] of the Admission Document are correct, accurate and complete;

16.4.2   to the best of his/her knowledge, information and belief save as disclosed in paragraph [6] of Part [5] of the Admission Document, there are no contracts to which [the Company / any member of the Group] is a party and which are, and no obligation which is, material for disclosure in the Admission Document;

16.4.3   to the best of his/her knowledge, information and belief, save as disclosed in paragraph [9] of Part [5] of the Admission Document, there are no legal or arbitration proceedings, active, pending, or threatened against, or being brought by, the Company [or any member of the Group] which are having or may have a significant effect on the Company's financial position;

16.4.4   the Admission Document complies in all respects with the provisions of the AIM Rules for Companies published by the London Stock Exchange;

16.4.5   the Admission Document contains all such other information as the Directors consider necessary to enable investors to form a full understanding of the assets and liabilities, financial position, profits and losses and prospects of the Company and its Ordinary Shares and the rights attaching to the Ordinary Shares and the other matters contained in the Admission Document;

16.4.6   the statements in the Admission Document could properly be made and he/she was satisfied that all statements of fact contained in the Admission Document were true and accurate in all material respects and not misleading, that all expressions of opinion, intention and expectation contained therein were fair and honestly held and made after due and careful consideration;

16.4.7 to the best of his knowledge, information and belief, having taken all reasonable care to ensure that such was the case, there were no other facts relating to the Company not disclosed in the Admission Document the omission of which would make any statement therein misleading or which in the circumstances of the proposed Placing might be material to be disclosed; and

16.4.8 he/she accepts responsibility for the Admission Document accordingly.

17   Financial Services and Markets Act 2000 and the Financial Services Act 2012

17.1   The attention of the Directors was drawn to sections 89 and 90 of the Financial Services Act 2012 which make it a criminal offence for a Director to:

17.1.1 make any statement which he knows to be false or misleading in a material respect;

17.1.2 make a statement which is false or misleading in a material respect, being reckless as to whether it is; or

17.1.3 dishonestly conceal any material facts whether in relation to a statement he makes or otherwise,

and, in doing so, to intend that (or be reckless as to whether) another person will be induced to enter or offer to enter into, or refrain from entering into, an investment agreement, such as that made with applicants for shares under the Placing, or to exercise or refrain from exercising, any rights conferred by an investment; and

17.1.4 do any act or engage in any course of conduct which creates a false or misleading impression as to the market in or the price or value of any investment, provided he does so intending to create that impression and:

(a) thereby induce another person to acquire, dispose of subscribe for or underwrite those investments, or to refrain from doing so, or to exercise or refrain from exercising any rights conferred by those investments; or

(b) know (or is reckless as to whether) the impression is false or misleading and intends to (or knows that the impression is likely to) result in a gain either for himself or another or cause loss to another or expose the other to risk.

17.2   The Directors were also reminded of the market abuse regime set out in Part VIII of the Financial Services and Markets Act 2000 which applies to "qualifying investments" (including shares traded on AIM) and sets out various forms of behaviour which constitute market abuse including (i) insider dealing, (ii) improper disclosure of inside information, (iii) improper use of information which is not generally available to the market, (iv) market manipulation, (v) market deception, (vi) dissemination of false or misleading information and (vii) misleading the market/market distortion. The market abuse regime applies to on and off market behaviour. Those who commit the civil offence of market abuse can be punished by, inter alia, an unlimited fine or public censure.

18   Approval of proposals and documents

18.1   After careful consideration **it was resolved** that the Placing be approved and **it was further resolved** that (subject to the Escrow Condition referred to below in minute 18.1.13 and such final amendments as may be agreed by the Committee of the Board to be appointed pursuant to minute 20):

18.1.1   the Admission Document be approved and the Nomad be authorised to arrange for bulk printing;

18.1.2   the Verification Notes be approved and adopted for the purpose of verifying the contents of the Admission Document;

18.1.3   the Placing Agreement be approved and any one Director in the presence of a witness, or any two Directors or one Director and the Secretary be authorised to execute the same on behalf of the Company;

18.1.4   any Director, the Secretary or CoSols be authorised to initial for the purpose of identification any of the documents referred to in the Placing Agreement as being "in the agreed form";

18.1.5   the Responsibility Letter and the Nomad Comfort Letter be approved and signed by each of the Directors;

18.1.6   the Company would comply with the terms of the continuing obligations contained in the AIM Rules for Companies of the London Stock Exchange and the AIM Compliance Manual be and is hereby adopted by the Company;

18.1.7   the various reports and letters prepared by the Reporting Accountants be noted;

18.1.8   the various letters prepared by CoSols be noted;

18.1.9   each of the Service Agreements [and bonus arrangement letters] and the Appointment Letters be approved and the Chairman be authorised to sign the same on behalf of the Company;

18.1.10 the form of the share certificate be and it is hereby approved;

18.1.11 the Estimate of Expenses be approved and that the Nomad [or the Broker] be authorised to arrange the payment of such expenses to the relevant persons out of the proceeds of the Placing, subject to the Company having been informed first of the exact amounts of each invoice;

18.1.12 the Press Announcement be approved and subject as set out below the Nomad is hereby authorised and directed to arrange for its release at or around 7.30 a.m. on [   ] 20[   ];

18.1.13 the Application be approved and the Nomad be authorised to deliver the same together with the Nomad Declaration, the AIM fee and an electronic copy of the Admission Document to the London Stock Exchange and do all such acts and things as the Nomad considers necessary in relation thereto in order to facilitate Admission;

but on the basis that all executed documents (apart from the Service Agreements and bonus arrangement letters) are signed but not delivered and held in escrow subject to the Nomad having agreed with the Company (which [   ] or [   ] is authorised to do on behalf of the Company) that they will release the Press Announcement at or around 7.30 a.m. on [   ] 20[   ] (**"Escrow Condition"**).

19   Publication of the admission document

It was resolved that subject to satisfaction of the Escrow Condition, the Admission Document be delivered to the London Stock Exchange and made available publicly, free of charge, at the offices of [the Nomad] for one month from [   ] 20[   ].

20   Appointment of committee

It was resolved that a committee (the **"Committee"**) comprising any two Directors be established with full authority to take all steps and approve, execute or procure to be executed all such documents, acts and things considered by the Committee to be necessary or desirable to have approved, executed or done for the purpose of implementing the Proposals and all matters ancillary thereto including, without limitation, approving any minor amendments to the Admission Document prior to its publication, and the performance of all the Company's obligations under or arising out of the agreements relating to the Placing and all other documents approved at this meeting, including (but not limited to) the allotment of Ordinary Shares pursuant to the Placing.

21   Allotment of ordinary shares

21.1   [The Broker] tabled a final list of places who had conditionally agreed to subscribe for the new Ordinary Shares being placed by the Company [and to purchase the Ordinary Shares being sold by the Vendors]. **It was resolved** that [   ] Ordinary Shares be allotted and issued [and, as appropriate, the transfers of [   ] Ordinary Shares being sold by the Vendors be approved] to those persons identified on the final list of places in those numbers and against those names as set out on such list, subject only to Admission.

21.2   The Secretary was instructed to liaise in due course with the Company's registrar to arrange for the register of members to be made up, for the issue and despatch to places of appropriate share certificates or, where applicable, the crediting of CREST accounts, as soon as possible and for the appropriate return of allotments Form SH01 to be filed with the Registrar of Companies. The Secretary was also instructed to provide to the Nomad a copy of these minutes or an extract thereof to the extent required by the London Stock Exchange as proof of allotment of the Ordinary Shares being the subject of the Placing.

22   WEBSITE

It was noted that pursuant to Rule 26 of the AIM Rules for Companies that from Admission the Company was required to maintain a website which included certain information specified in Rule 26. The Chairman confirmed that the Company's website would be updated from Admission to include the necessary information.

23   FILING

The Secretary was instructed to arrange for any necessary forms or returns to be filed with the Registrar of Companies.

There being no further business, the meeting then terminated.

....

CHAIRMAN

Index

This index has been prepared using Sweet and Maxwell's Legal Taxonomy. Main index entries conform to keywords provided by the Legal Taxonomy except where references to specific documents or non-standard terms (denoted by quotation marks) have been included. These keywords provide a means of identifying similar concepts in other Sweet and Maxwell publications and online services to which keywords from the Legal Taxonomy have been applied. Readers may find some minor differences between terms used in the text and those which appear in the index. Suggestions to *sweetandmaxwell.taxonomy@thomson.com*.

All indexing is to heading number